THE ETIOLOGY
OF BULIMIA NERVOSA

Series in Applied Psychology: Social Issues and Questions

Stevan E. Hobfoll, *Editor-in-Chief*

THE ETIOLOGY OF BULIMIA NERVOSA: THE INDIVIDUAL AND FAMILIAL CONTEXT

Edited by

Janis H. Crowther
Daniel L. Tennenbaum
Stevan E. Hobfoll
Mary Ann Parris Stephens

Kent State University, Ohio

●HEMISPHERE PUBLISHING CORPORATION

A member of the Taylor & Francis Group
Washington   Philadelphia   London

1 2 3 4 5 6 7 8 9 0   B R B R   9 8 7 6 5 4 3 2 1

This book was set in Janson by Hemisphere Publishing Corporation. The editors were Mary McCoy and Joyce Duncan; the production supervisor was Peggy M. Rote; and the typesetter was Shirley J. McNett. Cover design by Sharon M. DePass.
Printing and binding by Braun-Brumfield, Inc.

A CIP catalog record for this book is available from the British Library.

Library of Congress Cataloging-in-Publication Data

The Etiology of bulimia nervosa: the individual and familial context/edited by Janis H. Crowther . . . [et al.].
  p.   cm.—(Series in applied psychology)
  Based on the 1990 Kent Psychology Forum sponsored by the Applied Psychology Center at Kent State University.
  Includes bibliographical references and index.

  1. Bulimia—Etiology—Congresses. I. Crowther, Janis H.
II. Kent State University. Applied Psychology Center. III. Kent Psychology Forum (2nd: 1990: Kent State University) IV. Series:
Series in applied psychology (New York, N.Y.)
  [DNLM: 1. Bulimia—etiology—congresses. 2. Bulimia—genetics—congresses.   WM 175 E84 1990]
RC552.B84E84   1992
6616.85'263071—dc20
DNLM/DLC
for Library of Congress   91-35329
                                                          CIP
ISBN 1-56032-206-3
ISSN 1048-8146

CONTENTS

II   INDIVIDUAL FACTORS

7   Overview   129
Deborah S. Rosch and Kristen L. Shepherd

8   Chronic Dieting and Eating Disorders: A Spiral Model   133
Todd F. Heatherton and Janet Polivy

9   Body-Image Disorder: Definition, Development, and Contribution to Eating Disorders   157
James C. Rosen

CONTRIBUTORS

ILANA ATTIE, Northshore University Hospital, Cornell University Medical College, Manhasset, New York 11030.

JEANNE BROOKS-GUNN, Institute for Study of Exceptional Children, Educational Testing Service, Princeton, New Jersey 08541.

PEGGY A. CRAWFORD, Department of Psychology, Kent State University, Kent, Ohio 44242.

JANIS H. CROWTHER, Department of Psychology, Kent State University, Kent, Ohio 44242.

TODD F. HEATHERTON, Department of Psychology, Harvard University, Cambridge, Massachusetts 02138.

STEVAN E. HOBFOLL, Applied Psychology Center, Department of Psychology, Kent State University, Kent, Ohio 44242.

CRAIG JOHNSON, Department of Psychology, Laureate Psychiatric Hospital, Tulsa, Oklahoma 74147.

CHRIS M. LAWRENCE, Department of Psychology, University of Missouri-Columbia, Columbia, Missouri 65211.

MICHAEL P. LEVINE, Department of Psychology, Kenyon College, Gambier, Ohio 43022.

J. SCOTT MIZES, Department of Psychiatry, MetroHealth Medical Center, Cleveland, Ohio 44109.

JANET POLIVY, Department of Psychology, University of Toronto, Mississaugua, Ontario, Canada L5L 1C6.

ANNE L. POWELL, Department of Psychology, University of Missouri-Columbia, Columbia, Missouri 65211.

DEBORAH S. ROSCH, Department of Psychology, Kent State University, Kent, Ohio 44242.

JAMES C. ROSEN, Department of Psychology, University of Vermont, Burlington, Vermont 05405.

KRISTEN L. SHEPHERD, Department of Psychology, Kent State University, Kent, Ohio 44242.

NANCY E. SHERWOOD, Department of Psychology, Kent State University, Kent, Ohio 44242.

LINDA SMOLAK, Department of Psychology, Kenyon College, Gambier, Ohio 43022.

MARY ANN PARRIS STEPHENS, Department of Psychology, Kent State University, Kent, Ohio 44242.

RUTH H. STRIEGEL-MOORE, Department of Psychology, Wesleyan University, Middletown, Connecticut 06457.

DANIEL L. TENNENBAUM, Department of Psychology, Kent State University, Kent, Ohio 44242.

MARK H. THELEN, Department of Psychology, University of Missouri-Columbia, Columbia, Missouri 65211.

DANA WATTS, Department of Psychology, Kent State University, Kent, Ohio 44242.

EVE M. WOLF, School of Professional Psychology, Ellis Institute, Wright State University, Dayton, Ohio 45435.

STEPHEN WONDERLICH, Department of Neuroscience, University of North Dakota, Fargo, North Dakota 58102.

DEANNE L. ZOTTER, Department of Psychology, Kent State University, Kent, Ohio 44242.

PREFACE

Bulimia nervosa, an eating disorder characterized by episodic bingeing and purging, came to the attention of health professionals in the late 1970s. First recognized as a diagnostic entity in the Third Edition of the *Diagnostic and Statistical Manual* published by the American Psychiatric Association in 1980, bulimia nervosa has been the topic of a growing body of research that has focused on its epidemiology, description, and treatment. In planning the Second Annual Kent Psychology Forum and this accompanying volume, we hoped to make a unique contribution to the etiological literature on bulimia nervosa. Since etiological models of bulimia nervosa recognize that characteristics of the individual and her family may increase a young woman's risk for bulimia nervosa, particularly within the developmental context of puberty, it was our goal to bring together scholars whose work evolves from a developmental psychopathology perspective with scholars whose research focused on individual or familial characteristics that might be precursors to bulimia nervosa. The result is a thought-provoking integration of theory and research—with a bit of speculation—regarding the etiology of eating problems and eating disorders, particularly bulimia nervosa. We believe that *The Etiology of Bulimia Nervosa: The Individual and Familial Context* has met our goals.

Like its predecessor in this series, *Stress and Coping in Later-Life Families,* this book is unique with respect to the processes involved in its development. In large part, the volume is a product of the 1990 Kent Psychology Forum, where the volume's contributors presented the ideas regarding the etiology of bulimia nervosa represented in their chapters and participated in wide-ranging discussions of their ideas and the ideas of other experts in the field. As

a result, each chapter not only has been written by one of the leading researchers in the field, but also has benefited from the input of other chapters' contributors.

The Kent Psychology Forum was sponsored by the Applied Psychology
Center at Kent State University. The primary mission of the Applied Psychology Center is the facilitation and dissemination of applied psychological research. From its inception, the forum evolved as one means of achieving these
goals. However, the forum differs from typical research conferences, which
seek large registration and broad topic coverage. Instead, the forum seeks to
limit participation to a small group of invited scholars and active professionals
who share an interest in a specific research area. The intent is to foster intense
exchanges on theory and research in various arenas of applied psychology.

The 1990 forum on the etiology of bulimia nervosa was the second in a
series of three forums that focus in various ways on families and health, broadly
defined. The chair of the second forum was Janis H. Crowther, and co-chairs
were Daniel L. Tennenbaum, Stevan Hobfoll, and Mary Ann Parris Stephens.
All of the participants met for three days in October 1990 at Quail Hollow
Resort in northeastern Ohio. We hope that the forum produced not only the
ideas represented in this volume, but productive and collaborative working
relationships as well.

Because this volume approaches the theory and empirical research on the
etiology of bulimia nervosa from a unique perspective—that of focusing on
developmental, familial, and individual factors that may be involved in the
etiology of this disorder—this volume will be of interest to individuals in psychology, psychiatry, nursing, public health, and social work. In addition, because of the nature of the volume and its implications for prevention and intervention, this volume will also be of interest to mental health professionals who
are developing and offering prevention and intervention services to young
women. This book could also serve as a text in a graduate level psychopathology course focusing on eating disorders.

One final note: contributors throughout this volume tend to refer to eating
disorder subjects as girls or women. It was not our intent to ignore men with
eating disorders; the use of these terms only reflects the fact that women constitute the majority of cases of bulimia nervosa.

Janis H. Crowther
Daniel L. Tennenbaum
Stevan E. Hobfoll
Mary Ann Parris Stephens

ACKNOWLEDGMENTS

We acknowledge the contributions of several people whose efforts and resources made the Kent Psychology Forum and this accompanying volume possible. We are very grateful to the Ohio Board of Regents, whose Academic Challenge Award led to the creation of the Applied Psychology Center, whose purpose is the facilitation and dissemination of applied psychological research. We also thank our colleagues in the Department of Psychology at Kent State University who were instrumental in the development of the concept of the forum and who provided many tangible and intangible forms of support during the forum and the preparation of this volume. Special thanks go to Judy Jerkich and Joan Lash, for their organizational abilities and secretarial assistance, and to Mark Kuhnert and Nancy Sherwood for their careful proofreading of the chapters in this volume.

EPIDEMIOLOGY OF BULIMIA NERVOSA

Janis H. Crowther
Kent State University

Eve M. Wolf
Ellis Institute and Wright State University

Nancy E. Sherwood
Kent State University

Bulimia nervosa has been the focus of considerable attention in both the scientific and popular literature since 1980 when it was introduced as a diagnostic entity in the third edition of the *Diagnostic and Statistical Manual* (*DSM-III*; American Psychiatric Association [APA], 1980). Among the cardinal features of bulimia nervosa are cyclical episodes of bingeing and purging (the latter including self-induced vomiting), laxatives, diuretics, and strict dieting or fasting to counteract the weight gain associated with excessive caloric consumption. Central to this disorder are the feelings of loss of control over eating during a binge and a persistent overconcern with weight and shape (APA, 1987).

Although eating disorders generally are thought to be characteristic of modern society, some evidence has shown that eating-disordered symptomatology existed during ancient and medieval times (Wilson, Hogan, & Mintz, 1983). During ancient times, the Egyptians believed that food was a predominant etiological factor in disease and, thus, deliberately purged on a monthly basis, and the Romans were renowned for their vomitoriums (Bliss & Branch, 1960). During the high Middle Ages, many young women, motivated by religious conviction, engaged in rigorous fasts of some duration, surviving by eating only tiny portions of food with enough nutritional value to sustain life (Brumberg, 1988). Although anorexia nervosa was recognized as a clinical entity during the late 1800s (Gull, 1873; Lasegue, 1873), one of the earliest descriptions of binge eating was offered by Stunkard in 1959. As reports of a syndrome characterized primarily by episodes of uncontrolled eating began emerging in the 1970s, various diagnostic terms were introduced, including compulsive eating (Ondercin, 1979), the dietary chaos syndrome (Palmer, 1979), bulimarexia (Boskind-Lodahl & Sirlin, 1977), bulimia nervosa (Russell, 1979), and bulimia (APA, 1980).

Most researchers agreed that bulimia nervosa is a complex psychological disorder with a multifactorial etiology (e.g., Johnson & Connors, 1987; Mizes, 1985). To understand its cause more clearly, models are needed that not only incorporate individual, familial, and sociocultural factors but also recognize that these factors, individually or in combination, may have differential effects in those young women who subsequently develop bulimia nervosa. By way of introduction, we address the following questions. First, how has the diagnosis of bulimia nervosa evolved? Second, what is the prevalence of bulimia nervosa among various populations? Finally, given that most young women today experience a sociocultural milieu that emphasizes the importance of physical attractiveness and a thin, tubular physique, how can we best begin to understand the roles of developmental, familial, and individual factors in increasing a young woman's vulnerability to this disorder?

BULIMIA NERVOSA: AN EVOLVING DISORDER

In the revision of *DSM-III* (*DSM-III-R*; APA, 1987), several changes were made in the diagnostic terminology and criteria for the eating disorders, particularly for bulimia nervosa. First, the diagnostic term *bulimia* was replaced with the term *bulimia nervosa*. At least one of the reasons for this change involved the confusion over the use of the term bulimia (Fairburn & Garner, 1986). It had been used interchangeably in the eating-disorder literature to refer both to the symptom of binge eating and the more severe clinical syndrome characterized by a constellation of symptoms including cyclical episodes of bingeing and purging (Fairburn & Garner, 1986). Yet the symptom of bulimia (referring to binge eating) is far more prevalent than the syndrome of bulimia (e.g., Crowther, Post, & Zaynor, 1985; Pyle et al., 1983); it occurs among underweight, normal-weight, and overweight populations (Wolf & Crowther, 1983); and in the absence of purging as an extreme weight-control method, the symptom of bulimia did not necessarily distinguish eating-disordered populations from normal-weight and overweight populations.

Second, although the diagnostic criteria of recurrent binge episodes and a feeling of lack of control over eating during a binge were maintained in *DSM-III-R*, the remaining *DSM-III* diagnostic criteria were eliminated. These included the individuals' awareness that their eating patterns were abnormal, the presence of depression or self-deprecating thoughts after eating binges, and the presence of at least three of the following:

(1) consumption of high-caloric, easily ingested food during a binge; (2) inconspicuous eating during a binge; (3) termination of such eating episodes by abdom-

inal pain, sleep, social interruption, or self-induced vomiting; (4) repeated attempts to lose weight by severely restrictive diets, self-induced vomiting, or the use of cathartics or diuretics; [or] (5) frequent weight fluctuations greater than ten pounds due to alternating binges and fasts. (APA, 1980, pp. 70–71)

The original diagnostic criteria were criticized for being overinclusive primarily because of their emphasis on bulimia as a symptom of uncontrolled overeating as opposed to bulimia nervosa as a clinical syndrome (Fairburn & Garner, 1986). These criteria were also criticized for neglecting the extreme concerns about weight and shape and maladaptive weight-control measures including self-induced vomiting, the use of laxatives or diuretics, or rigid dieting or fasting, which are characteristic of clinical samples of bulimic individuals. Interestingly, under the *DSM-III* diagnostic criteria, an individual could receive a diagnosis of bulimia without ever engaging in repeated weight-control measures or without engaging in binge eating with any prescribed frequency. The current diagnostic criteria for bulimia nervosa have addressed these issues by requiring a minimum frequency of binge episodes, the regular use of extreme methods of weight control, and the presence of overconcern with body shape and weight (APA, 1987).

Currently, the *DSM-III-R* criteria for bulimia nervosa (APA, 1987) are as follows:

A. Recurrent episodes of binge eating (rapid consumption of a large amount of food in a discrete period of time).

B. A feeling of lack of control over eating behavior during the eating binges.

C. The person regularly engages in either self-induced vomiting, use of laxatives or diuretics, strict dieting or fasting, or vigorous exercise in order to prevent weight gain.

D. A minimum average of two binge eating episodes a week for at least three months.

E. Persistent overconcern with body shape and weight. (pp. 68–69)

A related issue involves the complicated interrelationship between bulimia nervosa and anorexia nervosa. Whereas bulimia nervosa is characterized by episodes of excessive overeating accompanied by a subjective loss of control, anorexia nervosa is an eating disorder whose central feature is the maintenance of extremely low body weight. Accompanying this refusal to maintain a normal weight are severe body-image disturbance, an intense fear of gaining weight, and amenorrhea (APA, 1987). Several lines of research raised questions regarding whether or not anorexia nervosa and bulimia nervosa represent clearly different forms of psychopathology. First, two anorectic subgroups have been identified: restricting anorexics, who exert excessive control over their caloric intake, and bulimic anorexics, who may engage in both bingeing and purging (e.g., Casper, Eckert, Halmi, Goldberg, & Davis, 1980; Garfinkel, Moldofsky, & Garner, 1980). Second, many bulimics report a history of anorexia nervosa (e.g., Vandereycken & Meerman, 1984). Finally, there is reason to believe that there are more similarities between bulimic anorexics and normal-weight bulimics than between restricting and bulimic anorexics (e.g., Wonderlich, this volume, ch. 6). Although distinctions between the two disorders often have been made historically on the basis of weight, research on the epidemiology of bulimia nervosa may need to pay particular attention to the differential diagnosis of these two disorders in the definition of a case.

EPIDEMIOLOGY OF BULIMIA NERVOSA

Methodological Issues

Over the past 10 years, much research has been generated in attempts to establish accurate prevalence rates for bulimia nervosa and associated bulimic behaviors. As Johnson and Connors (1987) noted:

> *Epidemiological studies are necessary to generate information concerning prevalence rates, variation of these rates in different populations, and identification of risk factors which increase the likelihood of developing the disorder. This information is vital for planning treatment and prevention strategies to meet the needs of the affected or at risk population. However, the information is all predicated on the ability to define what constitutes a "case" of the disorder and to distinguish clearly between "cases" and "normals." (p. 14)*

Unfortunately, epidemiological studies on bulimia have been plagued by problems of case definition. Primarily, two areas of controversy have had impact on case-definition problems in bulimia prevalence research. The first controversy relates to the definition of binge eating. Although most researchers agree that binge eating refers to the consumption of a large amount of food in a relatively short period of time, there is disagreement as to whether the subjective definition of binge eating should be operationalized in terms of the amount of food consumed or the length of time. Moreover, researchers varied in including loss of control over eating as part of the operational definition of binge eating (Pyle & Mitchell, 1986).

The second area of controversy in bulimia research relates to problems in choosing the proper inclusion criteria to define the bulimic syndrome (Pyle & Mitchell, 1986). With the inclusion of bulimia as a psychiatric disorder in the *DSM-III* (APA, 1980), uniform diagnostic criteria were introduced. However, many researchers viewed the *DSM-III* criteria as overly broad and used modified *DSM-III* criteria in their epidemiological research (e.g., Crowther et al., 1985; Pyle, Halvorson, Neuman, & Mitchell, 1986), most commonly including a frequency criterion and the use of extreme weight-control measures as cardinal features of this disorder. Finally, with the publication of *DSM-III-R* (APA, 1987), the syndrome was renamed bulimia nervosa, and the diagnostic criteria were changed. Thus, one reason for the wide differences in the reported estimates of the prevalence of bulimia may be differences in the criteria used.

In addition to definitional problems, other methodological limitations and inconsistencies have confounded the interpretation of prevalence data. These methodological problems have been grouped into three major categories: sampling issues, method of assessment, and scope of assessment (e.g., Connors & Johnson, 1987; Fairburn, 1984). Prevalence estimates may reflect significant differences among the subjects sampled. Different subject groups have included junior high, high school, and college students; attenders at various clinics; magazine readers; and women interviewed while shopping. In addition, there may be significant differences among apparently homogeneous samples on such variables as age, socioeconomic status, and racial composition. Other factors such as geographical location, size of community or school, and social climate may also create variability among samples (Connors & Johnson, 1987). Additional sampling issues relate to external validity. That most prevalence studies have been conducted on student populations in the United States seriously limits generalizability. Moreover, in some studies, it is open to question whether the samples have been representative of the populations from which they were drawn (Fairburn, 1984). This is particularly a factor in studies with relatively low return rates on questionnaires in which no follow-up was conducted to determine who was noncompliant and why (Connors & Johnson, 1987).

Numerous researchers highlighted problems in methods of assessment. Pyle and Mitchell (1986) noted that although prevalence studies should involve the administration of a standardized, validated questionnaire to a sample representative of the general population, ideally through a structured interview, most prevalence studies have been limited to the use of self-report questionnaires. Self-report questionnaire studies are limited by a number of problems including the fact that researchers must select wording that subjects will understand and that correctly represents the diagnostic criteria. Questionnaires are often limited to diagnostic inclusion criteria to maintain brevity and maximize response rate, thereby sacrificing detail necessary to measure lifetime prevalence of the disorder, associated psychopathological and risk factors, and more complex behaviors and attitudes (Pyle & Mitchell, 1986). There have been potential problems with the actual questionnaires used in many of the studies. Several new questionnaires have been developed for prevalence studies but have not been adequately assessed with regard to their reliability or validity (Fairburn, 1984; Pyle & Mitchell, 1986). Few questionnaires have been validated by administering them to eating-disordered populations to determine their specificity for identifying that particular disorder (Pyle & Mitchell, 1986). Additional assessment problems include differences in the time period included in the assessment (e.g., current behavior, past month, past year) and social desirability factors. For example, controversy persists about whether subjects overreport on questionnaires in an attempt to please researchers or underreport in an attempt to keep their eating problems secret (Connors & Johnson, 1987; Pyle & Mitchell, 1986).

Fairburn (1984) noted three major limitations regarding the scope of assessment in epidemiological research on bulimia. First, primary emphasis has been on the assessment of eating habits, typically neglecting subjects' attitudes toward food, body weight, and shape. Second, some studies provided inadequate information on the frequency of various eating habits, apparently failing to recognize the difference in the clinical significance of ever having engaged in a given behavior (e.g., bingeing or self-induced vomiting) versus engaging in the behavior regularly at present. Finally, most studies focused only on the statistical significance of their findings, thereby neglecting the clinical significance. For example, just because subjects have abnormal eating habits in the statistical sense does not mean they regard them as a problem, or desire or are in need of treatment. Along these lines, Fairburn (1984) noted that although cross-sectional research yielding retrospective data on the duration of key features of bulimia is important, it needs to be supplemented with information obtained from longitudinal studies to distinguish transitory abnormalities from more enduring problems.

Prevalence of Bulimia in Secondary School Students

The 17 studies reviewed in Table 1 report differing estimates of the prevalence of bulimia in junior high and high school students. When one examines only studies that used *DSM-III* inclusion criteria (at times slightly modified), these 11 studies yield prevalence rates ranging from 1.2% to 16% in girls (Crowther et al., 1985; Greenfeld, Quinlan, Harding, Glass, & Bliss, 1987; Gross & Rosen, 1988; Howat & Saxton, 1987; Johnson, Lewis, Love, Lewis, & Stuckey, 1984; Lachenmeyer & Muni-Brander, 1988; Lakin & McClelland, 1987; Maceyko & Nagelberg, 1985; Stein & Brinza, 1989; VanThorre & Vogel, 1985; Whitaker et al., 1989). When one eliminates studies that used measures that have not been shown to operationalize the *DSM-III* criteria adequately, for example, the Eating Attitudes Test (EAT; Garner & Garfinkel, 1979) and the Eating Disorder Inventory (EDI; Garner, Olmstead, & Polivy, 1983), the remaining studies yield prevalence rates ranging from 1.2% to 9.7% of girls. Six of the 17 studies using *DSM-III* criteria provided prevalence data on boys (Greenfeld et al., 1987; Gross & Rosen, 1988; Lachenmeyer & Muni-Brander, 1988; Lakin & McClelland, 1987; Maceyko & Nagelberg, 1985; Whitaker et al., 1989) that ranged from 0% to approximately 4.4%. It should be

TABLE 1 Prevalence in secondary school students

Reference	Subjects	Response rate	Inclusion criteria[a]				Screening instrument[b]				Prevalence findings
			DSM-III	Mod. DSM	DSM-III-R	Other	SRQ	EAT	EDI	Other	
Carter & Duncan (1984)	421 girls	NR				X	X	X			7.1% reported binge eating and self-induced vomiting
Johnson et al. (1984)	1,268 girls	98.1%		X			X				4.9% met criteria for bulimia
Moss et al. (1984)	151 10th-grade girls	NR				X		X			6.6% reported binge eating and self-induced vomiting
Crowther et al. (1985)	363 girls	34.0%		X			X				7.7% met criteria for bulimia
Maceyko & Nagelberg (1985)	257 boys and girls	80.0%		X			X				7.1% of girls and no boys met criteria for bulimia
VanThorre & Vogel (1985)	1,093 girls	100.0%	X						X		16% were probably bulimic; equally distributed in white and black groups
Hendren et al. (1986)	592 girls	NR				X	X				18% reported at least one major eating disorder symptom
Killen et al. (1986)	1,728 10th-grade boys and girls	100.0%				X	X				13% reported use of extreme weight-control measures
Leichner et al. (1986)	5,150 males and females (7th grade to college)	94.0%				X		X			22% of females and 5% of males had EAT scores ≥30
Greenfeld et al. (1987)	761 boys and girls	79–89%	X				X				4% of girls and 0.8% of boys met criteria for bulimia
Howat & Saxton (1987)	1,457 high school and college males and females	97.0%	X							X	6.7% of females and 0.21% of males met criteria for bulimia

(*Table continues on next page*)

TABLE 1 Prevalence in secondary school students (*continued*)

Reference	Subjects	Response rate	Inclusion criteria[a]				Screening instrument[b]				Prevalence findings
			DSM-III	Mod. DSM	DSM-III-R	Other	SRQ	EAT	EDI	Other	
Lakin & McClelland (1987)	126 boys and girls	70.4%	X							X	7.1% of girls and 1.8% of boys met criteria for bulimia
Gross & Rosen (1988)	1,373 boys and girls	85.0%		X			X	X	X		9.6% of girls met criteria for bulimia (2.2% with and 7.4% without purging); 1.2% of boys met criteria for bulimia (0.1% with and 1.1% without purging)
Lachenmeyer & Muni-Brander (1988)	1,261 boys and girls	NR	X				X	X			8.6% of girls and 4.4% of boys met criteria for bulimia; 7.6% of low SES and 5.2% of high SES met criteria for bulimia
Brown et al. (1988)	1,262 girls aged 15–19 years	NR				X	X				9% reported bingeing and self-vomiting
Stein & Brinza (1989)	547 junior high and high school girls	78.7%	X			X				X	2.4% of junior high and 4.4% of high school girls met cutoff for bulimia; interview yielded prevalence > 1.7%
Whitaker et al. (1989)	5,596 boys and girls	91.0%				X	X	X			1.2% of girls and 0.4% of boys met criteria for bulimia

Note. DSM-III-R = *Diagnostic and Statistical Manual of Mental Disorders* (3rd edition, revised). NR = not reported. SRQ = self-report questionnaire developed by authors; EAT = Eating Attitudes Test; EDI = eating disorder inventory; Mod. *DSM* = modified *DSM-III* criteria; SES = socioeconomic status.

[a]Other refers to other criteria stipulated by authors.

[b]Other refers to the use of another published questionnaire (e.g., Binge Scale, Bulimia Test) or use of an interview.

noted that to date, to our knowledge, no published studies on secondary school populations have reported prevalence findings using the *DSM-III-R* (APA, 1987) criteria for bulimia nervosa.

Although there is undoubtedly some variability in the true prevalence of bulimia in adolescent samples, Table 1 suggests that some inconsistency in findings may be the result of the diverse diagnostic criteria used, problems with the screening measures, and varying response rates (Stein & Brinza, 1989). Even among studies that reportedly used *DSM-III* criteria, modifications in these criteria varied. In different studies, subjects were required to binge eat at least once weekly (e.g., Johnson et al., 1984; Maceyko & Nagelberg, 1985), a minimum of once every 2 weeks (Crowther et al., 1985), and at least once per month (Gross & Rosen, 1988). Crowther et al. (1985) provided an excellent illustration of how minor modifications in diagnostic criteria can affect prevalence rates (Stein & Brinza, 1989). When criteria included binge eating "at least once every 2 weeks," a prevalence rate of 7.7% resulted. When the criteria were modified to include "at least weekly binge eating," 5.2% of the subjects met these more stringent diagnostic criteria. The prevalence rate decreased to 2.8% when these criteria were further modified to require the presence of at least weekly binge eating and purging only by means of self-induced vomiting or the use of laxatives.

Many of the studies in Table 1 are limited by the types of self-report measures used. Eleven of the 17 studies used questionnaires developed specifically by the authors for their research. Almost half of the studies relied solely on newly developed questionnaires to gather prevalence data on bulimia. However, validity and reliability data on many of these questionnaires remain to be established. Several studies used the EAT (Garner & Garfinkel, 1979) and the EDI (Garner et al., 1983) to make diagnostic decisions yet these measures are not specific to *DSM-III* (or *DSM-III-R*) diagnostic criteria for bulimia. The Bulimia Test (BULIT; Smith & Thelen, 1984) is a more specific alternative that was used in 2 of the studies; however, normative data on using the BULIT with junior high and high school studies have not yet been published (Stein & Brinza, 1989).

Two of the most recent prevalence reports are noteworthy. In response to the fact that most prevalence studies sampled populations drawn only from urban areas, Stein and Brinza (1989) examined the prevalence of bulimia in female junior high and high school students residing in an agricultural community within a large, rural catchment area. Although these authors screened participants with the Anorexia-Bulimia Inventory, which they are in the process of developing, they also used the BULIT to strengthen their judgments. The authors then conducted follow-up interviews with subgroups of clinical and control participants screened for bulimia by the self-report measures. Clearly, this method of assessment is more rigorous than that found in much of the prevalence research. Their results indicated a low level of correspondence between self-report and interview data. In a final study, Whitaker et al. (1989) conducted a survey of a county-wide high school population. Although the authors used their Eating Symptoms Inventory to assess *DSM–III* criteria, their sample size (N = 5,596) and survey completion rate (91%) were exemplary. Interestingly, both of these studies yielded fairly low prevalence rate for bulimia among high school students.

Prevalence of Bulimia or Bulimia Nervosa in College Students

Table 2 summarizes 18 studies on the prevalence of bulimia or bulimia nervosa among college students. These reports reflect a great deal of variability in prevalence findings; figures range from 0.79% to 19% of the women sampled. Although this discrepancy in figures appears quite dramatic, the range can be greatly reduced simply by examining inclusion criteria more closely. When one separates studies based predominantly on *DSM–III* criteria from those based on *DSM–III–R*, prevalence rates for *DSM–III* range from 1.6% to 19% of women (Gray & Ford, 1985; Halmi, Falk, & Schwartz, 1981; Healy, Conroy, & Walsh, 1985; Herzog, Norman, Rigotti, & Pepose, 1986; Katzman, Wolchik, & Braver, 1984; Nevo, 1985; Pope, Hudson, Yurgelun-Todd, & Hudson, 1984; Pyle et al., 1983; Pyle et al., 1986; Schotte & Stunkard, 1987; Stangler & Printz, 1980; Thelen, Mann, Pruitt, & Smith, 1987; Whitehouse & Button, 1988; Zuckerman, Colby, Ware, & Lazerson, 1986), whereas reported rates for *DSM–III–R* range only from 0.79% to 3.8% of women (Drewnowski, Hopkins, & Kessler, 1988; Drewnowski, Yee, & Krahn, 1988; Mintz & Betz, 1988; Schotte & Stunkard, 1987; Striegel-Moore, Silberstein, Frensch, & Rodin, 1989). Clearly, one result of the narrower definition of bulimia nervosa provided by *DSM–III–R* appears to be lower and less variable prevalence rates reported by various researchers. Yet it should also be noted that 13 of the studies in Table 2 used *DSM–III* or modified *DSM–III* criteria, 1 study used *DSM–III* or *DSM–III–R* diagnostic criteria, and only 4 studies to date are based solely on *DSM–III–R* criteria. Thus, one may see more variability as the number of reports based on *DSM–III–R* increases.

In contrast to the reported findings in college-aged women, bulimia has been reported only in a minority of college men sampled; *DSM–III* prevalence figures range from 0% to 5% (Gray & Ford, 1985; Halmi et al., 1981; Healy et al., 1985; Pope, Hudson, Yurgelun-Todd, & Hudson, 1984; Pyle et al., 1983; Pyle et al., 1986; Schotte & Stunkard, 1987; Stangler & Printz, 1980; Whitehouse & Button, 1988; Zuckerman et al., 1986). To date, only three studies examined the prevalence of bulimia nervosa in college men (Drewnowski, Hopkins, & Kessler, 1988; Schotte & Stunkard, 1987; Striegel-Moore et al., 1989). Using *DSM–III–R* criteria, prevalence figures ranged from 0.1% to 0.2%.

TABLE 2 Prevalence in college students

| Reference | Subjects | Response rate | Inclusion criteria | | | Screening instrument[a] | | | | Prevalence findings |
			DSM-III	Mod. DSM	DSM-III-R	SRQ	BULIT	INT	Other	
Stangler & Printz (1980)	500 men and women		X						X	5.3% of women and 1.1% of men met criteria for bulimia through review of records at university clinic
Halmi et al. (1981)	355 men and women in summer school	66.0%	X			X				19% of women and 5% of men met criteria for bulimia
Pyle et al. (1983)	1,355 men and women	98.3%		X		X				7.8% of women and 1.4% of men met *DSM-III* criteria A, B, and D; 4.5% of women and 0.4% of men met these criteria plus weekly binge eating; 1% of women and 0.3% of men met these criteria plus weekly purging
Katzman et al. (1984)	485 women (105 more closely screened)	71.0%		X		X				3.9% met criteria for bulimia, with at least eight 1,200-calorie binges and two extreme weight-control attempts in past month
Pope et al. (1984)	310 high school, 750 college-aged men and women	50–85%	X			X				6.5–18.6% of women and no men met criteria for a history of bulimia
Gray & Ford (1985)	339 men and women	54.0%	X			X				13% of women and 4% of men met criteria for bulimia

(*Table continues on next page*)

11

TABLE 2 Prevalence in college students (*continued*)

Reference	Subjects	Response rate	Inclusion criteria			Screening instrument[a]				Prevalence findings
			DSM-III	Mod. DSM	DSM-III-R	SRQ	BULIT	INT	Other	
Healy et al. (1985)	1,063 men and women	95.0%	X			X				2.7% of women and no men met criteria for bulimia
Nevo (1985)	689 women	90.0%	X			X		X		11% (14% of white and 2.7% of Asian-American samples) met criteria for bulimia; with interview, 4.6–11% met criteria (6–14% of whites)
Herzog et al. (1986)	550 women (medical, business, law students)	49.8%		X		X				10.2% met criteria for bulimia with at least weekly binge/purge episodes and 5-pound fluctuations
Pyle et al. (1986)[b]	1,389 freshmen men and women	95.9%	X			X				8% of women and 1 of 660 men met criteria for bulimia; 3.2% of women met criteria with at least weekly bingeing and purging
Zuckerman et al. (1986)	907 men and women	75.0%		X		X				8% of women and 0.7% of men met criteria for bulimia; 4% of women and 0.4% of men met criteria with at least weekly bingeing
Schotte & Stunkard (1987)	1,965 men and women	97.3%	X		X	X		X		1.3% of women met either DSM-III or DSM-III-R criteria; 0.79% of women and 0.1% of men met DSM-III-R criteria

Study	Sample	Response rate	SRQ	BULIT	INT	Other	Results
Thelen et al. (1987)	1,858 women	NR	X	X			2.0–3.8% met criteria for bulimia
Whitehouse and Button (1988)	578 men and women	NR	X	X		X	1.6% of women met criteria for bulimia; no men met EAT cutoff so none were interviewed
Drewnowski, Yee, & Krahn (1988)	931 freshman women (fall), 599 (spring)	41.9% (fall) 64.3% (spring)			X		2.9% in fall and 3.3% in spring met criteria for bulimia nervosa
Drewnowski, Hopkins, & Kessler (1988)	1,005 male and female college and graduate students	56.4%			X	X	1% of women and 0.2% of men met criteria for bulimia nervosa
Mintz & Betz (1988)	682 women	NR	X	X			3% met criteria for bulimia nervosa
Striegel-Moore et al. (1989)	1,040 men and women baseline; 949 follow-up	74.5% baseline; 70.5% follow-up	X	X			3.8% of women and 0.2% of men met criteria for bulimia nervosa; figures virtually unchanged at follow-up

Note. DSM-III-R = Diagnostic and Statistical Manual of Mental Disorders (3rd edition, revised); NR = not reported; Mod. *DSM* = modified *DSM-III* criteria; SRQ = self-report questionnaire developed by authors; BULIT = Bulimia Test; INT = interview.
[a]Other refers to the use of other published scales or procedures, including record reviews.
[b]Note three-fold increase from 1983 study.

A review of the studies in Table 2 suggests that, in addition to inconsistencies in inclusion criteria, there is wide variability in response rates and screening instruments used. Thirteen of 18 studies used questionnaires newly developed by the authors to screen for bulimia or bulimia nervosa. Of the remaining 5 studies, 1 used an unpublished questionnaire developed by another author, 1 used a record review of diagnoses (given after a diagnostic interview), 1 used telephone interviews, and 1 used the EAT, which has not demonstrated sufficient specificity as a diagnostic screening device for bulimia. Only 1 of the 18 studies used the BULIT, which has demonstrated some validity and reliability in screening college students for the symptoms of bulimia; this study was conducted by the scale's authors. A promising trend is that 4 of the 18 studies used some type of interview in the screening process. Although some investigators reported significant discrepancies in data obtained from questionnaires versus interviews, continued work with interviews appears to be a positive step. It is hoped that, with the advent of *DSM-III-R*, research will progress in developing reliable and valid screening procedures for bulimia nervosa and for consistently using them in epidemiological research.

A final methodological issue to be noted in prevalence research on college students is that there is inconsistency in whether researchers report the mean age of their samples. At least one third of the studies in Table 2 did not report this datum, which is crucial in reconciling discrepant findings. For example, according to one hypothesis, the vast difference in prevalence findings in the studies by Halmi et al. (1981) and Pyle et al. (1983) may be due to the fact the Halmi et al. summer school students were, on the average, about 7 years older than the Pyle et al. students, perhaps allowing more time for cases of bulimia to have developed (Pope, Hudson, Yurgelun-Todd, & Hudson, 1984). (Interestingly, other hypotheses include differences in the samples and diagnostic criteria used in the respective studies.)

Prevalence of Bulimia or Bulimia Nervosa in Community Samples

Table 3 summarizes the results of 11 studies that have addressed the prevalence of bulimia or bulimia nervosa in community samples. Although interesting findings have emerged and researchers should be applauded for their efforts in leaving the university or school system and addressing bulimia in the community at large, definitive conclusions cannot be drawn because of the sheer paucity of studies and methodological problems inherent in conducting survey research in community settings. Prevalence rates in community surveys ranged from 1% to 13% of females sampled using *DSM-III* criteria (Ben-Tovim, 1988; Ben-Tovim, Subbiah, Scheutz, & Morton, 1989; Cullberg & Engstrom-Lindberg, 1988; Hart & Ollendick, 1985; Martin & Wollitzer, 1988; Pope, Champoux, & Hudson, 1987; Pope, Hudson, & Yurgelun-Todd, 1984;

TABLE 3 Prevalence in community samples

Reference	Subjects	Response rate	Inclusion criteria				Screening instrument[a]				Prevalence findings
			DSM-III	Mod. DSM	DSM-III-R	Russell	SRQ	EAT	EDI	Other	
Cooper & Fairburn (1983)	369 women at family planning clinic	96.1%				X	X				1.9% met criteria for bulimia nervosa
Pope, Hudson, & Yurgelun-Todd (1984)	200 female shoppers	98.7%	X				X				10.3% met criteria for lifetime diagnosis; 3% met criteria plus weekly bingeing and purging
Zinkand et al. (1984)	176 male and female medical patients	95.0%	X					X			10.9% met criteria for bulimia
Hart & Ollendick (1985)	139 female employees and 234 college students	46.0% (employee); 100.0% (student)	X				X			X	1% of bank employees and 5% of college of college students met criteria for bulimia
Cooper et al. (1987)	331 women at family planning clinic	90.0%				X	X				1.8% met criteria for bulimia nervosa
Pope et al. (1987)	394 women at bingo	97.0%		X	X		X				11.9–24.7% met DSM-III or modified DSM-III-R criteria; 4.3–17.5% only met modified DSM-III-R; higher rates with lower income

(Table contines on next page)

15

TABLE 3 Prevalence in community samples (*continued*)

Reference	Subjects	Response rate	Inclusion criteria				Screening instrument[a]				Prevalence findings
			DSM-III	Mod. DSM-III	DSM-III-R	Russell	SRQ	EAT	EDI	Other	
Ben-Tovim (1988)	389 female shoppers	66.0%	X	X	X		X				12.7% met *DSM-III* criteria
	220 female medical patients	94.0%									0.67% met *DSM-III* criteria with monthly binge/purge
	792 high school girls	74.1%									1.7% met criteria A, B, C, and modified D of draft *DSM-III-R*
Cullberg & Engstrom-Lindberg (1988)	4,651 men and women aged 16–24 years		X							X	0.5% of women met criteria for bulimia through case-finding procedures
Martin & Wollitzer (1988)	277 female medical patients	52.0%		X			X				3.7% met criteria for bulimia with history of weekly purging
Ben-Tovim et al. (1989)	312 female shoppers	66.0%	X	X	X		X				13% met *DSM-III* criteria
	220 female medical patients	94.0%									1.9% met *DSM-III* criteria plus self-induced vomiting
	356 high school girls	74.0%									1.4% of medical and high school samples met draft *DSM-IIIR*
King (1989)	729 male and female patients	96.0%				X	X	X		X	1.1% of women and 0.5% men met criteria for bulimia nervosa

Note. DSM-III-R = Diagnostic and Statistical Manual of Mental Disorders (3rd edition, revised); Mod. *DSM* = modified *DSM-III* criteria; SRQ = self-report questionnaire developed by authors; EAT = Eating Attitudes Test; EDI = Eating Disorder Inventory.
[a]Other refers to the use of interview or case-finding procedures.

Zinkard, Cadoret, & Widmer, 1984) and from 1.4% to 1.7% of females using *DSM-III-R* (Ben-Tovim, 1988; Ben-Tovim et al., 1989; Pope et al., 1987). Similar to the *DSM-III-R* findings, 3 studies using Russell's (1979) criteria for bulimia nervosa produced prevalence rates in female samples ranging from 1.1% to 1.9% (Cooper, Charnock, & Taylor, 1987; Cooper & Fairburn, 1983; King, 1989). Thus, the findings are consistent with Fairburn and Cooper's (1984) conclusion that bulimia constitutes a significant undetected source of psychiatric morbidity and is by no means confined to student populations.

The studies in Table 3 illustrate a variety of methodological issues in bulimia prevalence studies on community samples. The limited representativeness of subject samples is a major problem in all of the studies. One can only speculate about the nature of the bias introduced by sampling female attenders at family planning clinics, female bank employees, female shoppers, female family practice patients, and females attending bingo tournaments. Varied inclusion criteria were used including *DSM-III*, several modified versions of *DSM-III*, modifications of *DSM-III-R*, and Russell's (1979) criteria. Screening instruments were most commonly self-report questionnaires newly developed by the authors for their research or eating-related measures not specific to the diagnosis of bulimia. Men have clearly been neglected in community studies; only one study reported cases of bulimia nervosa in a male sample (King, 1989). Finally, two studies included high school students in their community samples (Ben-Tovim, 1988; Ben-Tovim et al., 1989), thereby clouding the issue of the prevalence of this disorder in nonstudent adults.

PURPOSE OF THIS VOLUME

As this overview suggests, unlike anorexia nervosa, which was recognized as a clinical entity as early as the 1800s, bulimia nervosa is an eating disorder of relatively recent origin. Epidemiological research conducted primarily on adolescent and young adult samples suggests that the prevalence of bulimia nervosa ranges from 1% to 16% in junior and senior high school populations, from 1% to 13% in college-aged populations, and from less than 1% to 13% in community samples. Although changes in diagnostic criteria make it difficult to determine whether prevalence rates are increasing (as research by Pyle et al., 1986, suggests), it is clear that bulimia nervosa constitutes a significant disturbance for a variety of the populations sampled. Moreover, this research clearly indicates that risk for bulimia nervosa is associated with sex and race. Women are significantly more likely than men to develop bulimia nervosa; women make up 90% to 95% of all patients (Striegel-Moore, Silberstein, & Rodin, 1986). Additionally, most bulimia nervosa patients are white (e.g., Herzog, 1982; Johnson, Stuckey, Lewis, & Schwartz, 1982). Although bulimia nervosa has been identified among Asian and black women (e.g., Gray, Ford, & Kelly, 1987; Lacey &

Dolan, 1988; Nevo, 1985), the disorder remains underrepresented in minority populations.

Researchers generally agree that being young, female, and white in today's society increases one's risk for developing bulimia nervosa; however, there is considerably less agreement regarding the strength of association between other hypothesized risk factors and the disorder. For example, it has been suggested that low self-esteem, various personality characteristics, depression, body-image dissatisfaction, and chronic dieting may contribute to a young women's vulnerability to bulimia nervosa. Similarly, various familial factors, including socioeconomic status, family history of eating disorders, obesity, affective disorder, and substance abuse, and parental and familial pathology may also play a role in the development of this disorder. Although considerable research has documented the presence of many of these characteristics in populations with bulimia nervosa and even in individuals with subclinical eating disorders, there has been very little case control or prospective research that has investigated the role of both individual and familial factors in the cause and course of bulimia nervosa (e.g., Fairburn & Beglin, 1990). Furthermore, rather than investigating these factors in isolation, researchers must develop models that foster understanding and yield testable hypotheses concerning the dynamic interaction among various individual and familial risk factors.

The primary purpose of this volume is to bring together theory and research in three major areas pertaining to the cause of bulimia nervosa. Given that epidemiological research has documented the presence of bulimia nervosa in female high school populations, researchers must then focus on much younger female populations to identify the risk factors for this disorder before it emerges. If researchers focus on girls in their late elementary school and junior high school years, they must consider the role of the family and the impact of puberty because both are prominent influences on the lives of these young girls. Thus, the first section of this volume focuses on those familial and developmental factors that may be helpful to our understanding of the cause of bulimia nervosa. The second section focuses in more detail on various characteristics of the female adolescent that may have been influenced by familial and developmental factors and further increase her vulnerability to this disorder. Finally, as our understanding of the factors that increase a young woman's risk for bulimia nervosa increases, we can begin to focus on prevention. Thus, the final section of this volume focuses on primary prevention and directions for future research.

Figure 1 illustrates the relationships between the major constructs that are discussed further in the following chapters. Although sociocultural factors are not the focus of this volume, their inclusion in Figure 1 is intended to convey the fact that adolescent women today (and their mothers and sisters) are developing within a sociocultural milieu that values thinness and physical attractiveness and that stigmatizes obesity. In a now classic article, Garner, Garfinkel,

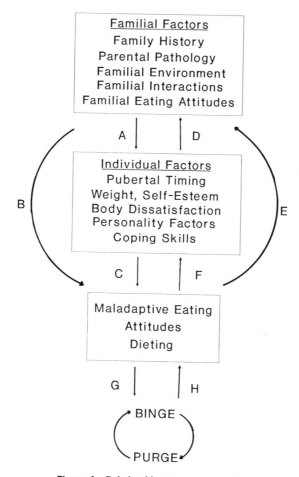

Sociocultural Milieu

Figure 1 Relationships among constructs.

Schwartz, and Thompson (1980) demonstrated that over time the average woman has experienced increases in weight, whereas the exemplars of female beauty (including beauty contestants and Playboy centerfolds) have moved toward an increasingly thin beauty ideal. Through the mass media, young women not only are exposed to a beauty ideal that is nearly impossible to attain but they are bombarded with articles on how to diet and exercise to try to achieve the ideal (Striegel-Moore et al., 1986). Although, it can be argued that most young women are exposed to these sociocultural pressures to achieve the thin beauty ideal, Figure 1 attempts to explain why only a very small percentage of young women develop bulimia nervosa.

In Figure 1, the boxes represent the general constructs that may increase risk for bulimia nervosa, and the arrows suggest possible causal pathways between the constructs of interest. These constructs and the hypothesized causal pathways between them are the foci of many of the chapters in this volume. Thus, the top two boxes are included in Figure 1 to denote those familial factors and individual factors that may increase young women's risk for maladaptive eating attitudes and behaviors (the bottom box). Included in the top box are those familial factors that may create risk for some form of psychopathology in the daughter (path A) as well as those factors that may contribute directly to the development of symptomatic eating attitudes and behaviors (path B). For example, maladaptive familial interactions may create risk for psychological maladjustment in the daughter (e.g., anxiety, depression, low self-esteem), whereas parental modeling of body dissatisfaction and dieting or communication of dissatisfaction with the daughter's body image may create risk for eating-specific psychopathology.

Included in the second box are those individual physiological and psychological characteristics, including the timing of puberty, body weight, body dissatisfaction, low self-esteem, affective instability, and inadequate coping repertoires, that may also increase risk for maladaptive eating attitudes and dieting behaviors (path C). Paths D, E, and F recognize that the causal pathways are not unidirectional. For example, an adolescent daughter who is experiencing psychological maladjustment or symptomatic eating problems may cause familial problems or exacerbate those familial characteristics that initially contributed to her pathology (paths D and E). Similarly, an adolescent girl with maladaptive eating attitudes who fails to achieve her weight goals may experience more difficulties with self-esteem and body image (path F).

Integral to this model is the theory and research supporting causal relationships between maladaptive eating attitudes and restrictive dieting behaviors (box C) and bulimic behaviors (e.g., Attie & Brooks-Gunn, this volume, ch. 3; Heatherton & Polivy, this volume, ch. 8) and causal relationships between the onset of bingeing and the onset of purging (e.g., Crowther et al., 1985; Johnson & Connors, 1987). Path G depicts the causal pathway linking restrictive dieting to binge eating and purging, whereas path H suggests that, once established, bingeing and purging may also maintain or exacerbate maladaptive eating attitudes and dieting behaviors.

Fairburn and Beglin (1990) argued that epidemiological research needs to shift its focus away from studies of the prevalence of bulimia nervosa to studies of the nature, cause, and course of the full spectrum of eating disorders. It is the intent of this volume to further our understanding of the complex interrelationships among developmental, familial, and individual factors that may be relevant to the etiology of bulimia nervosa. Each chapter in some way focuses on one or more of the constructs subsumed in the boxes as well as the hypothesized causal pathways between them. Ideally, by exploring these familial and individual factors in more detail, we may begin to clarify the many ways in which these factors increase young women's vulnerability to the development of bulimia nervosa.

REFERENCES

American Psychiatric Association. (1980). *Diagnostic and statistical manual of mental disorders* (3rd ed.). Washington, DC: Author.

American Psychiatric Association. (1987). *Diagnostic and statistical manual of mental disorders* (3rd ed., revised). Washington, DC: Author.

Ben-Tovim, D. I. (1988). DSM-III, draft DSM-III-R, and the diagnosis and prevalence of bulimia in Australia. *American Journal of Psychiatry, 145,* 1000–1002.

Ben-Tovim, D. I., Subbiah, N., Scheutz, B., & Morton, J. (1989). Bulimia: Symptoms and syndromes in an urban population. *Australian and New Zealand Journal of Psychiatry, 23,* 73–80.

Bliss, E. L., & Branch, C. H. H. (1960). *Anorexia nervosa: Its history, psychology and biology.* New York: Hoeber.

Boskind-Lodahl, M., & Sirlin, J. (1977, March). The gorging-purging syndrome. *Psychology Today,* pp. 50–52, 82–85.

Brown, T. A., Cash, T. F., & Lewis, R. J. (1988). Body-image disturbances in adolescent female binge-purgers: A brief report of the results of a national survey in the U.S.A. *Journal of Child Psychology and Psychiatry, 30,* 605–613.

Brumberg, J. J. (1988). *Fasting girls: The emergence of anorexia nervosa as a modern disease.* Cambridge, MA: Harvard University Press.

Casper, R., Eckert, E., Halmi, K., Goldberg, S., & Davis, J. (1980). Bulimia: Its incidence and clinical importance in patients with anorexia nervosa. *Archives of General Psychiatry, 37,* 1030–1035.

Carter, J. A., & Duncan, P. A. (1984). Binge-eating and vomiting: A survey of a high school population. *Psychology in the Schools, 21,* 198–203.

Connors, M. E., & Johnson, C. L. (1987). Epidemiology of bulimia and bulimic behaviors. *Addictive Behaviors, 12,* 165–179.

Cooper, P. J., Charnock, D. J., & Taylor, M. J. (1987). The prevalence of bulimia nervosa: A replication study. *British Journal of Psychiatry, 151,* 684–686.

Cooper, P. J., & Fairburn, C. G. (1983). Binge-eating and self-induced vomiting in the community: A preliminary study. *British Journal of Psychiatry, 142,* 139–144.

Crowther, J. H., Post, G., & Zaynor, L. (1985). The prevalence of bulimia and binge eating in adolescent girls. *International Journal of Eating Disorders, 1,* 29–42.

Cullberg, J., & Engstrom-Lindberg, M. (1988). Prevalence and incidence of eating disorders in a suburban area. *Acta Psychiatric Scandinavia, 78,* 314–319.

Drewnowski, A., Hopkins, S. A., & Kessler, R. C. (1988). The prevalence of bulimia nervosa in the US college student population. *American Journal of Public Health, 78,* 1322–1325.

Drewnowski, A., Yee, D. K., & Krahn, D. D. (1988). Bulimia in college women: Incidence and recovery rates. *American Journal of Psychiatry, 145,* 753–755.

Fairburn, C. G. (1984). Bulimia: Its epidemiology and management. In A. J. Stunkard & E. Stellar (Eds.), *Eating and its disorders* (pp. 235–258). New York: Raven Press.

Fairburn, C. G., & Beglin, S. J. (1990). Studies of the epidemiology of bulimia nervosa. *American Journal of Psychiatry, 147,* 401–408.

Fairburn, C. G., & Cooper, P. J. (1984). Binge-eating, self-induced vomiting and laxative abuse: A community study. *Psychological Medicine, 14,* 401–410.

Fairburn, C. G., & Garner, D. M. (1986). The diagnosis of bulimia nervosa. *International Journal of Eating Disorders, 5*(3), 403–419.

Garfinkel, P., Moldofsky, H., & Garner, D. (1980). The heterogeneity of anorexia nervosa: Bulimia as a distinct subgroup. *Archives of General Psychiatry, 37,* 1036–1040.

Garner, D. M., & Garfinkel, P. E. (1979). The Eating Attitudes Test: An index of the symptoms of anorexia nervosa. *Psychological Medicine, 9,* 273–279.

Garner, D. M., Garfinkel, P. E., Schwartz, D., & Thompson, M. (1980). Cultural expectations of thinness in women. *Psychological Reports, 47,* 483–491.

Garner, D. M., Olmstead, M. P., & Polivy, J. (1983). Development and validation of a multidimensional eating disorder inventory for anorexia nervosa and bulimia. *International Journal of Eating Disorders, 2,* 15–34.

Gray, J. J., & Ford, K. (1985). The incidence of bulimia in a college sample. *International Journal of Eating Disorders, 4,* 201–210.

Gray, J. J., Ford, K., & Kelly, L. M. (1987). The prevalence of bulimia in a Black college population. *International Journal of Eating Disorders, 6*(6), 733–740.

Greenfeld, D., Quinlan, D. M., Harding, P., Glass, E., & Bliss, A. (1987). *International Journal of Eating Disorders, 6,* 99–111.

Gross, J., & Rosen, J. C. (1988). Bulimia in adolescents: Prevalence and psychosocial correlates. *International Journal of Eating Disorders, 7,* 51–61.

Gull, W. W. (1873). Anorexia nervosa (apepsia/hysterica, anorexia hysterica). In M. R. Kaufman & M. Helman (Eds.), *Evolution of psychosomatic concepts: Anorexia nervosa: A paradigm* (pp. 132–138). New York: International Press.

Halmi, K. A., Falk, J. R., & Schwartz, E. (1981). Binge-eating and vomiting: A survey of a college population. *Psychological Medicine, 11*, 697–706.

Hart, K. J., & Ollendick, T. H. (1985). Prevalence of bulimia in working and university women. *American Journal of Psychiatry, 142*, 851–854.

Healy, K., Conroy, R. M., & Walsh, N. (1985). The prevalence of binge-eating and bulimia in 1063 college students. *Journal of Psychiatric Research, 19*, 161–166.

Hendren, R. L., Barber, J. K., & Sigafoos, A. (1986). Eating-disordered symptoms in a nonclinical population: A study of female adolescents in two private schools. *Journal of the American Academy of Child Psychiatry, 25*, 836–840.

Herzog, D. (1982). Bulimia: The secretive syndrome. *Psychosomatics, 23*, 481–483.

Herzog, D. B., Norman, D. K., Rigotti, N. A., & Pepose, M. (1986). Frequency of bulimic behaviors and associated social maladjustment in female graduate students. *Journal of Psychiatric Research, 20*, 355–361.

Howat, P. M., & Saxton, A. M. (1987). The incidence of bulimic behavior in a secondary and university school population. *Journal of Youth and Adolescence, 17*, 221–231.

Johnson, C., & Connors, M. E. (1987). *The etiology and treatment of bulimia nervosa: A biopsychosocial perspective.* New York: Basic Books.

Johnson, C., Lewis, C., Love, S., Lewis, L., & Stuckey, M. (1984). Incidence and correlates of bulimic behavior in a female high school population. *Journal of Youth and Adolescence, 13*, 15–26.

Johnson, C., Stuckey, M., Lewis, L., & Schwartz, D. (1982). Bulimia: A descriptive survey of 316 cases. *International Journal of Eating Disorders, 11*, 1–16.

Katzman, M. A., Wolchik, S. A., & Braver, S. L. (1984). The prevalence of frequent binge eating and bulimia in a nonclinical college sample. *International Journal of Eating Disorders, 3*, 53–62.

Killen, J. D., Taylor, B., Telch, M. J., Saylor, K. E., Maron, D. J., & Robinson, T. N. (1986). Self-induced vomiting and laxative and diuretic use among teenagers: Precursors of the binge-purge syndrome? *Journal of the American Medical Association, 255*, 1447–1449.

King, M. B. (1989). Eating disorders in a general practice population: Prevalence, characteristics and follow-up at 12 to 18 months. *Psychological Medicine Monograph Supplement, 14*, 1–34.

Lacey, J. H., & Dolan, B. M. (1988). Bulimia in British Blacks and Asians: A catchment area study. *British Journal of Psychiatry, 152*, 73–79.

Lachenmeyer, J. R., & Muni-Brander, P. (1988). Eating disorders in a nonclinical adolescent population: Implications for treatment. *Adolescence, 23*, 303–312.

Lakin, J. A., & McClelland, E. (1987). Binge eating and bulimic behaviors in a school-age population. *Journal of Community Health Nursing, 4*, 153–164.

Lasegue, E. C. (1873). On hysterical anorexia. *Medical Times Gazette, 2,* 265.

Leichner, P., Arnett, J., Rallo, J. S., Srikameswaran, S., & Vulcano, B. (1986). An epidemiological study of maladaptive eating attitudes in a Canadian school age population. *International Journal of Eating Disorders, 5,* 969-982.

Maceyko, S. J., & Nagelberg, D. B. (1985). The assessment of bulimia in high school students. *Journal of School Health, 55,* 135-137.

Martin, J. R., & Wollitzer, A. O. (1988). The prevalence, secrecy, and psychology of purging in a family practice setting. *International Journal of Eating Disorders, 2,* 515-519.

Mintz, L. B., & Betz, N. E. (1988). Prevalence and correlates of eating disordered behaviors among undergraduate women. *Journal of Counseling Psychology, 35,* 463-471.

Mizes, J. S. (1985). Bulimia: A review of its symptomatology and treatment. *Advances in Behavior Research and Therapy, 7,* 91-142.

Moss, R. A., Jennings, G., McFarland, J. H., & Carter, P. (1984). Binge eating, vomiting, and weight fear in a female high school population. *The Journal of Family Practice, 18,* 313-320.

Nevo, S. (1985). Bulimic symptoms: Prevalence and ethnic differences among college women. *International Journal of Eating Disorders, 4,* 151-168.

Ondercin, P. (1979). Compulsive eating in college women. *Journal of College Student Personnel, 20,* 153-157.

Palmer, R. L. (1979). The dietary chaos syndrome: A useful new term? *British Journal of Medical Psychology 52,* 187-190.

Pope, H. G. Champoux, R. F., & Hudson, J. I. (1987). Eating disorder and socioeconomic class: Anorexia nervosa and bulimia in nine communities. *Journal of Nervous and Mental Disease, 175,* 620-623.

Pope, H. G., Hudson, J. I., & Yurgelun-Todd, D. (1984). Anorexia nervosa and bulimia among 300 suburban women shoppers. *American Journal of Psychiatry, 141,* 292-294.

Pope, H. G., Hudson, J. I., Yurgelun-Todd, D., & Hudson, M. S. (1984). Prevalence of anorexia nervosa and bulimia in three student populations. *International Journal of Eating Disorders, 3,* 45-51.

Pyle, R. L., Halvorson, P. A., Neuman, P. A., & Mitchell, J. E. (1986). The increasing prevalence of bulimia in freshman college students. *International Journal of Eating Disorders, 5,* 631-647.

Pyle, R. L., & Mitchell, J. E. (1986). The prevalence of bulimia in selected samples. In S. C. Feinstein, A. H. Esman, J. G. Looney, A. Z. Schwartzberg, A. D. Sorosky, & M. Sugar (Eds.), *Adolescent psychiatry: Volume 13, Developmental and clinical studies.* Chicago: University of Chicago Press.

Pyle, R. L., Mitchell, J. E., Eckert, E. D., Halvorson, P. A., Neuman, P. A.,

& Goff, G. M. (1983). The incidence of bulimia in freshman college students. *International Journal of Eating Disorders, 2,* 75–85.

Russell, G. F. M. (1979). Bulimia nervosa: An ominous variant of anorexia nervosa. *Psychological Medicine, 9,* 429–448.

Schotte, D. E., & Stunkard, A. J. (1987). Bulimia vs. bulimic behaviors on a college campus. *Journal of the American Medical Association, 258,* 1213–1215.

Smith, M. C., & Thelen, M. H. (1984). Development and validation of a test for bulimia. *Journal of Consulting and Clinical Psychology, 52,* 863–872.

Stangler, R. S., & Printz, A. M. (1980). DSM-III: Psychiatric diagnosis in a university population. *American Journal of Psychiatry, 137,* 937–940.

Stein, D. M., & Brinza, S. R. (1989). Bulimia: Prevalence estimates in female junior high and high school students. *Journal of Clinical Child Psychology, 3,* 206–213.

Striegel-Moore, R. H., Silberstein, L. R., Frensch, P., & Rodin, J. (1989). A prospective study of disordered eating among college students. *International Journal of Eating Disorders, 8,* 499–509.

Striegel-Moore, R. H., Silberstein, L. R., & Rodin, J. (1986). Toward an understanding of risk factors of bulimia. *American Psychologist, 41,* 246–263.

Stunkard, A. J. (1959). Eating patterns of obese persons. *Psychiatric Quarterly, 33,* 184–192.

Thelen, M. H., Mann, L. M., Pruitt, J., & Smith, M. (1987). Bulimia: Prevalence and component factors in college women. *Journal of Psychosomatic Research, 31,* 73–78.

Vandereyecken, W., & Meerman, R. (1984). *Anorexia nervosa: A clinician's guide to treatment.* Berlin: Walter de Gruyter.

VanThorre, M. D., & Vogel, F. X. (1985). The presence of bulimia in high school females. *Adolescence, 20,* 45–51.

Whitaker, A., Davies, M., Shaffer, D., Johnson, J., Abrams, S., Walsh, B. T., & Kalikow, K. (1989). The struggle to be thin: A survey of anorexic and bulimic symptoms in a non-referred adolescent population. *Psychological Medicine, 19,* 143–163.

Whitehouse, A. M., & Button, E. J. (1988). The prevalence of eating disorders in a U.K. college population: A reclassification of an earlier study. *International Journal of Eating Disorders, 7,* 393–397.

Wilson, C. P., Hogan, C. C., & Mintz, I. L. (1983). *Fear of being fat: The treatment of anorexia nervosa and bulimia.* New York: Jason Aronson.

Wolf, E., & Crowther, J. (1983). Personality and eating habit variables as predictors of severity of binge eating and weight. *Addictive Behaviors, 8,* 335–344.

Zinkand, H., Cadoret, R. J., & Widmer, R. B. (1984). Incidence and detection of bulimia in a family practice population. *Journal of Family Practice, 18,* 555–560.

Zuckerman, D. M., Colby, A., Ware, N. C., & Lazerson, J. S. (1986). The prevalence of bulimia among college students. *American Journal of Public Health, 76,* 1135–1137.

I

DEVELOPMENTAL AND FAMILIAL FACTORS

2

OVERVIEW

Peggy A. Crawford
Dana Watts
Kent State University

As Crowther, Wolf, and Sherwood emphasized in chapter 1, there is consensus among researchers that the cause of bulimia nervosa is multifactorial, encompassing sociocultural, familial, and individual elements. However, as researchers identified the presence of a constellation of eating problems and eating disorders among younger adolescent girls, including junior high and high school populations, the roles of the family and the impact of pubertal development assume greater prominence in etiological models because these factors are influential in the lives of young adolescent girls. The four chapters in Part I examine the roles of developmental and familial factors in the cause of eating problems and eating disorders in general and bulimia nervosa specifically.

Attie and Brooks-Gunn (ch. 3) argue that a developmental perspective be used to investigate dieting, bingeing, and the more severe clinical syndromes of bulimia nervosa and anorexia nervosa because these eating problems and eating disorders tend to have their onset during middle to late adolescence and are closely tied to the biological and psychosocial changes that occur during this developmental period. Their premise is that eating problems emerging in adolescence are associated with the convergence of physical changes and psychosocial challenges with which young adolescents must cope. Integral to their developmental perspective is the use of prospective research designs in which individuals at risk are followed as they negotiate normative developmental tasks. They maintain that adolescent girls who are vulnerable to eating problems and eating disorders, either because of biological or intrapsychic predisposing characteristics or the particular familial environment or social context in which they find themselves, may accommodate to the challenges of adolescence with eating and weight-related problems.

The major contribution of Attie and Brooks-Gunn is their delineation of six developmentally focused issues that researchers should be considering. These include identifying the developmental processes and psychosocial tasks that are involved in the developmental emergence of eating problems and eating disorders; identifying individual characteristics and social relationships that may confer vulnerability to eating problems and eating disorders; determining whether there is a continuum of eating and weight-related psychopathology; determining how often and at what point in development eating problems and disorders may coevolve with other forms of psychopathology; determining whether there are different developmental pathways for eating problems in young women; and determining whether there are developmental changes in the meaning and expression of eating problems over time. They address these issues within the context of data drawn from their own research, clearly illustrating the contributions of developmental and familial factors in the onset of eating problems in young adolescent women.

The major focus of Levine and Smolak (ch. 4) is the presentation of a model that focuses on the combination of cumulative, normal developmental stressors with specific personality characteristics to explain a partial continuum of eating-related problems ranging from nonpathological dieting to subclinical eating disturbances to eating disorders. The crux of their model is that all points along this continuum begin with stressors—developmentally normative events such as weight gain and changes in social relationships—that trigger increases in the salience of body image and, consequently, body dissatisfaction. Although either weight gains or changes in social relationships can lead to dieting, the two will have additive effects such that the likelihood of dieting is greater when they co-occur within the same year. Levine and Smolak predict that the combination of weight gain and social changes will lead to subclinical eating disturbances if, in addition to body dissatisfaction, the individual has goals for slenderness that are limited by biological predispositions. Two additional variables—a threat to achievement status and the superwoman complex—are required if the adolescent is to develop an eating disorder. Clearly, one of the strengths of their model is its ability to account for the large disparity in the prevalence of dieting and the prevalence of eating disorders among young adolescent women.

Thelen, Lawrence, and Powell (ch. 5) focus on eating problems and eating disorders among children. They suggest that maladaptive eating-related attitudes and behaviors may be shaped during the early years, and the presence of body-image dissatisfaction and dieting behaviors before puberty may place a child at risk for the development of an eating disorder. They note that although there has been limited research on the prevalence and correlates of eating-related problems and eating disorders among elementary school-aged children, their review of the research literature suggests that eating-related problems and anorexia nervosa may occur before puberty. Interestingly, Thelen, Lawrence, and Powell note that, although bulimic symptoms have been identified among prepubertal children, their literature review did not identify any cases of bulimia nervosa among this population.

The major contribution of the chapter by Thelen, Lawrence, and Powell is its discussion of the familial and sociocultural factors that may increase a child's risk for subsequent eating problems or eating disorders, including familial histories of eating and weight-related disorders, familial overconcern with food and weight, conflicts over food, disturbed parent–child relationships, and children's adoption of sociocultural preferences for slender body ideals. They argue that we need not only additional research on the nature and scope of eating problems and eating disorders among children that uses developmentally appropriate measures but also research that examines from whom, where, and at what age children acquire eating attitudes, body-image perceptions, and dieting behaviors.

In contrast to the previous three chapters, which focus in some way on eating problems as precursors to eating disorders, Wonderlich (ch. 6) examines the empirical evidence for an association between various familial relationships and bulimia nervosa. The major contribution of his chapter may lie in his premise that one means of understanding the heterogeneity of familial environments within eating-disordered populations may be through examining the covariation of eating-disordered individuals' personality characteristics and their family transactions. Given the comorbidity of personality disorders and eating disorders, Wonderlich cites research suggesting that eating-disordered individuals' perceptions of their family environment may differ depending on the amount and type of personality disturbance accompanying the eating disorder, and he suggests that personality variables may serve as valuable descriptive indicators for subtyping various family patterns in the eating disorders. His interesting discussion of the heritability of some personality traits and their potential influence on the structure and process of family transactions raises complex questions regarding the interplay of genetic and familial factors in the cause of bulimia nervosa.

Across these chapters run several common themes. The first concerns the timing of the emergence of eating problems and eating disorders. Inherent in the chapters by Attie and Brooks-Gunn, Levine and Smolak, and Thelen and his associates is the assumption that with time, eating and weight-related problems may develop into eating disorders in a subset of vulnerable individuals. However, although all of these authors argue for a developmental perspective, they emphasize different periods during which these eating problems and eating disorders emerge. Attie and Brooks-Gunn and Levine and Smolak focus on adolescence as the developmental period during which eating problems and eating disorders are likely to emerge. They argue that adolescent developmental milestones, such as puberty or entering middle school, bring together a host of physical and psychological challenges to which the vulnerable adolescent may respond with eating problems. In contrast, although they note that there has not been extensive research on elementary school-aged children, Thelen and his associates provide empirical evidence that body dissatisfaction, dieting, atypical eating disorders, and anorexia nervosa may occur in at least some children before puberty.

The second theme concerns the role of familial factors in the cause of eating problems and eating disorders. Each of these four chapters addresses the etiological role of the family. However, there is considerable variability across the four chapters regarding the emphasis placed on familial factors. Wonderlich places the greatest emphasis on familial factors, noting that bulimic individuals and, to some extent, their parents perceive their families as disengaged, hostile, disorganized, and conflictual. From both a theoretical and empirical perspective, he discusses in depth the dynamic role that familial environments and specific familial interaction patterns may play in the etiology of bulimia nervosa, particularly in their interactions with various personality disturbances, and the maintenance and course of the disorder.

From somewhat different theoretical perspectives, Attie and Brooks-Gunn, Levine and Smolak, and Thelen and associates also recognize the role of familial factors. Noting that parent–child relationships tend to change during adolescence, Attie and Brooks-Gunn cite some of their own research indicating that familial relationships, particularly divergent mother–daughter perceptions of familial cohesion and support, were related to adolescent daughters' eating problems. Interestingly, Attie and Brooks-Gunn, Levine and Smolak, and Thelen and associates emphasize potential maternal influences on daughters' eating problems or actual eating disorders. Attie and Brooks-Gunn cite research suggesting that a mother who is preoccupied with her own weight and restrains her own eating places her high school daughter at risk for eating problems. In their model, Levine and Smolak argue that familial investment in weight, shape, and dieting behavior may increase body salience and body dissatisfaction, and they cite data indicating that a mother's investment in her own slenderness and parental investment in daughter's slenderness emerged as predictors of nonpathological dieting and eating disturbance, respectively. Similarly, Thelen and associates note that, in comparison to mothers of controls, the mothers of bulimic daughters were more likely to perceive their daughters as being or having been overweight and were more likely to have encouraged their daughters to diet or exercise, although it is not known at what point in their daughters' development this encouragement occurred.

The final theme running throughout these chapters is the need for prospective research. For example, both Attie and Brooks-Gunn and Thelen and associates argue for research that investigates the base rates of eating problems and eating disorders in childhood with a view toward identifying age and sex trends as well as the likelihood that eating and weight-related symptoms will persist or remit over time. Both Attie and Brooks-Gunn and Thelen and associates cite the need for prospective research designs to test specific etiological hypotheses regarding the development of eating problems and eating disorders. Recognizing that the research investigating the familial environments and familial interactions of families with a bulimic member is largely cross-sectional in nature and, thus, leaves unanswered the question of causality, Wonderlich also notes that longitudinal research is needed to clarify the direction of association between familial factors and bulimic symptomatology. As their chapters indicate, Attie and Brooks-Gunn and Levine and Smolak are currently engaged in such research endeavors. With their research and that of others, we may be optimistic regarding progress in the identification of risk factors that distinguish young women who develop eating disorders from those who do not.

3

DEVELOPMENTAL ISSUES
IN THE STUDY OF EATING PROBLEMS
AND DISORDERS

Ilana Attie
North Shore University Hospital and Cornell University Medical College

Jeanne Brooks-Gunn
Educational Testing Service and Teachers College, Columbia University

Despite substantial evidence supporting a biopsychosocial model of eating disorders, current research lacks a developmental framework for integrating findings from sociocultural, biogenetic, personality, family, and behavioral studies. Developmental psychopathology offers a conceptual paradigm within which to examine how eating problems (dieting, binge eating) and eating disorders (anorexia nervosa, bulimia nervosa) develop within each of these domains and the complex associations among them (Attie, Brooks-Gunn, & Petersen, 1990). A developmental perspective on the study of psychopathology takes into account the continuities and discontinuities between normal growth and psychopathology, age-related changes in modes of adaptation and symptom expression, behavioral reorganizations that occur around salient developmental transitions, internal and external sources of competence and vulnerability, and the effects of development on pathology and of pathology on development (Achenbach, 1990; Carlson & Garber, 1986; Cicchetti, 1984; Cicchetti & Schneider-Rosen, 1986; Rutter, 1986). Integral to this approach is the combined use of cross-sectional and longitudinal studies aimed at delineating patterns of continuity and change as these are manifested across the life span. Comparative studies elucidate similarities and differences in risk factors that contribute to the emergence of various forms of psychopathology or to the development of particular patterns of adaptation in specific groups (i.e., defined by gender, age, or probabil-

Portions of this chapter were presented at the Kent Psychology Forum entitled "The Etiology of Bulimia Nervosa: The Individual and Familial Context" (October, 1990). We thank Janis Crowther for her thoughtful comments and Rosemary Deibler for her help in preparation of the chapter.

ity of exhibiting a disorder). Especially useful are prospective research designs in which individuals are followed as they negotiate developmental tasks and major life transitions.

In this discussion, we draw on concepts in developmental psychopathology to consider several research problems in the study of eating disorders: (1) Which developmental processes and psychosocial tasks are involved in the developmental emergence of eating problems and eating disorders?; (2) What individual characteristics and social relationships render a child or adolescent vulnerable to eating problems or disorders, and by what mechanisms do these risk factors lead to the emergence of disorders?; (3) Is there a continuum of eating and weight-related psychopathology, from eating problems that are more widespread (i.e., dieting and bingeing) to the clinical syndromes of anorexia nervosa and bulimia nervosa?; (4) How often, in what groups, and at what point in development do eating disorders and problems coevolve with other forms of psychopathology?; (5) Do developmental pathways for eating problems differ for young women in different contexts? and (6) Are there developmental changes in the meaning and expression of eating problems over time?

This chapter has two aims. The first is to discuss these research problems with regard to the challenges they pose for developmental psychopathologists. The second is to present findings from our research group in which we explore the emergence of eating problems in groups at risk and compare girls in different social contexts with regard to antecedents and correlates.

We have conducted several series of studies. The first set consists of two prospective studies of upper-middle-class adolescent girls believed to be at risk for eating problems because of their social class background. The early adolescent follow-up is a study of about 120 girls seen yearly from the transition into adolescence through middle adolescence (Brooks-Gunn, 1987, 1989; Brooks-Gunn & Warren, 1989; Paikoff, Brooks-Gunn, & Warren, 1991). The late adolescent follow-up is a study of about 200 girls seen three times: during middle school, during high school, and during college (Attie & Brooks-Gunn, 1989; Carlton-Ford, Paikoff, & Brooks-Gunn, 1991; Paikoff, Brooks-Gunn, & Carlton-Ford, 1991). In the second set, adolescent athletes, some of whom engage in endeavors requiring low body weight for aesthetic reasons (classical ballet dancers and figure skaters) and some of whom do not (swimmers), are compared with girls not engaged in athletic endeavors (Brooks-Gunn, Burrow, & Warren, 1988; Brooks-Gunn & Warren, 1985; Gargiulo, Attie, Brooks-Gunn, & Warren, 1987). About 70 classical ballet dancers have been followed longitudinally (see the description of the late adolescent follow-up; Brooks-Gunn, Rock, & Warren, 1989). A third set, not discussed extensively in this chapter, involves young adult ballet dancers in national companies who are at very high risk for eating disorders. For example, across a series of our studies, about one third of the dancers have frank eating disorders (Brooks-Gunn, Warren, & Hamilton, 1987; Hamilton, Brooks-Gunn, & Warren, 1985; Warren,

Brooks-Gunn, Hamilton, Hamilton, & Warren, 1986). Currently, a more comparative study is underway; over 100 young women are being seen, one half of whom are dancers and one half of whom are not. In each group, one half of the young women have been amenorrheic for at least 5 months. Because amenorrhea and eating problems are closely linked (with amenorrhea a criterion for some eating disorders) this sample includes a large number of eating-disordered individuals (Dhuper, Warren, Brooks-Gunn, & Fox, 1990; Lancelot, Brooks-Gunn, Warren, & Newman, 1991).

WHAT DEVELOPMENTAL PROCESSES ARE GERMANE TO THE STUDY OF THE EMERGENCE OF EATING DISORDERS AND PROBLEMS?

Using the developmental study of childhood and adolescent depression as a model, research examined the emergence and prevalence of normal and abnormal mood states, psychobiological markers, age-related responses to specific stressors such as separation and loss, the development of a depressive attributional style, continuities between childhood and adult depression, and in some children interaction with a depressed parent (Brooks-Gunn & Petersen, 1991; Rutter, Izard, & Read, 1986). In eating disorders, an analogous set of developmental dimensions is more difficult to define. Do we focus on age-related signs and symptoms of eating pathology such as early feeding difficulties, eating rituals, or initial dieting attempts? Although early maladaptive eating patterns may be precursors to later eating problems or disorders in some children (Maloney, McGuire, & Daniels, 1988; Marchi & Cohen, 1990), in other children they may simply reflect transient responses to developmental stress. Moving beyond the study of behaviors with phenotypic similarities, the task is to identify underlying psychological or coping processes and their developmental transformations. These may include the development of body image, sexuality, self-esteem and body esteem, autonomy, and social competence. Ultimately, it will not be a single developmental process that is significant but its role in combination with other vulnerabilities such as patterns of family interaction. From a developmental perspective, it is the adolescent's ability to organize experience, particularly at critical transitions, that will most likely predict subsequent adaptive or maladaptive functioning (Cicchetti & Schneider-Rosen, 1986; Sameroff & Seifer, 1990).

Eating disorders and to a lesser extent eating problems (dieting, bingeing) occur modally at two developmental transitions: during the passage into adolescence and during the movement out of adolescence into young adulthood. A developmental approach requires that we study the emergence of eating problems in the context of developmental challenges confronting most adolescents during these transitions. Normative challenges of the early adolescent transition include the integration of a changing body image into one's self-representation; the loosening of childhood ties to parents and moves toward greater psychological and physical autonomy; the development of sexual relationships; the internalization of achievement values; and the organization of a relatively stable and cohesive self-structure for the regulation of mood, impulse, and self-esteem. Late adolescent challenges include the establishment of intimacy, the pursuit of an education and an occupation, and the development of an identity apart from the family (Attie et al., 1990). One question that emerges is how, for some adolescents, the experience of the body and the eating function become bound up with the negotiation of these phase-specific tasks (Ritvo, 1984).

Because it is unlikely that a single developmental model can account for psychopathological outcomes as heterogeneous as eating disorders, we need to consider multiple pathways to the development of anorexia nervosa, bulimia nervosa, and subclinical eating disorders. Although adolescent transitions are assumed to represent periods of highest risk, particularly for vulnerable females, there are several atypical presentations. The presence of eating disorders in subgroups of males is one such deviation. The greatly increased prevalence in certain social contexts, such as ballet schools or athletic groups, is another. The emergence of eating disorders at "off-time" developmental points, (i.e., in prepubertal children or in adults) also requires alternative or modified developmental pathways. Furthermore, the developmental trajectories that lead to chronic dieting and bingeing may be different from those that predispose to anorexia nervosa and bulimia nervosa, although the two may appear phenotypically similar at certain points (e.g., periods of high dieting).

In the discussion that follows, we present some of our data from the late adolescent follow-up, specifically that which is relevant to an examination of possible developmental pathways to eating problems in nonclinically referred girls (Attie & Brooks-Gunn, 1989). Our objective is to test the proposition that the emergence of eating and weight-related problems in female adolescents represents a mode of psychological accommodation to the challenges of adolescence. Of interest are the connections or lack of connections between normative (although dysfunctional) patterns of adaptation and abnormal patterns associated with severe psychological disturbance. In brief, 193 white upper-middle-class adolescents and their mothers were seen initially when the girls were in Grades 7 through 10 (age 14), with follow-up 2 years later (age 16). Girls were drawn from several private schools in New York City. The outcome of interest was problem eating, defined by mean scores on the total EAT-26 Scale (Garner, Olmstead, Bohr, & Garfinkel, 1982), an abbreviated version of the Eating Attitudes Test (EAT, Garner & Garfinkel, 1982). In addition to adolescents' self-reported behavior on body image, psychopathology, family functioning, and pubertal growth scales, we obtained mothers' self-reported eating behavior, body image, depression, and ratings of the family milieu. Regression models tested the relative contributions of grade in school, physical maturation indexes, body image, psychopathology, and family relationships to the prediction of eating problems, both longitudinally and concurrently (i.e., during the same test period). Mean levels of EAT-26 increased slightly over the 2 years of study. The modest correlation between Time 1 and Time 2 EAT-26 scores ($r = .44$, $p < .01$) suggested that considerable interindividual change occurred over the 2 years of study with respect to adolescents' self-reported eating problems.

Analyses of concurrent relationships at Time 1 point to the power of the proposed model in accounting for problem eating behavior at initial testing (see Attie & Brooks-Gunn, 1989). The findings suggest that eating problems emerge in response to physical changes of the pubertal period (specifically body fat and body image). Controlling for these variables, psychopathology was associated with problem eating, whereas family relationships were not. Two years later, when adolescents had completed their pubertal development, the pattern of influence among predictors had changed (see Attie & Brooks-Gunn, 1989). The more developmental factors (i.e., grade and physical maturation indexes) were no longer influential, whereas psychological dimensions, namely a negative body image and psychopathology, accounted for significant variance increments. Eating behavior was associated with affective overcontrol (i.e., depression) as opposed to undercontrol (aggression, delinquency).

Longitudinal analyses were performed using hierarchical regression models in which Time 1 EAT-26 scores were entered first. This procedure equates subjects on initial eating problems followed by sets of predictors entered according to the model discussed previously. Results showed that once initial eating scores were taken into account only Time 1 body image significantly and negatively predicted change in eating problems (i.e., a change in girls' relative standing with respect to her peers). Girls who early in adolescence felt most negatively about their bodies were significantly more likely to develop eating problems beyond what would be expected based on their earlier scores, controlling for variability in physical maturation, psychopathology, and family relationships. The absence of longitudinal effects for physical maturation, psychopathology, and family factors on EAT-26 scores implies that the factors associated with eating problems in later adolescence are relatively independent of those that initiate them. Perhaps at puberty a pattern of eating behavior is set in motion with the subsequent trajectory defined in part by pubertal transformations in body image (Attie & Brooks-Gunn, 1989).

WHAT INDIVIDUAL AND SOCIAL RISK FACTORS INCREASE VULNERABILITY FOR DEVELOPING AN EATING DISORDER?

The prospective study of vulnerable children is considered paradigmatic developmental psychopathology. In the case of anorexia nervosa, the low base rate (estimated at 1 per 100 adolescents) is one of the factors that may pose problems for prospective research. However, anorexia nervosa has a relatively short latency period (the incidence rising sharply and reaching a peak during adolescence), making it relatively accessible to prospective study. Bulimia nervosa has a less stable prevalence, estimated at one or two per 100 adolescents (Fairburn & Beglin, 1990; Johnson, Tobin, & Lipkin, 1989); the modal period of risk extends well into adulthood. Its detection among normal-weight individuals may be difficult because those afflicted tend to be secretive and do not "wear" their diagnosis.

The identification of risk variables, vulnerability, and protective processes is more problematic. At this relatively early stage of our understanding of the etiology of eating disorders, we have identified, at a descriptive level, certain variables that may constitute risk factors for the development of these disorders, including female gender, high socioeconomic status or upward mobility, specific social or vocational contexts (e.g., ballet, competitive schools), and a family or personal history of anorexia nervosa, bulimia nervosa, or affective illness. Additional risk variables for bulimia nervosa may include a family or personal history of obesity, substance abuse, and character pathology as well as a history of chronic restrained eating or anorexia nervosa.

As our understanding of the developmental antecedents and correlates of disordered eating is increased, the aim is to move from more static conceptualizations of risk factors (e.g., social class, gender, family history) to the study of the risk process itself in terms of underlying vulnerabilities, the changing nature of risk, important moderating factors, interactive or composite influences, and the impact of key life transitions (Rutter, 1990). For instance, epidemiologic studies indicate that high socioeconomic status or upward mobility confers increased vulnerability to the development of eating disorders independent of race or ethnic background (Andersen & Hay, 1985; Drewnowski & Yee, 1988). However, as noted by others (Richter & Weintraub, 1990), social class differences do not address the question of the proximal experiences to which children within a given social strata are exposed. Such an understanding demands the study of family and social relationships over time with a view toward identifying patterns of interaction, their progression across developmental periods, and the mechanisms by which they may lead to disorders in susceptible individuals.

For the adolescent girl, gender-related sources of risk include a culturally mediated focus on body shape and weight (Attie & Brooks-Gunn, 1987), the intensification of gender-specific expectations during the middle-school transition (Simmons & Blyth, 1987), conflicts between social role demands and the interpersonal focus of female identity formation (Josselson, 1973), and an increased risk of depression (Rutter, 1986; Strober & Katz, 1987). In addition, psychoanalysts suggest that gender differences in early psychosexual development render the negotiation of separation–individuation (and its reemergence in adolescence) potentially more conflictual and prolonged for girls in comparison to boys (Beattie, 1988). Descriptive and observational studies of family relationships in eating-disordered families provide some support for psychoanalytic conceptualizations, implicating current, ongoing family interactions (and not simply early relationships) in the maintenance of specific symptom patterns (Humphrey, 1986, 1988). Whether these current family transactions can be predicted from earlier patterns and whether they are causally linked to eating disorders requires prospective study of their coherence over time.

A cornerstone of research on young adolescents focuses on changes in parent–child relationships. Psychodynamic theories suggest that de-idealization of the parent occurs as a necessary step toward adolescent autonomy. Other theorists suggest that parent–child relationships are transformed during adolescence in terms of renegotiation from unilateral authority to mutuality. Actual research comparing younger and older adolescents (but usually not children on the verge of adolescence) suggests that time spent with parents, emotional closeness, and yielding to parents in decision making decrease whereas conflict increases during the first years of adolescence (see Paikoff & Brooks-Gunn, in press, for a review of this literature). Although parent–child conflict is seen in all dyads, mother–daughter pairs exhibit more intense and long-lasting conflict. Such changes often have positive consequences even though a minority of families experience a marked deterioration in parent–child relationships.

Of interest here is how parent–daughter relationships or changes in such relationships may render some girls at risk for eating problems. In our longitudinal study, daughters' perceptions of relationships with their parents were not associated with eating problems during middle school. At the high school data point (where maternal reports were also available), we found a discrepancy between mothers' and daughters' ratings of the family milieu (on the Family Environment Scale [FES]); only mothers' ratings predicted daughters' eating problems during follow-up testing (Attie & Brooks-Gunn, 1989).

This work has been extended to examine divergent perceptions within the mother–daughter dyad and their association with eating problems and depressive symptomatology. We studied family cohesion and conflict using both mothers' and daughters' FES ratings at the high school data point. We found that dyads varied substantially on their level of agreement. Divergence on family conflict was associated with daughters' depressive symptomatology, whereas divergence on family cohesion was associated with daughters' dieting behaviors (Carlton-Ford et al., 1991). The absolute difference between dyad members was more important than the direction of differences (i.e., mother higher than daughter or vice versa). Such divergences in perceptions of family functioning may be indicative of conflict or of a distant relationship between mother and daughter. In an extension of this work, we have added reproductive timing to the equation. We studied mother and daughter reproductive timing simultaneously because mothers in midlife are experiencing the end of the childbearing years just as their daughters are entering them. Of interest were the possible relationships between reproductive timing and family functioning, and between reproductive functioning and eating behavior. Family cohesion and conflict were not associated with timing of the daughters' menarche or the mothers' menstrual status. However, dieting behavior was. Early maturing girls whose mothers were premenopausal dieted less than early maturers whose mothers were menopausal. Perhaps girls whose mothers are menopausal are more conscious about possible weight gain (in part because of maternal concerns over this issue) and thus engage in more dieting behavior. Indeed, mothers of adolescent daughters were more likely to engage in dieting behavior when they were menopausal themselves. Maternal dieting was positively associated with maternal weight for height; the increased body fat probably reflects postmenopausal weight gain, lending credence to our hypothesis (Paikoff et al., in press).

Another source of vulnerability derives from the interaction between a biological predisposition toward an illness and adverse environmental factors affecting the individual. The possibility of a genetic predisposition to eating disorders has been researched in two types of studies: (1) studies that document the occurrence of eating disorders and other psychiatric illnesses among biological relatives of probands (Strober, Lambert, Morrell, Burroughs, & Jacobs, 1990) and (2) studies that examine concordance rates among twin pairs. In a recent family aggregation study, Strober et al. (1990) found evidence for the intergenerational transmission of anorexia nervosa, which was eight times as common in female first-degree relatives of anorectic woman compared with nonpsychiatric and psychiatric controls. Twin research on eating problems has not yet incorporated studies of twins adopted away, twins reared apart, or crossfostering. However, several studies report a higher concordance rate for monozygotic compared with dizygotic twins with anorexia nervosa (Holland, Hall, Murray, Russell, & Crisp, 1984) and, more recently, twins with bulimia nervosa (Fichter & Noegel, 1990; Hsu, Chesler, & Santhouse, 1990). Although findings with twins, together with Strober's family epidemiological work, lend support to a familial genetic contribution to eating disorders, its specific nature and relationship with familial environmental factors cannot be determined without further study.

What remains unanswered is why the vulnerable daughter (and not her sister or brother) develops an eating disorder—compared with other psychosomatic, affective, or addictive syndromes—and why she almost invariably does so postpubertally. Anorexia nervosa is rare in prepubertal children, and when it does emerge in childhood it is distinguished (from postpubertal anorexia nervosa) by an excess of males, the presence of early feeding difficulties, and a high incidence of coexisting depression (Fosson, Knibbs, Bryant-Waugh, & Lask, 1987; Jacobs & Isaacs, 1986). As in depression, the sex ratio of eating disorders appears to shift as a function of pubertal status. Although recent work in genetic epidemiology supports a familial transmission of risk for anorexia nervosa that is independent of a risk for depression (Strober et al., 1990), additional factors are needed to explain the emergence and possible coexistence of these disorders after the pubertal transition.

DOES A CONTINUUM OF EATING PSYCHOPATHOLOGY EXIST?

The issue of a continuum of eating pathology, from dieting to clinical syndromes, is complex given that most dieting adolescent and adult women do not go on to develop an eating disorder. Yet these normal dieters share many characteristics with eating-disordered individuals particularly in the realms of weight preoccupation, concern with appearance, and eating behaviors (Garner, Polivy, & Garfinkel, 1984; Polivy & Herman, 1987). With regard to the continuity issue, Sameroff and Seifer (1990) pointed out that "developmental psychopathologists make no prior assumptions about either continuity or discontinuity. They are concerned centrally with both the connections and lack of connections between normality and disorder" (p. 52). Importantly, normative is not synonymous with normality; dieting is pervasive among certain groups of women despite its deleterious effects on health and well-being (Attie & Brooks-Gunn, 1987; Polivy & Herman, 1987).

The study of eating pathology in both nonclinical and clinical samples has revealed three relatively independent, although interactive, dimensions along which behavior is organized: (1) normal versus pathological eating, (2) restricting versus bulimic mode, and (3) healthy versus more disturbed ego functioning (i.e., personality disordered). Although cross-sectional research has enabled us to define these dimensions and their interrelations better, longitudinal studies are needed to explore the emergence of eating behavior (at different levels of severity) as a function of developmental failures, vulnerabilities in personality, and family functioning. Although evidence of discontinuity certainly exists, there may be utility, conceptually and methodologically, to using a continuum classification to select individuals for prospective study (Lewis, 1990). For example, if we consider a continuum of eating pathology (cf. Polivy & Herman, 1987)—from normal eating to dieting to subclinical eating disorders to *Diagnostic and Statistical Manual of Mental Disorders* (third edition, revised) (*DSM–III–R*; American Psychiatric Association, 1987) disorders—individuals within each group could be compared with regard to antecedents, correlates, and outcomes.

Among nonclinically referred girls, we were interested in determining whether personality and family variables that tend to discriminate bulimic and nonbulimic patients with eating disorders also distinguish dieters from binge eaters in a normal adolescent sample. Using the high school data point from the late adolescent follow-up, exclusive dieters and binge eaters were compared with respect to psychosocial and family correlates. For these analyses, binge eaters were defined as those girls who scored above the 65th percentile on the

EAT-26 Bulimia Scale, and restricters were those scoring above the 65th percentile on the Diet Scale who did not have high Bulimia scores. In these discriminant function analyses, unlike the other analyses discussed in this chapter, dance and nondance samples were combined to have a large enough sample of dieters and binge eaters to analyze. Following Pedhauser (1982), discriminant loadings (i.e., structure coefficients) were considered meaningful if they reached at least .30 in magnitude. Given these modifications, these discriminant function analyses are viewed as exploratory and preliminary.

Discriminant function analyses provided a means of determining which of a number of psychological and social variables were most important in discriminating binge eaters from dieters. Four variables—body image, depressive symptoms, dating, and impulse control—were chosen for study on the basis of findings previously reported in the clinical literature. These variables produced a function that was statistically significant. Surprisingly, the variable that most contributed to the discrimination of binge eaters from dieters was low dating followed by body image and depression. Poor impulse control also correlated highly with the function that distinguished bingers from dieters, although the groups did not differ significantly on this dimension. When compared with exclusive dieters, then, binge eaters were more dysfunctional on all measures of psychological adaptation. Contrary to expectation, binge eaters were less socially competent than their dieting peers. Impairments in the regulation of mood, behavior, and self-esteem were also evident in this group's greater depression, decreased body image, and somewhat lessened impulse control.

Taken together, the findings suggest that deficient self-regulatory structures for managing affect and impulsivity, trends toward fatness, poor body image, and social incompetence are all associated with binge-eating tendencies. A true test of the continuum hypothesis (between binge-eating tendencies and bulimia nervosa) would require continued longitudinal study of the coherence or reorganization of these maladaptive patterns as girls negotiate the developmental demands of the late adolescent transition.

Family variables also distinguished problem eaters who diet exclusively from those with binge-eating tendencies. Families of both dieters and binge eaters were relatively lacking in cohesive and supportive family interactions as reflected in their worse Family Environment Scale relationship scores (see Attie & Brooks-Gunn, 1989). However, results of discriminant function analyses are consistent with clinical reports in suggesting greater family disturbance in the binge-eating group. Specifically, mothers' ratings of the systems dimension were significantly and negatively related to daughters' binge eating at follow-up; however, these structural family characteristics did not predict dieting. In discriminant analyses, families of binge-eating adolescents could be distinguished from families of dieting adolescents on the basis of their low levels of organization and control and their lack of interpersonal expressiveness. In some respects, then, the adolescent with binge-eating tendencies appears to be mirroring a more general pattern of familial inconsistency and disorganization characterized by little emphasis on the structuring of family activities, an absence of well-defined limits, lack of attention to family rules and responsibilities, and less direct and open expression of feelings.

Mothers' ratings of the family environment showed a relationship with daughters' eating as did mothers' weight-related concerns. These regression analyses were designed to partition unique variance proportions in daughters' eating behavior as a function of maternal eating behavior, body image, depression, and perceptions of the family environment. Although maternal EAT-26 scores approached significance ($p < .10$) only as a predictor of daughters' EAT-26 scores (Attie & Brooks-Gunn, 1989), they significantly predicted daughters' Diet scores (Attie, 1987). The findings suggest that having a mother who is preoccupied with thinness and who herself restrains eating places the normal high school adolescent at greater risk for restrained eating. Maternal eating behavior did not predict binge eating; rather, it was the relative absence of familial structure and positive affective involvement that ultimately tipped the balance of restrained eating toward the more internally dysregulated binge-eating pattern.

WHEN DO EATING DISORDERS COEVOLVE WITH OTHER FORMS OF PSYCHOPATHOLOGY?

The co-occurrence of eating disorders with other forms of psychopathology is a major focus of current research. Given the prevalence of depression among subgroups of eating-disordered patients, efforts have been made to elucidate the nature of this association (Strober & Katz, 1987, 1988). Recent work in genetic epidemiology reveals that anorexia nervosa and depression show independent familial transmission. The presence of depression among relatives of anorectic probands is accounted for by a subset of anorexics with coexisting depression (Strober et al., 1990). Moreover, there are suggestions that family environment differences reported between eating-disordered individuals and controls or among eating-disorder subtypes may in fact be accounted for by coexisting depression (Blouin, Zuro, & Blouin, 1990) or personality disorders (see Wonderlich, this volume, ch. 6). Although effects of comorbidity are receiving considerable attention, less is known about the developmental antecedents of the coexisting disorders or the specificity of risk factors for "pure" eating disorders compared with eating disorders that co-occur with other psychiatric syndromes or personality disorders.

In our work, we examined the co-occurrence of depressive symptoms and bulimia nervosa in two groups of young women: those who are classical ballet dancers and those who are not (Lancelot et al., 1991). We hypothesized that dancers, compared with nondancers, would be less likely to show psychopathology in areas other than eating and weight given the contextual demand for thinness within the dance profession. As predicted, nondancers diagnosed with bulimia nervosa according to more restrictive criteria (*DSM-III-R* vs. *DSM-III*) had higher mean depression scores (see Figure 1). We also expected that nondancers would be more likely to report a family history of bulimia nervosa and depression, given that their eating disorders may be less contextually driven. Indeed, the reported incidence of familial depression (but not bulimia nervosa) was higher for the nondancers than dancers, using a fairly gross measure of family history (see Lancelot et al., 1990). Similar results to those just described for depression and eating disorders were obtained for substance use (and familial history of substance abuse) and eating disorders; the links were stronger for nondancers than for dancers (see Figure 2; Holderness, Brooks-Gunn, & Warren, unpublished data).

Somewhat surprisingly, researchers have not investigated the co-occurrence of eating pathology with other psychopathology as a function of age or developmental transitions. Most of the research on co-occurrence focuses on young adult women and does not compare groups at risk for or presenting with different disorders. The work just presented with dancers illustrates the value of a comparative approach; we have made other dance–nondance comparisons that are more developmental in nature (see later discussion).

In an effort to map out developmental trajectories of the emergence of eating problems in relation to depressive symptoms, we have examined the association between these symptoms in a group of girls followed longitudinally from middle school to high school (Attie & Brooks-Gunn, 1989). Although eating problems and depressive affect (i.e., emotional tone) were not strongly related in young adolescents, they were significantly and positively correlated (controlling for physical maturation factors and body image) when the girls were older. The timing of large increases in depressive symptomatology and eating problems and comparisons between these developmental trajectories are currently being examined with yearly data collected over five years in the early adolescent study.

DO DEVELOPMENTAL TRAJECTORIES DIFFER FOR GIRLS IN DIFFERENT CONTEXTS?

Another approach to the study of developmental trajectories is to examine antecedents and correlates of eating problems in different contexts. We have studied one set of contextual influences: those involving athletic endeavors. Although sports are similar in that high standards of technical proficiency are demanded of all first-class athletes, they may differ in terms of requirements for body shape and size. Low weight is required of gymnasts, figure skaters, and dancers, all of whom are likely to be delayed maturers. In contrast, low weight is not demanded of swimmers, volleyball players, and other athletes (Malina, 1983). Requirements for thinness sometimes go beyond what is necessary for

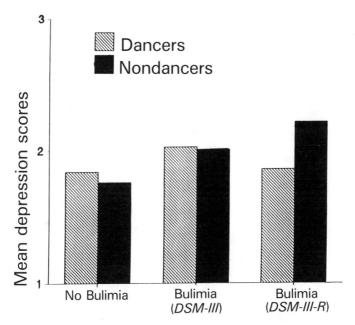

FIGURE 1   Mean depression scores for dancers (*n* = 50) and nondancers
(*n* = 56) with and without bulimia nervosa (Hopkins Symptom Checklist).
(*DSM–III–R-Diagnostic and Statistical Manual of Mental Disorders*, third
edition, revised. Figure is based on data from Lancelot, Brooks-Gunn,
Warren, & Newman, 1991.)

the performance of a certain athletic endeavor and become an aesthetic preference. The most obvious example is the ballet dancer who, unless she is very
thin, may not be accepted into a national company regardless of talent. The
demand for dancers to have very low weights is a fairly recent phenomenon
often attributed to Balanchine's aesthetic preferences. Although body size in
large part is genetically determined, it is influenced by environmental factors
(Garn & Clark, 1976; Stunkard et al., 1986). Diet, exercise, or a combination
of the two may affect body size (Stern & Lowney, 1986; Warren, 1980).

In one study, we compared adolescents dancers, swimmers, and figure
skaters with regard to physical characteristics and attitudes about eating (Brooks-
Gunn et al., 1988). It was expected that weight for height (as a measure of body
fat) would be lower in the two groups that have weight demands (figure skating
and ballet dancing) than in the group without such a demand (swimmers). In
addition, the dancers were expected to engage in more dieting behavior to maintain their low weight than the figure skaters given that in general the dancers
expend less energy in training than the skaters (about 200 kcal are expended in a
typical ballet class compared with about 500 kcal in swimming and skating based
on a weight of 50 to 53 kg; Cohen, Kim, May, & Ertel, 1982; McArdle, Katch,

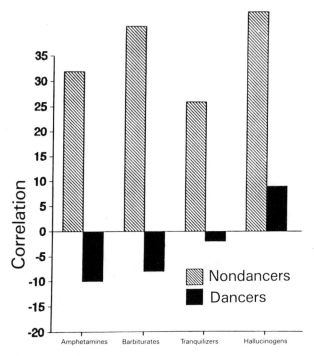

FIGURE 2   Correlations between bulimia nervosa (*Diagnostic and Statistical Manual of Mental Disorders*, third edition, revised) substance use, emotional distress (Hopkins Symptom Checklist) in dancers and nondancers. (From Holden, Brooks-Gunn, & Warren (1990). Unpublished manuscript. Used with permission of authors.)

& Katch, 1986). The swimmers, by contrast, were expected to exhibit little if any dieting behavior because low weight is not required and because caloric expenditure is relatively high. As expected, the dancers and skaters were comparatively leaner than the swimmers and nonathletes. The dancers and skaters also exhibited more restrained eating and binge–purge eating than the swimmers. The negative eating attitudes of the skaters and dancers were comparable to those reported for adult dancers. We postulate that skaters' and dancers' eating attitudes emerged in response to the low weights required by their professions. These findings are similar to those reported for male college wrestlers, nordic skiers, and swimmers; the wrestlers showed more negative eating attitude scores than the other two groups presumably because of weight requirements (Enns, Drewnowski, & Grinker, 1987; Malina, 1983). At the same time, skaters had lower and higher oral control scores than dancers. Oral control (i.e., self-control of eating) is negatively associated with weight, whereas dieting is positively associated with weight in other adolescent samples, suggesting that high dieting scores may reflect concerns with weight and unsuccessful dieting (Brooks-Gunn & Warren,

185). We hypothesize that the higher dieting scores of the dancers compared with the skaters are due to the fact that they expend less energy than skaters, and therefore may engage in more stringent dieting behavior to maintain equivalently low weights.

With an interest in exploring alternative developmental pathways, we compared the longitudinal sample of nonathletic upper-class girls to a group of girls attending selective national company ballet schools (see previous discussion of late adolescent follow-up). The dancers share an additional risk factor of being in a competitive environment that values leanness and delayed maturation. We hypothesized that puberty, family, and personality characteristics may be associated with eating concerns differently in the two contexts (Attie, 1987; Brooks-Gunn et al., 1989).

Longitudinal and concurrent regression analyses were performed on the combined sample of dancers and nondancers, and the regression models spoken of previously were modified to test for interaction effects (see Attie & Brooks-Gunn, 1989). Regressions on Time 1 eating measures yielded significant interaction effects, indicating that there is something different about the emergence of eating problems among dancers compared with nondancers (Attie, 1987). To interpret the interactions, their component variables were tested in a series of two-way analyses of variance, with eating-problem scores were dependent variables. As shown in Figure 3, the association between body image and EAT-26 clearly differed for the two groups. Although higher EAT-26 scores were associated with poor body image in both groups, dancers showed a dramatic rise in disturbed eating at low levels of body image. The association of maturational timing to eating problems differed in the two samples as well. Because of the paucity of early maturing dancers, a direct comparison of timing effects was not possible. Regardless of maturational status, dancers show more disturbed eating than nondance peers. In nondancers, there was a trend for early maturers to report higher EAT-26 scores than their later maturing peers.

Although dancers had more serious eating problems and weighed significantly less, they did not appear to be responding to the convergence of psychosocial changes of young adolescence. In contrast to the comparison sample, dancers' overall EAT-26 scores did not vary according to their grade in school, the timing of maturation (middle or late), or their self-reported psychopathology. On the whole, dancers were significantly more likely to diet and binge, and these eating patterns were more pronounced among those with worse body images. The results suggest that young dancers are likely to restrain eating regardless of differences in physical status or emotional adjustment.

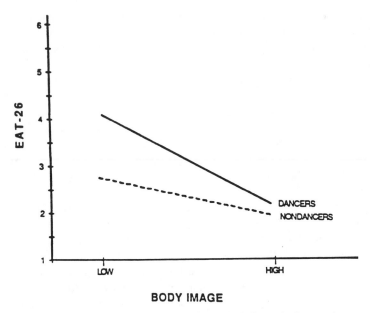

BODY IMAGE

FIGURE 3   Total Eating Attitudes Test (EAT-26) body image in dance and nondance samples: Time 1 concurrent analyses.

ARE THERE DEVELOPMENTAL CHANGES IN THE MEANING AND EXPRESSION OF EATING PROBLEMS OVER TIME?

Almost no research has addressed this issue. To begin with, few studies have charted the prevalence rates of eating problems or disorders from middle childhood through adolescence and young adulthood. Eating disorders or problems have only recently been studied in large groups of children in part because eating pathology was thought to be rare in prepubertal children and age-appropriate instruments had not been developed (Crowther, Post, & Zaynor, 1985; Irwin, 1981; Maloney et al., 1988; see Thelen et al., this volume, ch. 5). Contrast this situation with what is known about depression and depressive symptomatology in which age-related changes have been documented from an admittedly scanty and recent base (Brooks-Gunn & Petersen, 1991; Peterson, Brooks-Gunn, & Compas, in press; Rutter et al., 1986). For eating disorders, we are not yet able to piece together such estimates from disparate studies.

Given the lack of normative baseline information, it comes as no surprise that research has not addressed the question of whether the nature of eating problems differs as a function of age. Several approaches are germane to this issue. One technique involves the use of maximum likelihood factor analyses to see if particular constructs are similar or different in various age groups. Our group conducted such analyses with about 600 girls in seventh to twelfth grades; we found that although the latent construct underlying dieting and bingeing behavior (as assessed using a short form of the EAT-26) was similar for seventh to eighth, ninth to tenth, and eleventh to twelfth graders, the salience of the construct increased with grade in school (i.e., the size of the absolute factor loadings increased). Essentially, eating problems, specifically dieting and bingeing, became more important as girls progressed through the adolescent years (Brooks-Gunn et al., 1989).

Developmentally oriented clinical interviews are needed to explore age-related changes in the meaning of eating problems (Kovacs, 1986). We still do not know what young adolescents mean when they say they have been on a diet. Are they actually restricting food intake? How many have the self-regulatory systems in place to restrain eating to the point of experiencing hunger sensations? Are weight-loss efforts influenced by peer comparisons? As another example, purging seems to be less common in younger than older adolescents (Crowther et al., 1985). How much of this difference is a function of the entry into college or group living situations where modeling of purging behavior, unsupervised eating, and social contagion effects are more likely to occur (Striegel-Moore, Silberstein, & Rodin, 1986)? Does counterregulatory behavior or the spiral model for dieting proposed by Heatherton and Polivy (this volume, ch. 8) operate at younger as well as at older ages, and does cognitive competence play a role in any age-related changes? Alternatively, is some minimal level of repeated experience with failed diets needed for diet spirals to become established, experience that does not accrue for most young adolescents? In our adolescent samples of girls 14 years of age and older, diet and bingeing scores are associated with higher, not lower weights, suggesting that girls are learning that diets are not always successful. At the same time, oral control is associated with lower weights, suggesting that by age 14 self-regulatory systems may be operating. Whether these associations would be found for younger girls is not known.

Other measurement issues need to be addressed in a systematic manner to elucidate the changing meaning of disordered eating and eating problems with age. These include the time frames used by different-aged individuals when asked about eating behavior, the ability to identify affects associated with food intake, the domains of thinking and behavior tapped by different types of measures, the convergence or divergence of findings among different respondents (specifically the adolescent, parents, teachers, or clinicians), and a developmental understanding of terms such as binge, diet, and fat. Our point here is that a developmental psychopathology framework demands that age-related changes in the construction of a particular problem or disorder must be considered rather than assuming equivalence over age periods.

CONCLUSION

Perhaps the most challenging question raised by a developmental approach to the study of eating problems and eating disorders concerns the nature and degree of continuity, first, between early adaptational patterns and later eating disorders and, second, between dieting behavior and the clinical syndromes of anorexia nervosa and bulimia nervosa. A developmental perspective presumes an underlying coherence of individual functioning across periods of growth and transition despite changes in manifest behavior or symptomatology. However, research has yet to discover early patterns of developmental achievement and failure that might forecast subsequent eating pathology. To enhance our understanding of various developmental pathways, future studies need to address several areas including: (1) competent and incompetent adaptation to developmental tasks of early and late adolescent transitions; (2) the roles of social contexts and biological predispositions as mediators of risk; (3) the antecedents of comorbid conditions compared with pure eating disorders; (4) the impact of gender-specific socialization practices on the expression of both pathological and nonpathological eating-related outcomes; and (5) the establishment of expected base rates of eating-disordered symptoms from childhood through adulthood with a view toward identifying age and sex trends, modal points of developmental breakdown, and the likelihood that symptoms will persist or remit over time.

Another perspective on the continuity question concerns how eating disorders arise in the context of adolescent dieting. How can we differentiate the normal adolescent girl who is preoccupied with appearance and body weight and who also is struggling with developmental issues of autonomy, identity, and sexuality from one who will eventually develop an eating disorder? Can dieting and weight loss, in themselves, serve as precipitants for anorexia nervosa or bulimia nervosa in a nonspecifically vulnerable adolescent (Katz, 1985)? Are there other immediate precursors, apart from dieting, that may presage the onset of disorder?

Our research has focused on the emergence of eating problems that are more widespread given the low incidence of eating disorders. It is noteworthy that several of the personality and family factors associated with eating pathology in clinic samples were found to contribute to the emergence of self-reported dieting and binge eating in our sample of nonclinically referred private school girls (Attie & Brooks-Gunn, 1989). These data suggest some continuity, at least in antecedent factors, between eating disorders and eating problems. However, we still are left with the question of how a small number of problem eaters develop an eating disorder. Is it due to the greater concentration of vulnerability factors or to a greater intensity of such factors (i.e., a more negative body image, more severe depressive symptomatology, or more dysfunctional family interaction)? Do the relative timing and interactions among various risk factors make a difference? How do repeated dieting and binge-eating cycles, actual weight loss, and the physiological consequences of weight fluctuations contribute to subsequent, more severe problems? In our late adolescent follow-up, we hope to have the opportunity to explore some of these issues when the girls are seen for the third time as they finish college. Preliminary findings derived from clinical interviews with the first 100 young women suggest that perhaps as many as 8% have had frank eating disorders whereas another 20% have had subclinical eating problems. Such a high occurrence will allow us to examine continuities and discontinuities between eating problems during adolescence and eating disorders during young adulthood as well as the concatenation of risk factors that distinguish those adolescent girls who develop eating disorders from those who do not.

REFERENCES

Achenbach, T. (1990). What is "developmental" about developmental psychopathology? In J. Rolf, A. Masten, D. Cicchetti, K. H. Nuechterlein, & S. Weintraub (Eds.), *Risk and protective factors in the development of psychopathology* (pp. 29–48). Cambridge, England: Cambridge University Press.

American Psychiatric Association. (1987). *Diagnostic and statistical manual of mental disorders* (3rd edition, revised). Washington, DC: Author.

Anderson, A. E., & Hay, A. (1985). Racial and socioeconomic influences in anorexia nervosa and bulimia. *International Journal of Eating Disorders, 4,* 479–488.

Attie, I. (1987). *Development of eating problems in adolescence: A follow-up of girls at risk.* Unpublished doctoral dissertation, Catholic University of America.

Attie, I., & Brooks-Gunn, J. (1987). Weight concerns as chronic stressors in women. In R. C. Barnett, L. Biener, & G. K. Baruch (Eds.), *Gender and stress* (pp. 218–254). New York: Free Press.

Attie, I., & Brooks-Gunn, J. (1989). The development of eating problems in adolescent girls: A longitudinal study. *Developmental Psychology, 25*(1), 70–79.

Attie, I., Brooks-Gunn, J., & Petersen, A. C. (1990). The emergence of eating problems: A developmental perspective. In M. Lewis & S. Miller (Eds.), *Handbook of developmental psychopathology* (pp. 409–420). New York: Plenum Press.

Beattie, H. J. (1988). Eating disorders and the mother-daughter relationship. *International Journal of Eating Disorders, 7*(4), 453–460.

Blouin, A. G., Zuro, C., & Blouin, J. H. (1990). Family environment in bulimia nervosa: The role of depression. *International Journal of Eating Disorders, 9,* 649–658.

Brooks-Gunn, J. (1987). Pubertal processes and girls' psychological adaptation. In R. Lerner & T. T. Foch (Eds.), *Biological-psychosocial interactions in early adolescence: A life-span perspective* (pp. 123–153). Hillsdale, NJ: Erlbaum.

Brooks-Gunn, J. (1989). Pubertal processes and the early adolescent transition. In W. Damon (Ed.), *Child development today and tomorrow* (pp. 155–176). San Francisco: Jossey-Bass.

Brooks-Gunn, J., Burrow, C., & Warren, M. P. (1988). Attitudes toward eating and body weight in different groups of female adolescent athletes. *International Journal of Eating Disorders, 7*(6), 749–758.

Brooks-Gunn, J., & Petersen, A. C. (1991). The emergence of depression and depressive symptoms during adolescence. *Journal of Youth and Adolescence, 20*(2), 115–119.

Brooks-Gunn, J., Rock, D., & Warren, M. P. (1989). Comparability of constructs across the adolescent years. *Developmental Psychology, 25*(1), 51–60.

Brooks-Gunn, J., & Warren, M. P. (1985). Effects of delayed menarche in different contexts: Dance and nondance students. *Journal of Youth and Adolescence, 14*(4), 285–300.

Brooks-Gunn, J., & Warren, M. P. (1989). Biological contributions to affective expression in young adolescent girls. *Child Development, 60,* 372–385.

Brooks-Gunn, J., Warren, M. P., & Hamilton, L. H. (1987). The relationship of eating disorders to amenorrhea in ballet dancers. *Medicine and Science in Sports and Exercise, 19*(1), 41–44.

Carlson, G. A., & Garber, J. (1986). Developmental issues in the classification of depression in children. In M. Rutter, C. E. Izard, & P. B. Read (Eds.), *Depression in young people: Clinical and developmental perspectives* (pp. 399–434). New York: Guilford Press.

Carlton-Ford, S., Paikoff, R. L., & Brooks-Gunn, J. (1991). Models for assessing effects of disagreement on adolescents and their parents. In R. L. Paikoff & W. A. Collins (Eds.), *New directions for child development: Implications of disagreements about family functioning for adolescents and their parents.* San Francisco: Jossey-Bass.

Cicchetti, D. (1984). The emergence of developmental psychopathology. *Child Development, 55,* 1–7.

Cicchetti, D., & Schneider-Rosen, K. (1986). An organizational approach to childhood depression. In M. Rutter, C. Izard, & P. Read (Eds.), *Depression in young people: Developmental and clinical perspectives* (pp. 71–134). New York: Guilford Press.

Cohen, J. L., Kim, C. S., May, P. B., & Ertel, N. H. (1982). Exercise, body weight, and amenorrhea in professional ballet dancers. *Physician and Sports Medicine, 10*(4), 92–101.

Crowther, J. H., Post, G., & Zaynor, L. (1985). The prevalence of bulimia and binge eating in adolescent girls. *International Journal of Eating Disorders, 4,* 29–42.

Dhuper, S., Warren, M. P., Brooks-Gunn, J., & Fox, R. (1990). Effects of hormonal status on bone density in adolescent girls. *Journal of Clinical Endocrinology Society, 71*(5), 1083–1088.

Drewnowski, A., & Yee, D. K. (1988, August). *Adolescent dieting: Fear of fatness and role of puberty.* Paper presented at the 96th annual meeting of the American Psychological Association, Atlanta, Georgia.

Enns, M. P., Drewnowski, A., & Grinker, G. A. (1987). Body composition, body size estimation, and attitudes towards eating in male college athletes. *Psychosomatic Medicine, 49*(1), 56–64.

Fairburn, C. G., & Beglin, S. (1990). Studies of the epidemiology of bulimia nervosa. *American Journal of Psychiatry, 147,* 401–408.

Fichter, M. M., & Noegel, R. (1990). Concordance for bulimia nervosa in twins. *International Journal of Eating Disorders, 9*(32), 255–263.

Fosson, A., Knibbs, J., Bryant-Waugh, R., & Lask, B. (1987). Early onset anorexia nervosa. *Archives of Disease in Childhood, 62,* 114–118.

Gargiulo, J., Attie, I., Brooks-Gunn, J., & Warren, M. P. (1987). Girls' dating behavior as a function of social context and maturation. *Developmental Psychology, 23*(5), 730–737.

Garn, S. M., & Clark, D. C. (1976). Trends in fatness and the origins of obesity. *Pediatrics, 57*(4), 443–456.

Garner, D. M., & Garfinkel, P. E. (1979). The Eating Attitudes Test: An index of the symptoms of anorexia nervosa. *Psychological Medicine, 1,* 273–279.

Garner, D. M., Olmsted, M. P., Bohr, Y., & Garfinkel, P. E. (1982). The Eating Attitudes Test: Psychometric features and clinical correlates. *Psychological Medicine, 12,* 871–878.

Garner, D. M., Polivy, J., & Garfinkel, P. E. (1984). Comparison between weight preoccupied women and anorexia nervosa. *Psychosomatic Medicine, 46,* 255–266.

Hamilton, L. H., Brooks-Gunn, J., & Warren, M. P. (1985). Sociocultural influences on eating disorders in female professional dancers. *International Journal of Eating Disorders, 4*(4), 465–477.

Holland, A. J., Hall, A., Murray, R., Russell, G. F. M., & Crisp, A. H. (1984). Anorexia nervosa: A study of 34 twin pairs and one set of triplets. *British Journal of Psychiatry, 145,* 414–419.

Hsu, L. K. G., Chesler, B. E., & Santhouse, R. (1990). Bulimia nervosa in eleven sets of twins: A clinical report. *International Journal of Eating Disorders, 9,* 275–282.

Humphrey, L. L. (1986). Family relations in bulimic-anorexic and nondistressed families. *International Journal of Eating Disorders, 5,* 223–232.

Humphrey, L. L. (1988). Relationships within subtypes of anorexic, bulimic, and normal families. *Journal of American Academy of Child and Adolescent Psychiatry, 27*(5), 544–551.

Irwin, M. (1981). Diagnosis of anorexia nervosa in children and the validity of DSM-III. *American Journal of Psychiatry, 138,* 1382–1383.

Jacobs, B. W., & Isaacs, S. (1986). Pre-pubertal anorexia nervosa: A retrospective controlled study. *Journal of Child Psychology and Psychiatry, 27,* 237–250.

Johnson, C., Tobin, D. L., & Lipkin, J. (1989). Epidemiologic changes in bulimic behavior among female adolescents over a five-year period. *International Journal of Eating Disorders, 8*(6), 647–655.

Josselson, R. (1973). Psychodynamic aspects of identity formation in college women. *Journal of Youth and Adolescence, 2,* 3–52.

Katz, J. L. (1985). Some reflections on the nature of eating disorders: On the need for humility. *International Journal of Eating Disorders, 4,* 617–626.

Kovacs, M. (1986). A developmental perspective on methods and measures in the assessment of depressive disorders: The clinical interview. In M. Rutter, C. E. Izard, & P. B. Read (Eds.), *Depression in young people: Developmental and clinical perspectives* (pp. 435–465). New York: Guilford Press.

Lancelot, C., Brooks-Gunn, J., Warren, M. P., & Newman, D. L. (1991). A comparison of DSM-III and DSM-IIIR bulimia classifications for psychopathology and other eating behaviors. *International Journal of Eating Disorders, 10*(1), 57–66.

Lewis, M. (1990). Models of developmental psychopathology. In M. Lewis & S. M. Miller (Eds.), *Handbook of developmental psychopathology* (pp. 16–25). New York: Plenum Press.

Malina, R. M. (1983). Menarche in athletes: A synthesis and hypothesis. *Annals of Human Biology, 10*(1), 1–24.

Maloney, M. J., McGuire, J. B., & Daniels, S. R. (1988). Reliability testing of a children's version of the eating attitude test. *Journal of American Academy of Child and Adolescent Psychiatry, 27*(5), 541–543.

Marchi, M., & Cohen, P. (1990). Early childhood eating behaviors and adolescent eating disorders. *Journal of the American Child and Adolescent Psychiatry, 29*(1), 112–117.

McArdle, W. D., Katch, F. I., & Katch, V. L. (1986). *Exercise physiology: Energy, nutrition, and human performance* (2nd ed., pp. 642–649). Philadelphia: Lea & Febiger.

Paikoff, R. L., & Brooks-Gunn, J. (1991). Do parent-child relationships change during puberty? *Psychological Bulletin, 110*(1), 47–66.

Paikoff, R. L., Brooks-Gunn, J., & Carlton-Ford, S. (in press). Effect of reproductive status changes upon family functioning and well-being of mothers and daughters. *Journal of Early Adolescence, 11,* 201–220.

Paikoff, R. L., Brooks-Gunn, J., & Warren, M. P. (1991). Effects of girls' hormonal status on depressive and aggressive symptoms over the course of one year. *Journal of Youth and Adolescence, 20*(2), 191–215.

Pedhauser, E. J. (1982). *Multiple regression in behavioral research: Explanation and prediction* (2nd ed.). New York: Holt, Rinehart, & Winston.

Petersen, A. C., Brooks-Gunn, J., & Compas, B. (in press). *Adolescent depression.* Washington, DC: Carnegie Corporation, Council on Adolescent Development.

Polivy, J., & Herman, C. P. (1987). Diagnosis and treatment of normal eating. *Journal of Consulting and Clinical Psychology, 55*(5), 635–644.

Richter, J., & Weintraub, S. (1990). Beyond diathesis: Toward an understanding of high-risk environments. In J. Rolf, A. S. Masten, D. Cicchetti, K. H. Nuechterlein, & S. Weintraub (Eds.), *Risk and protective factors in the development of psychopathology* (pp. 67–96). Cambridge, England: Cambridge University Press.

Ritvo, S. (1984). The image and uses of the body in psychic conflict. *Psychoanalytic Study of the Child, 39,* 449–469.

Rutter, M. (1986). The developmental psychopathology of depression: Issues and perspectives. In M. Rutter, C. E. Izard, & P. B. Read (Eds.), *Depression in young people: Developmental and clinical perspectives* (pp. 3–30). New York: Guilford Press.

Rutter, M. (1990). Psychosocial resilience and protective mechanisms. In J. Rolf, A. S. Masten, D. Cicchetti, K. H. Nuechterlein, & S. Weintraub (Eds.), *Risk and protective factors in the development of psychopathology* (pp. 181–214). Cambridge, England: Cambridge University Press.

Rutter, M., Izard, C. E., & Read, P. B. (1986). *Depression in young people: Developmental and clinical perspectives.* New York: Guilford Press.

Sameroff, A. J., & Seifer, R. (1990). Early contributors to developmental risk. In J. Rolf, A. S. Masten, D. Cicchetti, K. H. Nuechterlein, & S. Weintraub (Eds.), *Risk and protective factors in the development of psychopathology* (pp. 52–66). Cambridge, England: Cambridge University Press.

Simmons, R. G., & Blyth, D. A. (1987). *Moving into adolescence: The impact of pubertal change and school context.* New York: Adline De Gruyter.

Stern, J. S., & Lowney, P. (1986). Obesity: The role of physical activity. In K. D. Brownell & J. P. Foreyt (Eds.), *Handbook of eating disorders: Physiology, psychology and treatment of obesity, anorexia, and bulimia* (pp. 145–158). New York: Basic Books.

Striegel-Moore, R. H., Silberstein, L. R., & Rodin, J. (1986). Toward an understanding of risk factors for bulimia. *American Psychologist, 41*(3), 246–258.

Strober, M., & Katz, M. (1987). Do eating disorders and affective disorders share a common etiology? A dissenting opinion. *International Journal of Eating Disorders, 6,* 171–180.

Strober, M., & Katz M. (1988). Depression in the eating disorders: A review and analysis of descriptive, family, and biological findings. In P. Garfinkel & D. M. Garner (Eds.), *Diagnostic issues in anorexia nervosa and bulimia nervosa* (pp. 80–111). New York: Brunner/Mazel.

Strober, M., Lampert, C., Morrell, W., Burroughs, J., & Jacobs, C. (1990). A controlled family study of anorexia nervosa: Evidence of familial aggregation and lack of shared transmission with affective disorders. *International Journal of Eating Disorders, 9*(3), 239–253.

Stunkard, A. J., Sorensen, T. I. A., Hanis, C., Teasdale, T. W., Chakraborty, R., Schull, W. J., & Schulsinger, F. (1986). An adoption study of obesity. *New England Journal of Medicine, 314,* 193–198.

Warren, M. P. (1980). The effects of exercise on pubertal progression and reproductive function in girls. *Journal of Clinical Endocrinology and Metabolism, 51*(5), 1150–1157.

Warren, M. P., Brooks-Gunn, J., Hamilton, L. H., Hamilton, W. G., & Warren, L. F. (1986). Scoliosis and fractures in young ballet dancers: Relationships to delayed menarcheal age and secondary amenorrhea. *New England Journal of Medicine, 314*(21), 1348–1353.

4

TOWARD A MODEL OF THE DEVELOPMENTAL PSYCHOPATHOLOGY OF EATING DISORDERS: THE EXAMPLE OF EARLY ADOLESCENCE

Michael P. Levine
Linda Smolak
Kenyon College

At any given time, 2% to 3% of females past the age of 13 suffer from anorexia nervosa or bulimia nervosa or both (Fairburn, 1988; Johnson & Connors, 1987). Retrospective reports from clinical samples indicate that the bimodal ages of onset for these eating disorders are 14 and 18 years (Levine, 1987). At least nine times as many women as men suffer from eating disorders (Johnson & Connors, 1987). Moreover, there is a tendency for those women who develop eating disorders to come from upwardly mobile backgrounds that blend a concern for appearances, an investment in the outward manifestations of status, and an emphasis on achievement in a variety of roles (Striegel-Moore, Silberstein, & Rodin, 1986; Timko, Striegel-Moore, Silberstein, & Rodin, 1987).

The most influential models of risk for anorexia nervosa and bulimia nervosa emphasize the complex interplay of distal predispositions and proximal stressors (e.g., Garfinkel & Garner, 1982; Johnson & Connors, 1987). These multidimensional models highlight the heterogeneity within eating disorders of causality, psychopathology, and symptomatology, and as such they have made very significant contributions to the understanding and treatment of eating disorders. However, the complexity of their multidimensionality suggests the need for a more parsimonious approach that has clear implications for research on etiology and prevention. We believe that the data concerning age of onset, gender differences, and association with upper socioeconomic status point to the usefulness of a developmental model that emphasizes the role of normal or

An earlier version of this chapter was presented at the meeting of the Society for Research in Child Development, Kansas City, MO, April, 1989.

normative factors in the cause of eating disorders (Attie & Brooks-Gunn, this volume, ch. 3; Polivy & Herman, 1987).

Two additional trends lend credence to this conclusion. First, the increased prevalence of clinically significant eating disorders among female adolescents over the past 20 years (Gordon, 1990) has coincided with dramatic increases among this group in weight and shape consciousness, the idealization of slenderness, body dissatisfaction, and dieting (Cohn et al., 1987; Kelley & Patten, 1985; Rosen & Gross, 1987). In fact, these experiences may now be normative among middle-class and upper-class white adolescent girls (Hesse-Biber, 1989; Polivy & Herman, 1987). Second, the rise of eating disorders as a significant health issue in upwardly mobile women has paralleled significant changes in sex-role expectations and gender identity for that group (Silverstein, Peterson, & Perdue, 1986; Steiner-Adair, 1986; Timko et al., 1987).

Building on the work of Attie and Brooks-Gunn (1987, 1989), Simmons (Bush & Simmons, 1987; Simmons & Blyth, 1987), and Striegel-Moore (Rodin, Silberstein, & Striegel-Moore, 1985; Striegel-Moore, Silberstein, & Rodin, 1986), we offer both a general model of normative influences on the onset of eating problems and its specific application to early adolescence. We believe our developmental approach to eating problems merits attention because it addresses a number of important questions: (1) Why are women at greater risk than men? (2) What constitutes a risk period for eating disorders? (3) Why is early adolescence a particular risk period? (4) What are the critical differences between nonpathological dieting, subclinical eating disturbances, and eating disorders? (5) What determines whether women under stress will develop an eating disorder as opposed to no disorder or some other type of disorder?

GENERAL MODEL

As shown in Figure 1, our general model postulates that three classes of precipitating events interact with peer and family influences and with personal vulnerability to determine the onset of nonpathological dieting, subclinical eating disturbances, or frank eating disorders. Although the relationship between these three outcomes is complex and in need of further clarification, they can be conceptualized as points along what we call a *partial continuum* (Polivy & Herman, 1987). There is a continuum because nonpathological dieters, women with subclinical eating disturbances, and women with eating disorders have certain beliefs, attitudes, and behaviors that are similar and therefore can be compared in terms of severity. The adjective *partial* acknowledges a discontinuity in psychopathology and perhaps in psychosocial adjustment such that eating disorders are qualitatively different from the other two phenomena (Polivy & Herman, 1987; Thompson & Schwartz, 1982).

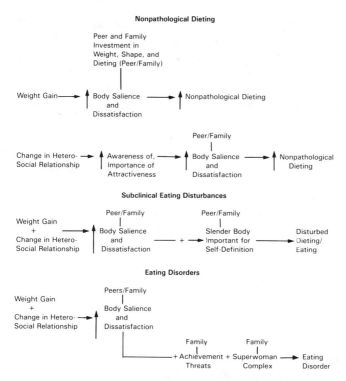

FIGURE 1 Developmental model of nonpathological dieting and eating problems.

Continuum of Eating Problems

Nonpathological dieting

At any given point in time, 50% to 70% of high school girls are trying to lose weight by dieting, although only 10% to 20% of these girls are statistically overweight (e.g., Kelley & Patten, 1985; Rosen & Gross, 1987). In most cases, such dieting is neither disturbed nor disordered. Many normal-weight girls yield to cultural pressures for body dissatisfaction and weight reduction but, fortunately, most do not or cannot sustain weight management in a manner that becomes pathological (Patton, 1988). A model of disordered eating must explain why the prevalence of self-reported dieting is extremely high relative to the prevalence of disturbed eating, eating disorders, and no dieting.

Subclinical eating disturbances

Numerous clinical reports and systematic studies have documented the existence of subclinical eating disorders in approximately 5% to 10% of postpubertal women (Button & Whitehouse, 1981; Garner, Olmsted, Polivy, & Garfinkel,

1984; Hesse-Biber, 1989; Johnson-Sabine, Wood, Patton, Mann, & Wakeling, 1988; Patton, 1988; Thompson & Schwartz, 1982). To highlight its distinction from eating disorders, we have renamed this heterogeneous category "eating disturbances."

For these women, low body weight in accordance with a slender ideal shape is central to self-concept and self-esteem. This type of weight and shape concern generates a morbid abhorrence of body fat, high levels of body dissatisfaction, and a powerful desire to become thinner. The behavioral results, in varying combinations for different women within this category, are unhealthy dieting, periodic binge eating, occasional purging, unstable self-esteem, and episodic anxiety about weight, shape, and food. These effects constitute serious problems (hence the label *disturbances*), but the number of symptoms or their severity is insufficient to meet the criteria for an eating disorder as outlined in the *Diagnostic and Statistical Manual of the American Psychiatric Association* (third edition, revised; *DSM–III–R*; American Psychiatric Association [APA], 1987). A developmental model must explain why some dieters proceed to develop subclinical eating disturbances whereas others do not (Patton, 1988).

Eating disorders

In our model, the term *eating disorders* refers to behaviors (e.g., frequency of binge eating), beliefs (e.g., that one is too fat even when obviously emaciated), and attitudes (e.g., principal definition of self in terms of weight and shape) that meet the *DSM–III–R* criteria for anorexia nervosa and bulimia nervosa (APA, 1987; Fairburn & Garner, 1988). At present, our model does not distinguish between anorexia nervosa and bulimia nervosa because we focus on the substantial similarities in their psychopathology (i.e., the shared nervosa; Fairburn & Garner, 1988; Garner, Olmsted, & Polivy, 1983). In both disorders there is a preoccupation with weight, shape, and self-control of food as crucial components of self-esteem, a fierce determination to be slender, an irrational fear of body fat, a distorted body image, and a sense of personal ineffectiveness.

As noted previously here, the difference between eating disorders and subclinical eating disturbances reflects both a continuity and discontinuity between them. There is continuity in that the weight–shape concerns, eating habits, and weight-management practices seen in eating disorders are more extensive, more severe, and more chronic (APA, 1987; Johnson & Connors, 1987). Consequently, eating disorders involve considerably more psychological distress and social maladjustment (e.g., Thompson & Schwartz, 1982).

The discontinuity is that the signs and symptoms of eating disorders, but not eating disturbances, are bound up with ego deficits such as extreme feelings of ineffectiveness, a disturbed awareness of internal processes such as hunger or emotions, interpersonal sensitivity and mistrust, and affective instability (Bruch, 1973; Garner et al., 1984; Johnson & Connors, 1987). In and of themselves, these ego deficits do not necessarily constitute a syndrome, but their presence implies that personality disorders or affective disorders will co-occur more frequently with eating disorders than with eating disturbances or non-pathological dieting (see Johnson & Wonderlich, this volume, ch. 10; Wonderlich, this volume, ch. 6).

As discussed in detail later, our model explains the qualitative differences between eating disorders and subclinical eating disturbances by emphasizing the interaction between cumulative stressors, weight and shape concerns, and a personality factor called the superwoman complex. One reason for focusing on the latter variable is the inadequacy of alternative explanations of discontinuity. Axis II character pathology (e.g., borderline personality disorder or avoidant personality disorder), depression, and sexual victimization are clearly important for an understanding of some cases of eating disorders, but there is compelling evidence that none of these is an etiological factor in most cases (Pope & Hudson, 1989; Smolak, Levine, & Sullins, 1990; Strober & Katz, 1988).

Body Salience and Body Dissatisfaction

The crux of our model is that all points along the partial continuum of eating disturbances and disorders begin with person–environment transactions that increase the salience of body image and, therefore, the likelihood of body dissatisfaction. Clinical experience and numerous studies indicate that body dissatisfaction is a crucial moderating variable for nonpathological dieting and for eating problems in those for whom body shape and weight are important components of self-concept (Fairburn & Garner, 1988; Polivy & Herman, 1987; Rosen, this volume, ch. 9; Striegel-Moore, Silberstein, & Rodin, 1986).

We postulate that the most frequent causes of increases in body salience and body dissatisfaction in women are (1) weight gain and (2) changes in heterosocial relationships in which physical attractiveness plays a role. Socialization pressures continue to insist that women build their identities around their bodies and interpersonal relationships (for reviews, see Attie & Brooks-Gunn, 1987; Striegel-Moore, Silberstein, & Rodin, 1986). By the fourth grade, girls begin expressing body dissatisfaction and fears about becoming fat (Thelen, Powell, Lawrence, & Kuhnert, 1990). Thus, messages about attractiveness and slimness reach girls early. Although the precise mechanisms by which these messages are transmitted are unknown, there is evidence that some parents place more pressure concerning weight and dieting on their daughters than other parents do. These daughters often respond with eating problems (Moreno & Thelen, 1990). Insomuch as thinness and dieting have become part of people's conception of what it means to be feminine (i.e., part of the gender schema for women), we expect family and peers to be powerful influences (e.g., Kelley & Patten, 1985; Liben & Signorella, 1987).

Women's roles have expanded and grown more complex in the past 25 years, but being attractive to and for others remains a significant aspect of being female (Timko et al., 1987). In fact, being attractive may now be more important than ever because it symbolizes qualities relevant to career success as well as social success (Larkin & Pines, 1979; Silverstein & Perdue, 1988). For women more so than men, and for the upper classes more so than the lower classes, attractiveness and fitness are defined by slenderness, and avoidance of body fat has become a principal source of personal satisfaction and indeed moral superiority (Attie & Brooks-Gunn, 1987; Garner, Rockert, Olmsted, Johnson, & Coscina, 1985). Thus, weight gains in women will likely increase the salience of body image and the intensity of body dissatisfaction even though accumulation of adipose tissue is a normal aspect of female maturation (Rodin et al., 1985; Warren, 1983).

Girls and women believe that attractiveness is important to heterosocial success and that men prefer thin rather than curvaceous or heavier women. Judgments of heterosocial success and physical attractiveness are intimately linked (Fallon & Rozin, 1985; Simmons & Blyth, 1987). Consequently, changes in heterosocial relationships are likely to heighten awareness of the importance of being attractive. This in turn increases the salience of body image, thereby increasing the probability of body dissatisfaction.

It is important to note that, although the changes that trigger increases in body salience and body dissatisfaction may be stressors, they are not necessarily traumatic or major life events (such as divorce or sexual abuse). In fact, our model assumes that weight gains and relationship changes across a woman's life span are more likely to be caused by developmentally normative events. Weight gains could arise from pubertal development, the first year of college ("the freshman 15"), or becoming pregnant. Changes in heterosocial relationships include the emergence of an interest in boys and dating during junior high school, the onset or intensification of sexual relationships during college, or the resumption of dating after a divorce.

Path to Nonpathological Dieting

According to our model, weight gains will positively correlate with increased body salience and dissatisfaction. This will lead to nonpathological dieting. Similarly, changes in social relationships that heighten awareness of physical attractiveness will be positively correlated with nonpathological dieting. If the two events are concurrent (which we define as occurring within the same year), their effect will be cumulative. Therefore, the likelihood of dieting will be even greater. Weight gains and relationship changes occur fairly frequently in the course of female development. Thus, our model can account for the high prevalence of dieting among postpubertal women.

Path to Subclinical Eating Disturbances

The model assumes that subclinical eating disturbances, as opposed to non-pathological dieting, are more likely when a vulnerable person encounters (or creates) a set of stressors that make up a cumulative threat to various interlocking aspects of self-concept (Simmons & Blyth, 1987). To reiterate, in our model, "cumulative" means that the stressful events occur within the same year. On the basis of this transactional perspective, we predict that the combination of weight gain and social changes will lead to disturbed eating if body salience and body dissatisfaction are great enough and if the individual has goals for slenderness that are well-defined but difficult to obtain because of biological predispositions.

A significant disparity between current weight (gain) and an unrealistic slender ideal is likely to create extreme dissatisfaction, anxiety about self-control, and periods of intense dieting (Garner et al., 1985). If the individual's weight set point is normally well above the ideal, the intense dietary restraint increases the probability of dietary disregulation in the form of binge eating and unhealthy methods of weight management, such as vomiting and use of laxatives (Garner et al., 1985; Polivy & Herman, 1987). In other words, the interaction between weight gain, heterosocial changes, and a slender ideal sets the stage for the dietary spiral described by Heatherton and Polivy (this volume, ch. 8).

Path to Eating Disorders

As discussed previously, eating disorders are more likely than disturbed eating to be generated and sustained by ego deficits and by intense feelings of dissatisfaction, ineffectiveness, and distress. Our model accounts for this by proposing that the development of eating disorders, as opposed to disturbed eating, requires two additional variables (see Figure 1). First, weight gain and changes in heterosocial relationships must coincide with a threat to achievement status. Thus, the girl or woman would be faced with two stressors (weight gain and relationship change) that directly increase body salience and body dissatisfaction and a third issue (achievement threats) that creates or intensifies an overall sense of ineffectiveness, loss of control, and distress.

The second variable is a personality characteristic called the superwoman complex (Boskind-White & White, 1983; Steiner-Adair, 1986; Timko et al., 1987). The woman with this characteristic builds her identity around high achievement in a variety of realms including, at a minimum, school or work, social relationships, and attractiveness and fitness. Success is important to her because it brings respect, status, and the opportunity for wealth, not just financial stability. One form of achievement is self-controlled attainment of the slender, ostensibly fit body valued as attractive by our culture. The superwoman sees physical attractiveness as important for career success as well. Dieting, exercising, and controlling herself become areas in which she can compete and excel (Rodin et al., 1985; Steiner-Adair, 1986; Striegel-Moore, this volume, ch. 12).

The superwoman does not reject all that is "feminine": She wants a good-looking, successful husband and attractive, gifted children. However, success in traditional feminine realms is not enough for her, possibly because she associates the traditional female role and its concomitant rounded shape with dependence, weakness, and passivity (Silverstein & Perdue, 1988; Steiner-Adair, 1986; Wooley & Wooley, 1985). The superwoman also wants to be successful in masculine roles involving autonomy, accomplishment, and individual power. Thus, the essence of the superwoman is the pursuit of excellence in multiple roles that cut across traditional conceptions of femininity and masculinity (Murnen, Smolak, & Levine, 1991). Consequently, superwoman constitutes a new gender category that is neither masculine nor feminine nor androgynous.

We hypothesize that the principal components of the superwoman complex—multiple and potentially contradictory roles, perfectionism, and an extreme need for external approval—are a compromise between sociocultural messages about the modern woman and ego deficits that have been implicated in the development of eating disorders. In other words, we suspect that the superwoman complex is a false self that emerges as a defense against identity confusion (Boskind-White & White, 1983; Steiner-Adair, 1986), family conflict (Wooley & Wooley, 1985), familial pressure to succeed, and a profound sense of personal ineffectiveness (Bruch, 1973; Johnson & Connors, 1987). Given this unstable foundation, the superwoman will always measure her success against the standards of her beliefs about what others expect of her and her perceptions of what others think of her. This external orientation leaves her extremely vulnerable to perceived loss of status in the eyes of family and peers.

The superwoman complex creates a unique vulnerability to the pathogenic effects of weight gains, changes in heterosocial relationships, and threats to achievement. Faced with the co-occurrence of these stressors, the superwoman is likely to become obsessively dissatisfied with her body shape and to feel distressed, out of control, and alone in her struggle. The most salient solution to these problems is dictated by the schema that in part nurtured them, namely to become thin, to control one's hunger and body, to diet perfectly, and even to purge oneself of past errors (Silverstein & Perdue, 1988). In the short term, "success" in these endeavors may well "solve" all three problems: weight management, protection of heterosocial relationships, and achievement. However, over time "successful" control of this type moves the person toward anorexia nervosa, whereas failure sets the stage for the cyclical dieting, bingeing, and purging of bulimia nervosa (Garner et al., 1985; Johnson & Connors, 1987).

Considerations of false self and coping style raise an important point about the origin of the superwoman complex. We believe that the superwoman complex, like other gender schema (Stangor & Ruble, 1987), is constructed by the individual as she interacts with her environment. Family, media, and peers do not directly cause the complex. However, these socialization agents do provide numerous cues and reinforcements concerning the relationships between attractiveness, slenderness, dieting, self-control, coping, and competitive success (Gordon, 1990). We postulate that some women with the ego problems discussed previously will selectively attend to these messages and organize them into a superwoman orientation. The outcome of this constructive process may be pathological, but we would do well to remember that the components of superwoman are in some respects both reasonable and effective within the current culture.

A number of studies linked concerns with achievement and feelings of failure with eating problems and body dissatisfaction (e.g., Hawkins, Turrell, & Jackson, 1982; Kagan & Squires, 1983). In a more direct test of the difference between disturbed eating and eating disorder, Silverstein and Perdue (1988) found that different variables predicted purging and underweight status (two potential indicators of serious eating-related problems) versus dieting and binge eating. In support of our model, two of the significant predictors of purging were a slender ideal figure and the importance of professional success, whereas three predictors of underweight status were a slender ideal, the importance of popularity, and the importance of intelligence. It is logical to suppose that concerns about success and perceived intelligence would be heightened by threats to achievement.

The upper classes seem most likely to endorse the superwoman role, and they are the group at greatest risk for eating disorders. Within the upper-middle class, those high school girls and college-age women who embrace the superwoman ideal are at greater risk for eating problems (Steiner-Adair, 1986; Timko et al., 1987), and they are more likely to translate their feelings of failure into feeling fat (Striegel-Moore, McAvay, & Rodin, 1986). Moreover, consistent with our model, college women who report that many roles are central to their identity are more likely to believe that a fit, slim, and attractive appearance is important (Timko et al., 1987). Similarly, clinical reports and research indicate a relationship between perfectionism and eating problems (Bruch, 1978; Garner et al., 1983; Hesse-Biber, 1989; Kimele, Slade, & Dewey, 1987).

In summary, the model shown in Figure 1 (bottom) assumes that a high-risk period for an eating disorder (as opposed to a subclinical eating disturbance or nonpathological dieting) is one in which a set of stressors, any or all of which may be developmentally normative, combine to promote body salience, body dissatisfaction, distress, and perceived loss of control. These effects are attributable in part to activation of personality characteristics that constitute vulnerability to disordered eating: investment in body shape as a major reflection of self, a slender body ideal, and the superwoman complex.

In the absence of the superwoman complex, the combination of multiple stressors and a slender ideal body shape increases the probability of subclinical eating disturbances but not eating disorders. In the absence of both a slender body ideal and the superwoman complex, the combination of weight gain, social relationship changes, and achievement threats will produce a different disorder (e.g., depression), adjustment problems, or successful coping.

EARLY ADOLESCENT TRANSITION

Early adolescence (ages 11 to 14) offers a unique opportunity for examining the development of eating problems within the framework of a model emphasizing changes in weight, in heterosocial relationships, and in achievement status. Early adolescence is a period marked by changes in virtually every developmental realm. Physical growth is more rapid than at any other point except the prenatal period and early infancy (Brooks-Gunn, 1987). New levels of cognitive functioning (formal operational thought) often emerge. Social roles and demands shift, particularly in regard to heterosocial and familial interactions (Simmons, Burgeson, Carlton-Ford, & Blyth, 1987; Steinberg, 1988). Issues concerning identity may also appear.

Change in these areas allows researchers to tease apart their independent and interactive influences (Brooks-Gunn, 1987). For example, one can examine the effects of pubertal change on heterosocial interactions, the effects of heterosocial transactions on interpretation and assimilation of pubertal changes, and how schemas concerning the body change as cognitive development and puberty proceed. These research opportunities are readily available because the changes in question are normative.

The early adolescent years provide an interesting application of the model because this is one time in which the three types of stressors hypothesized as crucial all normatively appear. There are significant weight and fat gains associated with puberty. The beginning of dating marks a major new challenge in the realm of social relationships. Changing from an elementary school to a middle school or a junior high school alters achievement demands.

In addition, research indicates that for some girls these events occur one at a time, whereas for others they co-occur (Simmons & Blyth, 1987). An accumulation of negative events has been associated with psychological and physical symptoms in adolescents, especially girls (Compas, Davis, Forsythe, & Wagner, 1987; Siegel & Brown, 1988). Furthermore, the specific coincidence of puberty, dating, and moving into junior high school has been associated with a variety of negative outcomes for young girls, including reductions in self-esteem, grade point average (GPA), and extracurricular activities (Simmons et al., 1987).

Figure 2 shows the specific application of our general model to early adolescence. We turn now to an examination of the three normative developmental challenges and demonstrate how, when mediated by superwoman attitudes (including a slender ideal body shape), they may be related to nonpathological dieting, subclinical eating disturbances, and eating disorders.

Puberty

During puberty, body shape is increasingly important in determining self-esteem. After puberty, girls are more aware of and more concerned about their bodies (Brooks-Gunn, 1987; Grief & Ulman, 1982). Most girls are pleased about some pubertal changes, notably breast development and height increases, but they are typically distressed about their weight gain and the amount of fat generated during normal maturation (e.g., Attie & Brooks-Gunn, 1987; Brooks-Gunn & Warren, 1988; Fabian & Thompson, 1989). Indeed, girls' body image is the only area of self-esteem to show consistent declines across

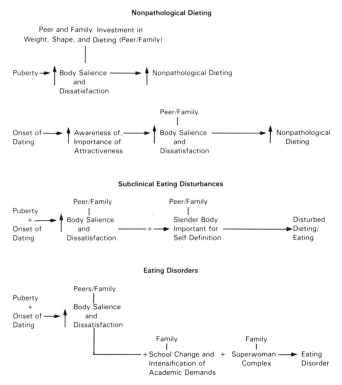

FIGURE 2 Developmental model of nonpathological dieting and eating problems in early adolescence.

the early adolescent years (Abramowitz, Petersen, & Schulenberg, 1984; Simmons & Blyth, 1987).

Among American girls, most of the pubertal process occurs during early adolescence. The average age of menarche, which occurs late in puberty, is 12.75 years, and the on-time range is 11.5 to 13 years. The greatest fat growth spurt coincides with menarche; typically, a seventh grader will be experiencing the most rapid single fat gain of her life (Brooks-Gunn, 1987).

Over the past 25 years, the ideal shape for women has moved progressively toward a prepubertal image of long legs, short torso, and thin hips (e.g., Attie & Brooks-Gunn, 1987; Silverstein et al., 1986). This means that normal biological growth moves the shape and weight of many females away from the prepubertal ideal (Faust, 1983). For females, this pernicious mismatch between culture and biology establishes the conditions for statistically and developmentally normative dissatisfaction with weight and shape regardless of actual weight for height (Polivy & Herman, 1987). This epidemic of female body dissatisfaction, usually accompanied by dieting, has been demonstrated in numerous studies (e.g., "Feeling Fat," 1984; Greenfield, Quinlan, Harding, Glass, & Bliss, 1987; Kelley & Patten, 1985; Klesges, Mizes, & Klesges, 1987). Moreover, weight–shape dissatisfaction and dieting are significantly correlated with pubertal status in early adolescence (Attie & Brooks-Gunn, 1989; Cohn et al., 1987; Gralen, Levine, Smolak, & Murnen, 1990).

Pubertal weight gain comes at a particularly bad time because it coincides with the early adolescent girl's growing desire to be popular and her growing concern with appearance, especially weight and body build (Simmons & Blyth, 1987). During early and middle adolescence, girls are also more likely to judge their own attractiveness in terms of popularity with boys (Simmons & Blyth, 1987).

Coupled with the normal development of fat deposits in puberty, this normative emphasis on opposite-sex popularity and attractiveness increases the probability of body salience and body dissatisfaction. The shape that girls believe is attractive to boys gets thinner over the period from early adolescence into the college years (Cohn et al., 1987; Fallon & Rozin, 1985; Gralen et al., 1990). At some point, perhaps as early as the eighth grade (Gralen et al., 1990), the disparity between a realistic increase in self-perceived current shape and a decrease in the shape seen as attractive to males becomes one component of the widespread body dissatisfaction (Fallon & Rozin, 1985).

Adjusting to the physical changes of puberty is a commonly cited developmental task of early adolescence (Havighurst, 1972; Simmons & Blyth, 1987). Our hypothesis is that, within the current culture of slenderness for women, nonpathological dieting will often be one facet of this adaptation.

Dating

Most adolescent girls begin dating between the ages of 13 and 14, probably as a function of pubertal maturation and sociocultural expectations that they begin acquiring the skills necessary for marriage (Dornbusch et al., 1981; Gargiulo, Attie, Brooks-Gunn, & Warren, 1987; Gralen et al., 1990; Magnusson, Stattin, & Allen, 1988; Simmons & Blyth, 1987). Research indicates that dating during early adolescence is more stressful for girls than for boys (Bush & Simmons, 1987; Simmons et al., 1987). This may be because females of all ages tend to emphasize intimacy over sex, whereas males are less oriented toward displays of caring (Gilligan, 1982; Rubin, 1985). Furthermore, girls and women may invest more of their identity in relationships so failures may be more devastating to them (Gilligan, 1982). Of course, we should not overlook the fact that heterosexual relations carry more risk for girls in the form of date rape, unwanted pregnancy, and even threats to one's reputation.

Dating, like puberty, is a normal developmental challenge requiring adaptation. Because of the link between attractiveness and heterosocial popularity, and because slenderness is an important aspect of attractiveness for females, one facet of adaptation is likely to be nonpathological dieting.

Additive Effects of Dating and Puberty

Either puberty or beginning to date could increase a girl's awareness of her body's shape, weight, or level of fat, and thus make her wish to be thinner. In fact, research indicates that puberty and beginning to date each makes an independent contribution to the likelihood of dieting in early adolescence (Gralen et al., 1990). It seems likely that their effects would be additive, as is the case for their documented effects on self-esteem (Simmons et al., 1987). That is, we believe the co-occurrence of puberty and first dates heightens the desire for a certain body type (narrow hipped, flat stomach) that most people believe can be achieved through dieting. We predict, therefore, an increase in the probability of nonpathological dieting when puberty and beginning to date occur independently and an even greater increase when they co-occur. If they co-occur and the girl's ideal body shape is (1) a very important goal for her and (2) unrealistically slender, than we predict the appearance of a subclinical eating disturbance but not an eating disorder.

Achievement Threats and the Superwoman Complex

In early adolescence, achievement threats are most likely academic problems such as a decline in GPA. However, these threats may also involve failure, or the threat of failure, in athletics, extracurricular activities, or other preprofessional activities. Such problems are particularly common when girls move from elementary to junior high school (Hirsch & Rapkin, 1987; Simmons et al., 1987). According to our model, achievement threats in early adolescence only predict disordered eating when (1) the threats coincide with puberty and first dating and (2) the girl holds unrealistically high ideals in a variety of areas (i.e., when she is a budding superwoman).

Threats to her high standards of achievement are likely to make the superwoman-to-be feel anxious, ineffectual, out of control, lonely, and perhaps even depressed. They may also cause her to feel fat (Striegel-Moore, McAvay, & Rodin, 1986). These negative effects are not caused by achievement threats per se. Rather, they represent a transaction between events and personal vulnerabilities to insecurity, disintegration, abandonment, and impulse-control problems (Johnson & Connors, 1987). We hypothesize that the negative effects of this transaction are likely to culminate in an eating disorder because of the body salience brought about by puberty and dating and because the superwoman complex incorporates a slender ideal and an overinvestment in control (Timko et al., 1987). Body salience may be heightened by familial values and conflicts concerning weight and shape (Garfinkel & Garner, 1982; Wooley & Wooley, 1985) and by family and peers who tease or pressure the girl about her chubby appearance (Fabian & Thompson, 1989; Moreno & Thelen, 1990). Moreover, socialization agents, including the media, generally emphasize the importance of a slim body for today's women. When confronted with complex, abstract problems, young adolescents tend to opt for the most salient solution (Baumrind, 1987). Thus, faced with the complexities of identifying and achieving the most appropriate appearance, young girls are likely to decide that thinness and weight control are the most straightforward solutions. This may be partially attributable to both direct messages and modeling cues from parents concerning the importance of slenderness and dieting (Moreno & Thelen, 1990).

TEST OF THE MODEL

As an initial test of our model (see Figure 2), 382 middle-school girls were given a set of questionnaires that assessed menarcheal status, dating status, perceived academic pressure, ideal body shape, body satisfaction, and weight-management behaviors. The girls were also asked about the level of weight–shape concerns and dieting among parents and peers. Three scales were then formed from those measures.

A four-item scale of parental investment in daughters' slenderness was produced by summing over the girl's report (all parental and peer measures were on 5-point Likert scales) of how concerned her mother and father were that she might be or become too fat as well as how important it is to her mother and father that she be thin (alpha = .82).

A three-item scale of mother's investment in their own slenderness was produced by summing over the girl's report of how often her mother is on a diet, how important it is to her mother to be thin, and how important physical appearance is to her mother (alpha = .69). The girls' perceptions of similar concerns for their fathers did not yield an internally consistent scale.

A three-item scale of peer investment in slenderness was produced by summing over the girl's report of how many of her friends would like to be thinner, how many of her friends are on a diet, and how often she and her friends talk about weight, weight loss, and dieting (alpha = .73).

To measure attitudes and behaviors associated with eating disorders, the girls also completed a child version of the Eating Attitudes Test (ChEAT; Maloney, McGuire, Daniels, & Specker, 1989; after Garfinkel & Garner, 1982). The ChEAT is not designed to determine the presence or absence of an eating disorder. Therefore, we considered higher scores to be indicative of greater eating disturbance and very high scores (≥ 27 = 90th percentile; Rosen, Silberg, & Gross, 1988) to be suggestive of eating disorder. We were unable to test the complete model because (1) we could not make diagnoses of eating disorders and (2) a measure of the superwoman complex, which we have developed (Murnen, Smolak, & Levine, 1991) and are currently testing for reliability and criterion validity, was not available.

To examine the effect of concurrent developmental stressors, girls were categorized as having experienced no changes (had never menstruated or dated), no simultaneous changes (had begun menstruating or dating, or had begun both but not within the same year), or two simultaneous changes (had begun menstruating and dating within the same year). Stepwise regressions indicated that, as predicted, girls who had experienced two changes simultaneously and who reported greater levels of academic pressure had the highest levels of disturbed eating. The predicted interaction between the three developmental stressors and slender body ideal also contributed significantly to the variance in ChEAT scores, as did peer investment in slenderness and parental investment in their daughter's slenderness, total adjusted R^2 = .27, $F(4, 205)$ = 19.96, $p < .0001$. A stepwise discriminant function analysis was then conducted to determine which combination of those variables entered into the multiple regression best discriminated between ChEAT scores high enough (≥ 27 = $\geq$90th percentile) to suggest an eating disorder and low ChEAT scores (≤ 16 = $\leq$75th percentile; Rosen et al., 1988). A function incorporating the interaction between simultaneous change and academic pressure, the interaction between simultaneous change and slender body ideal, peer investment in slenderness, and parental investment in daughter's slenderness resulted in correct classification of 84% of the cases.

As expected on the basis of our model, the predictors of nonpathological dieting differed from the predictors of eating disturbance. The most significant predictor of weight management was mother's investment in her own slenderness. Girls who had experienced two changes simultaneously did try harder to lose weight, but, as predicted, interaction effects (e.g., with ideal shape) were nonsignificant, total adjusted R^2 for the two significant predictors = .11, $F(2, 194)$ = 13.56, $p < .0001$.

These data provide considerable support for the utility of the vulnerability stressor model shown in Figures 1 and 2. Additional support is found in a multiple regression analysis of longitudinal data from 77 girls in the seventh grade who completed a comparable set of questionnaires for a study (Gralen et al., 1990) conducted while they were in the sixth grade. For this sample, the interaction between simultaneous changes in menarcheal and dating status, ideal body shape in the seventh grade, and academic pressure in the seventh grade was a more significant predictor of seventh-grade ChEAT score (and change in EAT score from sixth grade to seventh grade) than was EAT score in the sixth grade, total adjusted R^2 = .27, $F(2, 38)$ = 8.33, p = .001.

DISCRIMINANT ABILITY OF THE MODEL

Many of the proposed causes of eating disorders, such as sexual victimization, personality disorder, or distorted family dynamics, are remarkably similar to those of other disorders, especially depression. Our model, however, suggests that three types of events must co-occur to produce eating disorders. In addition, certain personality characteristics must lead to a particular interpretation of these events before eating disorders will develop. Finally, different combinations of the events and the personal characteristics will lead to different levels and types of eating problems.

Less than 5% of all postpubertal females suffer from a diagnosable eating disorder (Fairburn, 1988; Johnson & Connors, 1987), and the rate of disturbed eating is probably no greater than 10%. Therefore, any model attempting to predict these eating problems must identify a fairly small group of girls (and clearly a group smaller than those suffering from depression). Only 15% of the junior high school girls studied by Simmons et al. (1987) faced three or more concurrent stressors. Thus, our pool of potential eating disorders starts at about 15% of the girls. Within our model, this group would be further narrowed by the co-occurrence of the three specific stressors we name and the presence of the superwoman complex.

At the other end of the partial continuum of eating problems, less than 20% of the girls in the Simmons et al. (1987) study were not facing any of the developmental stressors. Thus, the group of girls facing at least one relevant developmental task is sufficiently large to account for the substantial percentage of girls who engage in at least casual dieting.

CONCLUSION

The proposed model emphasizes the synchrony of developmental stressors in combination with personal vulnerability to account for the continuum of eating problems in females. The focus on normative developmental events makes the model unique. Unlike most proposals concerning disturbed eating and eating disorders, the model offers specific predictions about the conditions leading to different types and levels of eating problems.

Early adolescence provides an interesting and important example of how our general model might be used to guide research. However, the model's usefulness is not limited to early adolescence. Anytime that weight gain, relationship changes, achievement threats, and unrealistic ideals coincide, there will be an increased risk of disturbed eating and eating disorders. Thus, other high-risk periods might be the transition to college, pregnancy and childbirth, and divorce (Dickstein, 1989).

REFERENCES

Abramowitz, R. H., Petersen, A., & Schulenberg, J. E. (1984). Changes in self-image during early adolescence. In D. Offer, E. Ostrov, & K. I. Howard (Eds.), *Patterns of adolescent self-image* (pp. 19–28). San Francisco: Jossey-Bass.

American Psychiatric Association. (1987). *Diagnostic and statistical manual of mental disorders* (3rd ed., rev.). Washington, DC: Author.

Attie, I., & Brooks-Gunn, J. (1987). Weight concerns as chronic stressors in women. In R. C. Barnett, L. Biener, & G. K. Baruch (Eds.), *Gender and stress* (pp. 218–254). New York: Free Press.

Attie, I., & Brooks-Gunn, J. (1989). Development of eating problems in adolescent girls: A longitudinal study. *Developmental Psychology, 25,* 70–79.

Baumrind, D. (1987). A developmental perspective on adolescent risk taking in contemporary America. In C. Irwin, Jr. (Ed.), *Adolescent social behavior and health* (pp. 93–126). San Francisco: Jossey-Bass.

Boskind-White, M., & White, W. C. (1983). *Bulimarexia: The binge/purge cycle.* New York: W. W. Norton.

Brooks-Gunn, J. (1987). Pubertal processes and girls' psychological adaptation. In R. M. Lerner & T. T. Foch (Eds.), *Biological-psychosocial interactions in early adolescence* (pp. 123–153). Hillsdale, NJ: Erlbaum.

Brooks-Gunn, J., & Warren, M. (1988). The psychological significance of secondary sexual characteristics in nine-to-eleven-year-old girls. *Child Development, 59,* 1061–1069.

Bruch, H. (1973). *Eating disorders: Obesity, anorexia nervosa, and the person within.* New York: Basic Books.

Bruch, H. (1978). *The golden cage: The enigma of anorexia nervosa.* Cambridge, MA: Harvard University Press.

Bush, D. M., & Simmons, R. G. (1987). Gender and coping with entry into early adolescence. In R. C. Barnett, L. Biener, & G. K. Baruch (Eds.), *Gender and stress* (pp. 185–217). New York: Free Press.

Button, E. J., & Whitehouse, A. (1981). Subclinical anorexia nervosa. *Psychological Medicine, 11,* 509–516.

Cohn, L. D., Adler, N. E., Irwin, C. E., Millstein, S. G., Kegeles, S., & Stone, G. (1987). Body-figure preferences in male and female adolescents. *Journal of Abnormal Psychology, 96,* 276–279.

Compas, B., Davis, G., Forsythe, C., & Wagner, B. (1987). Assessment of major and daily stressful events during adolescence: The Adolescent Perceived Events Scale. *Journal of Counseling and Clinical Psychology, 55,* 534–541.

Dickstein, L. J. (1989). Current college environments: Do these communities facilitate and foster bulimia in vulnerable students? *Journal of College Student Psychotherapy, 9,* 107–133.

Dornbusch, S., Carlsmith, J., Gross, R., Martin, J., Jennings, D., Rosenberg, A., & Duke, P. (1981). Sexual development, age, and dating: A comparison of biological and social influences upon one set of behaviors. *Child Development, 52,* 179–185.

Fabian, L. J., & Thompson, J. K. (1989). Body image and eating disturbance in young females. *International Journal of Eating Disorders, 9,* 63–74.

Fairburn, C. (1988, October). *Epidemiology: What we know and don't know.* Paper presented at the Seventh National Conference on Anorexia Nervosa and Bulimia Nervosa of the National Anorexic Aid Society, Columbus, OH.

Fairburn, C., & Garner, D. M. (1988). Diagnostic criteria for anorexia nervosa and bulimia nervosa: The importance of attitudes to weight and shape. In D. M. Garner & P. E. Garfinkel (Eds.), *Diagnostic issues in anorexia nervosa and bulimia nervosa* (pp. 36–55). New York: Brunner/Mazel.

Fallon, A. E., & Rozin, P. (1985). Sex differences in perceptions of body shape. *Journal of Abnormal Psychology, 94,* 102–105.

Faust, M. S. (1983). Alternative constructions of adolescent growth. In J. Brooks-Gunn & A. C. Petersen (Eds.), *Girls at puberty: Biological and psychosocial perspectives* (pp. 105–125). New York: Plenum Press.

Feeling Fat in a Thin Society. (1984, February). *Glamour Magazine,* pp. 198–201, 251–252.

Garfinkel, P. E., & Garner, D. M. (1982). *Anorexia nervosa: A multidimensional perspective.* New York: Brunner/Mazel.

Gargiulo, J., Attie, I., Brooks-Gunn, J., & Warren, M. P. (1987). Girls' dating behavior as a function of social context and maturation. *Developmental Psychology, 23,* 730–737.

Garner, D. M., Olmsted, M. P., & Polivy, J. (1983). Development and validation of a multidimensional eating disorder inventory for anorexia nervosa and bulimia. *International Journal of Eating Disorders, 2,* 15–34.

Garner, D. M., Olmsted, M. P., Polivy, J., & Garfinkel, P. E. (1984). Comparison between weight-preoccupied women and anorexia nervosa. *Psychosomatic Medicine, 46,* 255–266.

Garner, D. M., Rockert, W., Olmsted, M. P., Johnson, C., & Coscina, D. V. (1985). Psychoeducational principles in the treatment of bulimia and anorexia nervosa. In D. M. Garner & P. E. Garfinkel (Eds.), *Handbook of psychotherapy for anorexia nervosa and bulimia* (pp. 513–572). New York: Guilford Press.

Gilligan, C. (1982). *In a different voice: Psychological theory and women's development.* Cambridge, MA: Harvard University Press.

Gordon, R. A. (1990). *Anorexia and bulimia: Anatomy of a social epidemic.* Cambridge, MA: Basil Blackwell.

Gralen, S. J., Levine, M. P., Smolak, L., & Murnen, S. K. (1990). Dieting and disordered eating during early and middle adolescence: Do the influences remain the same? *International Journal of Eating Disorders, 9,* 501–512.

Greenfield, D., Quinlan, D. M., Harding, P., Glass, E., & Bliss, A. (1987). Eating behavior in an adolescence population. *International Journal of Eating Disorders, 6,* 99–111.

Grief, E., & Ulman, K. (1982). The psychological impact of menarche on early adolescent females: A review of the literature. *Child Development, 53,* 1413–1430.

Havighurst, R. (1972). *Developmental tasks and education* (2nd ed.). New York: David McKay.

Hawkins, R. C., Turell, S., & Jackson, L. J. (1982). Desirable and undesirable masculine and feminine traits in relation to students' dieting tendencies and body image dissatisfaction. *Sex Roles, 9,* 483–491.

Hesse-Biber, S. (1989). Eating patterns and disorders in a college population: Are college women's eating problems a new phenomenon? *Sex Roles, 20,* 71–89.

Hirsch, B. J., & Rapkin, B. D. (1987). The transition to junior high school: A longitudinal study of self-esteem, psychological symptomatology, school life, and social support. *Child Development, 58,* 1235–1243.

Johnson, C., & Connors, M. E. (1987). *The etiology and treatment of bulimia nervosa: A biopsychosocial perspective.* New York: Basic Books.

Johnson-Sabine, E., Wood, K., Patton, G., Mann, A., & Wakeling, A. (1988). Abnormal eating attitudes in London schoolgirls—A prospective epidemiological study: Factors associated with abnormal response on screening questionnaires. *Psychological Medicine, 18,* 615–622.

Kagan, D. M., & Squires, R. L. (1983). Eating disorders among adolescents: Patterns and prevalence. *Adolescence, 19,* 15–29.

Kelley, J. T., & Patten, S. E. (1985). Adolescent behaviors and attitudes toward weight and eating. In J. E. Mitchell (Ed.), *Anorexia nervosa and bulimia: Diagnosis and treatment* (pp. 191–204). Minneapolis: University of Minnesota Press.

Kimele, G., Slade, P. D., & Dewey, M. E. (1987). Factors associated with abnormal eating attitudes and behaviors: Screening individuals at risk of developing an eating disorder. *International Journal of Eating Disorders, 6,* 713–724.

Klesges, R. C., Mizes, J. S., & Klesges, L. M. (1987). Self-help dieting strategies in college males and females. *International Journal of Eating Disorders, 6,* 409–417.

Larkin, J. C., & Pines, H. A. (1979). No fat persons need apply: Experimental studies of the overweight stereotype and hiring preference. *Sociology of Work and Occupations, 6,* 312–327.

Levine, M. P. (1987). *Student eating disorders: Anorexia nervosa and bulimia.* Washington, DC: National Education Association.

Liben, L., & Signorella, M. (Eds.). (1987). *Children's gender schemata.* San Francisco: Jossey-Bass.

Magnusson, D., Stattin, J., & Allen, V. (1988). Differential maturation among girls and its relation to social adjustment: A longitudinal perspective. In *Life-span development and behavior* (Vol. 7, pp. 136–172). Hillsdale, NJ: Erlbaum.

Maloney, M. J., McGuire, J., Daniels, S. R., & Specker B. (1989). Dieting behavior and eating attitudes in children. *Pediatrics, 84,* 482–489.

Moreno, A., & Thelen, M. (1990, August). *Familial factors related to bulimia nervosa.* Paper presented at the annual meeting of the American Psychological Association, Boston, MA.

Murnen, S. K., Smolak, L., & Levine, M. P. (1991). *Development of a scale to measure adherence to the "Superwoman" construct.* Manuscript submitted for publication.

Patton, G. C. (1988). The spectrum of eating disorder in adolescence. *Journal of Psychosomatic Research, 32,* 579–584.

Polivy, J., & Herman, C. P. (1987). Diagnosis and treatment of normal eating. *Journal of Consulting and Clinical Psychology, 55,* 635–644.

Pope, H. G., Jr., & Hudson, J. I. (1989). Are eating disorders associated with borderline personality disorder? A critical review. *International Journal of Eating Disorders, 8,* 1–9.

Rodin, J., Silberstein, L. R., & Striegel-Moore, R. H. (1985). Women and weight: A normative discontent. In T. B. Sonderegger (Ed.), *Nebraska symposium on motivation: Vol. 32. Psychology and gender* (pp. 267–307). Lincoln: University of Nebraska Press.

Rosen, J. C., & Gross, J. (1987). Prevalence of weight reducing and weight gaining in adolescent girls and boys. *Health Psychology, 6,* 131–147.

Rosen, J. C., Silberg, N. T., & Gross, J. (1988). Eating Attitudes Test and Eating Disorders Inventory: Norms for adolescent girls and boys. *Journal of Consulting and Clinical Psychology, 56,* 305–308.

Rubin, L. (1985). *Just friends.* New York: Harper & Row.

Siegel, J., & Brown, J. (1988). A prospective study of stressful circumstances, illness symptoms, and depressed mood among adolescents. *Developmental Psychology, 24,* 715–721.

Silverstein, B., & Perdue, L. (1988). The relationship between role concerns, preferences for slimness, and symptoms of eating problems among college women. *Sex Roles, 18,* 101–106.

Silverstein, B., Peterson, B., & Perdue, L. (1986). Some correlates of the thin standard of bodily attractiveness for women. *International Journal of Eating Disorders, 5,* 895–905.

Simmons, R. G., & Blyth, B. A. (1987). *Moving into adolescence: The impact of pubertal change and school context.* Hawthorne, NJ: Aldine.

Simmons, R. G., Burgeson, R., Carlton-Ford, S., & Blyth, D. A. (1987). The impact of cumulative change in early adolescence. *Child Development, 58,* 1220–1234.

Smolak, L., Levine, M. P., & Sullins, E. (1990). Are child sexual experiences related to eating disordered attitudes and behaviors in a college sample? *International Journal of Eating Disorders, 9,* 167–178.

Stangor, C., & Ruble, D. (1987). Development of gender role knowledge and gender constancy. In L. Liben & M. Signorella (Eds.), *Children's gender schemata* (pp. 5–22). San Francisco: Jossey-Bass.

Steinberg, L. (1988). Reciprocal relation between parent-child distance and pubertal maturation. *Developmental Psychology, 24,* 122–128.

Steiner-Adair, C. (1986). The body politic: Normal female adolescent development and the development of eating disorders. *Journal of the American Academy of Psychoanalysis, 14,* 95–114.

Striegel-Moore, R., McAvay, G., & Rodin, J. (1986). Psychological and behavioral correlates of feeling fat in women. *International Journal of Eating Disorders, 5,* 935–947.

Striegel-Moore, R., Silberstein, L. R., & Rodin, J. (1986). Toward an understanding of risk factors for bulimia. *American Psychologist, 41,* 246–263.

Strober, M., & Katz, J. L. (1988). Depression in the eating disorders: A review and analysis of descriptive, family, and biological findings. In D. M. Garner & P. E. Garfinkel (Eds.), *Diagnostic issues in anorexia nervosa and bulimia nervosa* (pp. 80–111). New York: Brunner/Mazel.

Thelen, M., Powell, A., Lawrence, C., & Kuhnert, M. (in press). Eating and body image concerns among children. *Journal of Clinical Psychology.*

Thompson, M. G., & Schwartz, D. M. (1982). Life adjustment of women with anorexia nervosa and anorexic-like behavior. *International Journal of Eating Disorders, 2,* 47–60.

Timko, C., Striegel-Moore, R., Silberstein, L. R., & Rodin, J. (1987). Femininity/masculinity and disordered eating in women: How are they related. *International Journal of Eating Disorders, 6,* 701–712.

Warren, M. P. (1983). Physical and biological aspects of puberty. In J. Brooks-Gunn & A. C. Petersen (Eds.), *Girls at puberty: Biological and psychosocial perspectives* (pp. 3–28). New York: Plenum Press.

Wooley, S. C., & Wooley, O. W. (1985). Intensive outpatient and residential treatment for bulimia. In D. M. Garner & P. E. Garfinkel (Eds.), *Handbook of psychotherapy for anorexia nervosa and bulimia* (pp. 391–430). New York: Guilford Press.

5

BODY IMAGE, WEIGHT CONTROL, AND EATING DISORDERS AMONG CHILDREN

Mark H. Thelen
Chris M. Lawrence
Anne L. Powell
University of Missouri–Columbia

Eating disorders have become a significant problem in the Western world and have attracted the interest of many sectors of our society. This interest stems, in part, from what appears to be a high prevalence of bulimia nervosa and related behaviors. Whereas prevalence estimates of bulimia nervosa have ranged as high as 21.6% (Pertschuk, Collins, Kreisberg, & Fager, 1986), our own research indicated a prevalence of 2% and 3.8% in two populations of college women (Thelen, McLaughlin-Mann, Pruitt, & Smith, 1987). Prevalence estimates in the general population of females have ranged from 1% (Hart & Ollendick, 1985) to 10.7% (Pope, Hudson, & Yurgelun-Todd, 1984). Even if one takes the most conservative estimates of the prevalence of bulimia nervosa, it is still clear that this eating disorder is a significant problem that warrants our attention.

Researchers suggested a variety of causes that might be responsible for the onset of bulimia nervosa, including biological, psychological, and sociocultural factors (Striegel-Moore, Silberstein, & Rodin, 1986). Most researchers agree that multiple factors play a role in the cause of bulimia nervosa in most females. With the possible exception of psychoanalytic, object relations, and self-psychology theories, however, there is little theoretical work on childhood factors that might relate to eating disorders.

Most of the research to date has been with young females of at least adolescent age; little research has focused on eating problems and eating disorders among prepubertal girls. Some researchers suggested that physical changes at the onset of puberty play an important role in body-image problems, which are significant factors in eating disorders (Tobin-Richards, Boxer, & Peterson, 1983). Although relevant research has not been conducted, it is likely that the prevalence of bulimia nervosa among prepubertal girls is low. Nevertheless, eating-related attitudes, perceptions, and behaviors may be shaped during these early years, and these developments may place the child at risk of developing an eating disorder (Attie & Brooks-Gunn, 1989). We discuss recent research that suggests eating-related problems (e.g., body-image problems, dieting behavior, eating disorders) occur with significant frequency among preadolescent girls.

In this chapter, we review research on the occurrence of eating disorders and eating-related problems. We review other research, including our own work, that concerns eating problems in children. We also address variables that might significantly affect eating problems and eating disorders in children. These include peer and sociocultural factors, family influences, food difficulties, teasing related to obesity, and associated psychological problems. Finally, we address methodological issues and questions that might be pursued in future research.

With a few exceptions, the present chapter focuses on research pertaining to females because the prevalence of eating disorders is much higher among females than males. Because relatively little research is available concerning bulimia nervosa in children and because individuals with anorexia nervosa often exhibit bulimic behaviors (Casper, Eckert, Halmi, Goldberg, & Davis, 1980), some material on anorexia nervosa is included. Finally, because there is little theoretical work on childhood factors and eating disorders, the present chapter is focused on empirical rather than theoretical work.

OCCURRENCE OF EATING DISORDERS

Before discussing the occurrence of eating disorders among children, it is important to note some diagnostic issues related to eating disorders in children. The validity of the diagnosis of anorexia nervosa in children has been questioned. Irwin (1981) identified 13 children with possible anorexia nervosa. However, because of the smaller percentage of body fat on prepubescent girls, 54% of the subjects did not fulfill *Diagnostic and Statistical Manual of Mental Disorders* (third edition [*DSM–III*]; American Psychiatric Association, 1980) criteria for anorexia nervosa (weight loss of 25% of more). The revised version of *DSM–III* (*DSM–III–R*; American Psychiatric Association, 1987) criteria of 15% weight loss may result in fewer false negatives, however. In addition, Irwin (1981) noted that fluid intake is often restricted in anorexic children, whereas it is not in older anorexics. He suggested that this be an additional criterion. Finally, the cessation of menses is a criterion that is not applicable to prepubertal girls.

The issue of diagnosis of bulimia nervosa in children has not been addressed in the literature perhaps because there are no documented cases of bulimia nervosa in children. One problem that might occur when attempting to diagnose bulimia nervosa in children pertains to the validity of information obtained from children. It might be difficult for a child to acknowledge bingeing and especially difficult to report purging out of fear of detection and censure from parents. For both bulimia nervosa and anorexia nervosa, it is important to ensure that children understand the meaning of critical terms such as bingeing and restricting caloric intake when using self-report measures.

It is also important to discuss issues related to diagnosis because other disorders may be erroneously diagnosed as anorexia nervosa. Jaffe and Singer (1989) identified atypical eating disorders that occurred in young children. The 8 children (6 girls and 2 boys) were all prepubertal, ranging in age from 5 to 11 years; age at onset of the eating problems ranged from 1 to 8 years. These children displayed a number of eating behaviors that are associated with eating disorders such as slow eating, food rituals, hoarding, scavenging, and hiding of food. However, a number of behaviors that are necessary for a diagnosis of anorexia nervosa or bulimia nervosa were not apparent in these children. For example, no child expressed a fear of fatness, and only 1 child demonstrated a distorted body image, although this child was not opposed to gaining weight. All of the children experienced other psychological diagnoses in conjunction with their eating disturbance. The authors suggested that these children manifested a specific syndrome distinct from other eating disorders (Jaffe & Singer, 1989).

Eating disorders have been thought to be largely a disorder of adolescents and adults. The average age of onset of bulimia nervosa is between 17.7 and 21 years (Fairburn & Cooper, 1984; Mitchell, Hatsukami, Pyle, & Eckert, 1986; Russell, 1979). The mean age of onset for anorexia nervosa has been reported between 16.6 and 18.3 years (Crisp, Hsu, & Harding, 1980; Halmi, 1974; Nemiah, 1950; Theander, 1970). However, cases of eating disorders with an onset before the age of 16 and even before the advent of puberty have been reported (Theander, 1970). Up to this point, only cases of anorexia nervosa have been documented. In addition, no estimates are available on the prevalence or incidence of anorexia nervosa or bulimia nervosa for prepubertal children.

Anorexia Nervosa

A study conducted by Lesser, Ashender, Debuskey, and Eisenberg (1960) was one of the first to document anorexia nervosa before the age of 16 years. Of 15 subjects, 13 reported the age at onset before 16 years; 2 reported onset before age 11. Unfortunately, pubertal status was not documented in this study. Additionally, Goetz, Succop, Reinhart, and Miller (1977) reported 30 cases of anorexia nervosa in girls ranging in age from 9.5 to 16 years at the time of diagnosis, although age at onset and pubertal status were not reported.

Other studies more clearly identified the occurrence of anorexia nervosa before puberty. In a report of 15 subjects with anorexia, 9 had an onset before menarche (Blitzer, Rollins, & Blackwell, 1961). Warren (1968) also identified 20 girls with a primary diagnosis of anorexia nervosa; the age of onset was between 10 and 16 years. Of this population, 8 were prepubertal, and 4 showed some early pubertal development but were not yet menstruating. In addition,

Hawley, (1985) discussed the cases of 21 children who were 13 years of age or younger (range = 7.2–13.5 years) at the onset of anorexia nervosa. Of these subjects, 7 were prepubertal, 7 showed early development of secondary sexual characteristics but had not reached menarche, and 4 were postpubertal at the onset of the disorder. Silverman (1974) also identified 29 anorexic patients, 11 of whom were girls who had not yet menstruated before their first episode of anorexia. One study identified 48 children who were diagnosed with anorexia nervosa at an early age (Fosson, Knibbs, Bryant-Waugh, & Lask, 1987). These children, 35 girls and 13 boys, were between the age of 7.75 to 14.33 years at onset. Sexual development was assessed, indicating that 23 were prepubertal, 20 were pubescent, and 5 were postpubertal. Finally, Alessi, Krahn, Brehm, and Wittekindt (1989) published a case report of a 9-year-old who was diagnosed as anorexic, although the onset of eating problems coincided with the very beginnings of pubertal development.

Several factors commonly associated with eating disorders have been documented in young children with anorexia nervosa. A distorted body image was found in one group of anorexics when the onset of the disorder was determined to be before the occurrence of menarche (Blitzer et al., 1961). Half of another sample of anorexics were found to have a distorted body image, although this study did not differentiate between those who were prepubertal and those who were postpubertal at onset of anorexia nervosa (Fosson et al., 1987). Finally, a fear of fatness was documented in two studies of prepubertal children (Fosson et al., 1987; Warren, 1968). Perhaps as a result of the distorted body image and fear of obesity, food refusal was often present (Fosson et al., 1987). Preoccupation with food and with food-related behaviors as well as premorbid feeding difficulties and premorbid parental conflict with the child over food were also found (Blitzer et al., 1961).

As can be seen from the research reviewed here, the studies on prepubertal anorexia nervosa have often not included a postpubertal group to examine differences between the two groups. However, Jacobs and Isaacs (1986) conducted a controlled study that addressed the question of whether anorexia nervosa manifested itself differently in those subjects who were pre- versus postpubertal at onset of the disorder. In addition, a prepubertal neurotic group was included as a second control group. A number of variables were measured, including childhood feeding difficulties, family eating disturbance, sexual anxiety, and family disturbance and behavioral adjustment before onset of the disorder. The prepubertal anorectic group had a significantly higher level of childhood feeding difficulties and more feeding difficulties in close family members than both the postpubertal anorectic and prepubertal neurotic groups.

One unexpected finding in the studies addressing prepubertal anorexia nervosa is the greater number of boys at least compared with the number of adolescent boys in postpubertal anorectic groups. For example, Jacobs and Isaacs (1986) found only 1 postpubertal anorectic boy compared with 6 prepubertal anorexics. Fosson et al. (1987) identified 7 prepubertal and 6 pubescent boys but no postpubescent adolescent boys who were diagnosed as anorexic. Hawley (1985) identified 4 male anorexics who were prepubertal, which constituted 19% of his sample. Whereas there have been no direct studies addressing the different rates of anorexia in pre- and postpubescent boys, these studies suggested that the prevalence rates may differ for boys depending on their pubertal status. Several possible explanations exist for this disparity. It may be that prepubescent boys are more likely to become emaciated quickly, possibly because of the low rate of body fat, and are thus more likely to be diagnosed as anorexic after weight loss. It may also be that, as boys approach adolescence, they develop mechanisms other than food refusal to deal with their problems (Rosen & Gross, 1987). Given that issues with regard to body weight, dieting, and thinness are more relevant for females, the greater prevalence of eating disorders in older females is understandable. However, it remains unclear why the proportion of males to females appears to be greater for prepubertal anorexia nervosa than for postpubertal anorexia nervosa.

One of the most common questions addressed across studies conducted with younger eating-disordered subjects is the effect of age at onset on the prognosis of the disorder. To date, there is no consensus with regard to this question. Some studies demonstrated that early onset of anorexia nervosa is associated with better outcome (Goetz et al., 1977; Lesser et al., 1960). These authors concluded that anorexia nervosa in children is "probably commoner, milder, and more often spontaneously resolved than in older patients" (Lesser et al., 1960, p. 580). Eighteen patients with early onset anorexia nervosa who had been followed up at 8.7 years after treatment for anorexia nervosa were found to have a 0% mortality rate (Hawley, 1985). No deaths attributable to anorexia nervosa were found in a follow-up study of 30 anorectic subjects aged 9 to 16 years (Goetz et al., 1977). Goetz et al. concluded that there is a good prognosis for early onset of anorexia nervosa. However, several authors found that early-onset anorexia was not a good indicator of positive prognosis both physically and emotionally (Bryant-Waugh, Knibbs, Fosson, Kaminski, & Lask, 1988; Russell, 1985; Warren, 1968). For the most part, the studies addressing this particular question did not include control groups and were not methodologically sound. In many cases, age and pubertal status were confounded; therefore, it is impossible to determine what variables, if any, were related to a favorable or unfavorable prognosis.

Bulimia Nervosa

To date, no research has addressed the prevalence of bulimia nervosa in young children. As with anorexia, the consensus is that bulimia is a disorder that occurs in adolescents and adults. In the cases reports conducted with young anorexics, however, some bulimic symptoms were found to occur. For example, Fosson et al. (1987) found that 40% of their subjects exhibited self-induced vomiting, 33% exercised vigorously, 13% exhibited a binge-eating pattern, and 8% abused laxatives. However, it is unclear whether any of these subjects displayed the syndrome of bulimia nervosa. Lesser et al. (1960) reported that many of his subjects displayed periods of bulimia before becoming anorectic. Although the subjects were aged 10 to 16 years, pubertal status was not reported, and it is possible that bulimia occurred only in the older subjects.

Thus, it is unclear whether bulimia occurs rarely in preadolescent populations or if it simply goes undetected. It may be that, because anorexia nervosa often results in a marked loss of weight, it is more obvious to the parents or professionals. With bulimia nervosa, however, there is often no visible, noticeable symptom (such as significant weight loss) and, therefore, bulimia may be less likely to be diagnosed. In addition, bulimia nervosa generally requires secrecy to conceal the bingeing and purging. It may be that sufficient secrecy cannot be maintained by young children and, therefore, bingeing and purging do not develop in children. In addition, children do not have access to food or monetary resources that are required to engage in binge behavior. Future research with children should address other symptoms besides anorectic behaviors that indicate significant eating problems.

FACTORS ASSOCIATED WITH EATING DISORDERS IN CHILDREN

As has been emphasized previously, research on eating disorders in children is rare and consists mainly of case reports on anorexia nervosa. To date, little is known about the cause, maintenance factors, associated features, prognosis, or successful treatment approaches to childhood bulimia nervosa or anorexia nervosa. This section focuses on possible etiological factors in childhood anorexia, including food difficulties, the occurrence of obesity and teasing, psychological problems, and family difficulties. Although there appears to be some concomitant bingeing and purging with anorexia nervosa in children, bulimia nervosa as a distinct syndrome has not been documented among children. As a result, this disorder is not discussed.

Food Difficulties

Over half of a sample of 15 anorectic children ranging in age from 7 to 14 years had premorbid feeding difficulties, and approximately one quarter had a symbolic event such as having food stick in their throat before onset of anorexia nervosa (Blitzer et al., 1961). Premorbid parental conflict with the child over food was also present, reflecting some degree of difficulty with food (Blitzer et al., 1961). Jacobs and Issacs (1986) found that, as children, prepubertal anorexics (age not given) had higher levels of feeding difficulties as children than postpubertal anorexics. Warren (1968) determined that breast-feeding was prolonged in many of the 20 anorectic subjects in his study (age 10 to 16 years). However, only a few of his subjects were poor eaters or displayed food fads premorbidly. Premorbid eating difficulties may predispose some children to become anorectic because they are traumatized by food, or they may learn that food is an effective means of control in the family. However, the studies conducted have not used control groups so it is unclear whether premorbid food difficulties occur to a greater extent in those children who later develop anorexia nervosa compared with those who do not develop an eating disorder.

Obesity and Teasing

Little evidence exists that premorbid obesity plays a major role in anorexia nervosa. Premorbid obesity was found in only 20% of one sample of anorexic children aged 10 to 16 years (Warren, 1968). In another study, 1 of 15 anorectic children had a premorbid history of obesity (Blitzer et al., 1961). In addition, there were no differences between a neurotic group, a postpubertal anorectic group, and a prepubertal anorectic group on the prevalence of obesity or dieting among family members (Jacobs & Isaacs, 1986). However, Irwin (1981) described a 9-year-old anorectic girl for whom the precipitating factor for the disorder appeared to have been an incident in which she was teased by some boys about being fat. Therefore, obesity and particularly teasing about obesity may play a role in the onset of the disorder for only a subset of the patients (Fabian & Thompson, 1989; Warren, 1968).

Associated Psychological Problems

Other psychiatric disorders may be associated with eating disorders. It is unclear whether other disorders are related to cause, are simply an associated factor, or are a result of starvation. Alessi et al. (1989) reported a 9-year-old prepubertal girl who was diagnosed with anorexia nervosa and depression. In addition, other anorectic patients were described as exhibiting signs of depression (Blitzer et al., 1961; Fosson et al., 1987; Warren, 1968). Assuming a genetic or familial link, depression, anxiety, and alcohol abuse were found in relatives of 44% of children (younger than 15 years of age) with anorexia nervosa (Fosson et al., 1987). Thirty-five percent of the patients in another study had engaged in suicide attempts or self-inflicted harm (Jacobs & Isaacs, 1986). In addition, low self-esteem predicted eating disturbance among 12- to 13-year-old girls (Fabian & Thompson, 1989). Anxiety and obsessive-compulsive traits were found in many anorexics (9 to 16 years of age; Fosson et al., 1987; Goetz et al., 1977; Reinhart, Kenna, & Succop, 1972; Warren, 1968). One study found that many anorectic children (7 to 14 years of age) engaged in ceaseless physical activity (Blitzer et al., 1961), although it was not clear whether this was a weight-loss technique or a sign of hyperactivity. Only 10% of another sample (10 to 16 years of age) displayed signs of hyperactivity (Warren, 1968). In addition, premorbid behavior problems were more common among pre- versus postpubertal anorectic children (Jacobs & Isaacs, 1986). A few patients aged 10 to 16 years were described as schizoid (Lesser et al., 1960). However, in a sample of 9- to 16-year-old anorexics, none were found to be schizoid (Goetz et al., 1977). Reinhart et al. (1972) found that several of their subjects might have been schizophrenic as well, although Blitzer et al. (1961) did not find any schizophrenics in their sample. Hysterical personality was found in approximately half of two samples of anorexics who ranged in age from 9 to 16 years of age (Goetz et al., 1977; Lesser et al., 1960). Most of the patients in another sample (age not provided) were hysterical manipulative (Reinhart et al., 1972).

Some of the prepubertal anorexics were found to be socially withdrawn or shy. Warren (1968) found that all of his sample of 10- to 16-year-old anorexics were socially withdrawn. Sexual anxiety might have been present as well. Jacobs and Isaacs (1986) determined that a prepubertal group of anorectic children had higher levels of sexual anxiety than did a control group of neurotic children. Compared with older anorexics, a greater fear of puberty existed among younger anorexics. Blitzer et al. (1961) interpreted statements made by their 7- to 14-year-old anorectic patients and found that some expressed a fear of sexual maturity or oral impregnation. Incest fantasies were also sometimes expressed. However, Jacobs and Isaacs (1986) found that fears of oral impregnation were rarely expressed. In 2 of 15 children with anorexia nervosa, the occurrence of a pregnancy of someone in their environment appeared to precipitate the onset of the disorder (Blitzer et al., 1961). In conclusion, it appears that many anorectic girls display other signs of psychopathology ranging from social withdrawal to various forms of personality disorders.

Family Factors

The role of family factors in the etiology of prepubertal eating disorders is not yet well understood. In fact, although many factors have been identified, no factors have received strong empirical support. In this section, we illustrate the factors that have received some attention. Some of the mothers of anorexics aged 7 to 14 years were overconcerned with weight and might have been anorectic themselves (Blitzer et al., 1961). A family history of anorexia nervosa was found in first-degree relatives of 4 of 48 anorexics who were 11 to 14 years of age (Fosson et al., 1987). Jaffe and Singer (1989) determined that 3 of 8 children, who ranged from 5 to 11 years of age, with atypical eating disorders (i.e., a refusal to eat, although a need to be thin or a distorted body image was lacking) had mothers with an eating disorder. However, Warren (1968) did not find any cases of maternal anorexic nervosa in any of the mothers of his prepubertal anorectic subjects. The mother and father of a 9-year-old anorectic child were preoccupied with their own weight and often dieted. In addition, there was a strong emphasis placed on outward appearances (Alessi et al., 1989). Jacobs and Isaacs (1986) did not find any differences between an anorectic group and a neurotic group on the prevalence of obesity or dieting among family members. It is unclear whether the presence of an eating disorder or concern with weight or appearance among relatives predisposes a child to an eating disorder and whether this is specific to anorexia nervosa.

Other family characteristics, including marital conflict, parental psychopathology, and family dysfunction, may be related to juvenile anorexia nervosa. In 4 of 15 cases, marital conflict or conflict between the parents over their own problems regarding food appeared to predate the onset of anorexia nervosa (Blitzer et al., 1961). In addition, marital conflict was found in 7 of 8 children with an atypical eating disorder (Jaffe & Singer, 1989). Therefore, marital conflict may be only one of several predisposing factors and may be related to a number of childhood psychological disorders.

With respect to parental psychopathology and family dysfunction, 65% of the mothers of anorexics were found to be anxious, hypochondriacal, and overprotective (Warren, 1968). The parents of a 9-year-old anorectic child were very ambitious and described themselves as perfectionistic and obsessive (Alessi et al., 1989). Fosson et al. (1987) reported that family dysfunction was common in families of anorectic children. In addition, overinvolvement of family members was present in 82% of the cases. In another study, families of anorectic children displayed more overinvolvement than did families of neurotic children (Jacobs & Isaacs, 1986). Failure to resolve family conflict was present in almost 90% of the anorexics' (age = 1–14 years) families (Fosson et al., 1987). Inconsistent or inadequate parental control was present in 85% of the families. Communication difficulties were found in 75% of the cases. This also occurred more frequently in families with anorectic children than in families with neurotic children (Jacobs & Issacs, 1986). Parents were overprotective in 59% of the cases (Fosson et al., 1987). A disturbed father–child relationship was found more frequently among anorectic children's families than among those of neurotic children. No differences were found between pre- and postpubertal anorectic children or neurotic children in terms of a disturbed mother–child relationship. A disturbed mother–child relationship was found in more than 90% of the cases in all three groups (Jacobs & Isaacs, 1986).

In summary, many factors appear to be associated with the occurrence of anorexic nervosa in children. Some of these factors include teasing by peers regarding weight, eating disorders among relatives, a family history of depression, anxiety, alcohol abuse, marital conflict, family problems related to power struggles over food, overconcern among family members about weight, familial overinvolvement, shyness, perfectionistic tendencies, feeding difficulties as children, and sexual anxiety.

These conclusions regarding associated factors were, for the most part, based on case reports of groups of anorectic children. Most—an exception being Jacobs and Isaacs (1986) study—did not include control groups. In addition, most of the studies included mixed samples of pre- and postpubertal anorectic subjects. Finally, much of the information provided in these research reports was gleaned through unstructured clinical interviews that were retrospective in nature. Therefore, it is impossible to determine the specific factors related to the onset of prepubertal anorexia. As a result, the conclusions reached in this review should be viewed as tenuous. Despite the many methodological weaknesses inherent in these studies, however, rich information was provided about the possible etiological factors that may be involved in the early onset of anorexia nervosa. This information may point future researchers in the direction of several promising areas of research.

EATING-RELATED PROBLEMS IN CHILDREN

This section reviews research with children on eating-related problems that are seen as relevant to eating disorders. Foremost among these are dieting and body-image problems. Only one study concerned difficulties at meals and picky eating. In addition to research addressing anorexia nervosa and other eating disorders in children, our research (Lawrence, 1990; Lawrence, Thelen, & Powell, 1990; Moreno & Thelen, in press; Thelen, Powell, Lawrence, & Kuhnert, in press) and that of others (Maloney, McGuire, Daniels, & Specker, 1989; Marchi & Cohen, 1989) indicates that other eating-related problems and concerns can begin in childhood.

Moreno and Thelen (in press) obtained self-report data from 324 junior high school girls in the eighth and ninth grades (mean age = 13.75 years). Half of the subjects reported that they had been on a diet at some point in their lives. The reported age at first diet ranged from 3 years (.6%) to 15 years (1%). Sixty-four percent of those who had dieted reported that they had first dieted when they were 12 years of age or younger. Although it is likely that most of the 64% had not reached puberty when they first dieted, a measure of pubertal status was not taken.

Maloney et al. (1989) studied children in Grades 3 through 6. They reported that 55% of the girls wanted to be thinner and that 41% had tried to lose weight. Although no statistical analyses were conducted, there were appreciable increases in these percentages as a function of grade. Marchi and Cohen (1989) reported that 3.8% of children aged 1 to 10 had problem meals (e.g., unpleasantness at meals) and 29% were picky eaters.

A recent study was completed with nonobese second- , fourth- , and sixth-grade children (Thelen et al., in press). By means of a paper and pencil measure, the following variables were measured: dieting, which reflected the occurrence of dieting behavior; overweight, which dealt with the concern about being or becoming overweight; restraint, which assessed concern with the negative effects of eating food; and a real–ideal difference score, which reflected the difference between the silhouettes that subjects chose to depict their perceived body type and their ideal body type. The results highlighted gender differences and pivotal age differences between the second and fourth grades. Among fourth- and sixth-grade children, girls indicated more concern than boys about being or becoming overweight, more concern about the effects of eating food, a greater desire to be thinner than their perceived body figure, and a history of more dieting behavior. There were no gender differences among the second-grade children. Analyses for grade effects revealed that fourth- and sixth-grade girls were more concerned about being or becoming overweight and were more dissatisfied with their body image than were second-grade girls. No grade differences were found among the boys. The authors discussed the results in terms of societal pressure on children, especially girls, concerning their body weight.

Another study conducted by one of the present authors addressed dieting and body-image issues with third- and sixth-grade samples (Lawrence, 1990). Subjects received a body-image questionnaire derived from an earlier questionnaire administered by Thelen et al. (in press). The four factors addressed by the body-image questionnaire were the same factors derived in the original study: dieting, overweight, restraint, and a real–ideal difference score. Results indicated that white girls indicated more dieting and more concern about being or becoming overweight than did black girls, white boys, and black boys. This difference occurred regardless of the age of the child. Across both age groups, whites indicated more restrained eating behavior than did blacks. In addition, boys and blacks indicated that they desired a figure that was larger than their perceived body figure, whereas girls and whites desired a smaller figure than their own perceived figure. Finally, blacks desired a figure that was larger than their perceived current figure, whereas whites indicated a desire to be thinner than their current perceived figure. What was notable about these results was the lack of an interaction with grade. Thus, for third-grade white girls, dieting and body-image issues were as salient as they were for sixth-grade white girls. Because many sixth graders have entered or are anticipating entering puberty, one might expect differences between the two grades based on the puberty hypothesis that with puberty comes concerns with body image and perhaps increased dieting as a result. However, the present study found that this was not the case. Third-grade white girls were just as concerned with their body and were as likely to diet as were sixth-grade white girls. A previous study found that fourth- and sixth-grade girls indicated greater dieting behaviors and concern about body image than did second graders (Thelen et al., in press). It may be that the development of these concerns occurs between the second and third grades (Lawrence, 1990).

CHILDHOOD FACTORS ASSOCIATED
WITH BODY DISSATISFACTION
AND DIETING

Little research exists that examines the factors in childhood that are associated with body dissatisfaction and dieting. Current theory and research suggest that sociocultural influences, peer influences, and family factors may exert an influence during childhood and thereby cause body dissatisfaction and dieting.

Sociocultural Factors

In recent years, there has been an increasing trend in Western societies to value an ideal figure for women that is lean and thin (Furnhan & Alibhai, 1983; Garner, Garfinkel, Schwartz, & Thompson, 1980; Mazur, 1986; Morris, Cooper, & Cooper, 1989). Playboy centerfolds and Miss America winners have become increasingly thinner since 1960 (Garner et al., 1980) as have fashion models (Morris et al., 1989). Societal emphasis and value placed on thinness have been hypothesized to have resulted in an increase in body dissatisfaction and eating disorders among women (e.g., Schwartz, Thompson, & Johnson, 1982).

The sociocultural emphasis on thinness and the role it has played in eating disorders among women is well accepted. What is less clear is the age at which girls develop an awareness of sociocultural norms regarding weight and become dissatisfied with their weight. It has been suggested that puberty marks the beginning of body dissatisfaction (Tobin-Richards et al., 1983). However, some research indicated that body dissatisfaction among nonobese girls occurs before adolescence (Lawrence, 1990; Thelen et al., in press). In addition, age-matched pre- and postpubertal girls were not found to differ in terms of their body esteem (Fabian & Thompson, 1989). Therefore, it appears that some preadolescent children may be aware of the sociocultural emphasis on thinness and may be dissatisfied with their bodies.

What are the specific factors that place a child at risk for developing a negative body image in childhood? The first two risk factors are being female and white. Striegel-Moore et al. (1986) also cited evidence that girls learn from families, schools, and the mass media that their appearance is especially important. An important component of appearance is body shape and weight. Girls may pay more attention to judging weight in others than do boys. For example, girls (age range = 5–6 years) were better able to determine average weight and thin peers than were boys (Lerner & Gellert, 1969). Furthermore, Leon, Bemis, Meland, and Nussbaum (1978) reported that girls (8 to 13 years of age) were more accurate at judging an adult women's weight than were boys in judging an adult man's weight. The researchers suggested that girls pay more attention to the weight of other girls. These differences may reflect social learning differences because girls were reinforced for being thin. Lawrence (1990) found that third- and sixth-grade white girls were more concerned about being or becoming overweight, desired a smaller figure than their own, and indicated more dieting than did black girls, black boys, and white boys. Simmons and Rosenberg (1975) concluded that white girls are more self-conscious, place more emphasis on interpersonal relationships, and care more about their looks. Therefore, girls, especially white girls, appear more likely to pay special attention to cultural ideals regarding weight and attempt to emulate them.

At what age do girls become aware of sociocultural ideals regarding weight? Lerner and Gellert (1969) found that none of the 5- to 6-year-old girls desired to look like a chubby peer, whereas 4 wanted to look like the thin peer and 8 wanted to look like the average peer. The researchers concluded that cultural ideals of being thin or average weight as opposed to overweight were present in kindergarten children. Similarly, Lerner and Schroeder (1971) determined that kindergarten male and female subjects demonstrated a preference to look like the average figure and an aversion toward the chubby figure. Cavior and Lombardi (1973) found that, among boys and girls who were 5 to 8 years of age, the sociocultural criteria for judging physical attractiveness used by older individuals began to be developed at the age of 6 years and became fully developed by the age of 8 years. Similarly, Staffieri (1967) found that a preference to attain a mesomorph body build appeared at the age of 7 years in boys and was fully evident at the age of 8 years. However, girls were not included in this study. Thus, it appears that there is a developmental progression in terms of the awareness of sociocultural norms and acceptance of these norms. Unfortunately, none of these studies examined the presence of the awareness of the norms and the acceptance of these norms in the same study.

Another related question is the age at which children become aware of their own appearance. Five- to 6-year-old girls were better able to correctly identify their own body build than were boys, although this finding was not statistically significant (Lerner & Gellert, 1969). Staffieri (1967) found that 10-year-old boys were more accurate in their perception of their body type than were 7-year-old boys. Furthermore, Mendelson and White (1985) found that overweight children (mean age = 10 years) were less satisfied with their weight than normal-weight peers, indicating some accuracy in body-image perception. In contrast to these findings, however, 8- to 9-year-old children were found to overestimate their body size to a greater degree than were 12- to 13-year-old boys and girls (Leon et al., 1978). Unfortunately, there is not enough information from these studies to determine unequivocally developmental progressions in accuracy in body-build perceptions. Research should be conducted over a wide range of ages to determine the development of accurate and distorted body images.

In summary, there appears to be a developmental progression beginning at the age of 6 years to adolescence in which the accuracy of self-perception, the recognition of sociocultural ideals, and the preference for the culturally accepted ideals of physical attractiveness increase. In addition, from our data and those of others, it appears that puberty is not a necessary condition for body dissatisfaction to occur. With the change in the cultural stereotype of the ideal female body, even young, normal-weight girls are reporting dissatisfaction with their bodies.

Peer Influence

Peers may also exert an influence on body-image disturbances and dieting behavior. Negative attention from peers about one's weight may be related to body dissatisfaction. Fabian and Thompson (1989) found that greater frequency and negative consequences of teasing were related to a negative body image in premenarcheal 12- to 13-year-old girls. Furthermore, girls who are thin may be viewed more positively by their peers. Although there is no evidence to support this proposition, Staffieri (1967) and Lerner and Korn (1972) did find that boys as young as 6 years of age had common stereotypes (all positive) of the mesomorph image. In addition, Lerner, Karabenick, and Meisels (1975) reported that children in kindergarten through third grade acted differently toward children of differing weights, maintaining a greater distance away from the heaviest children. Another study found that the normal-weight figure was selected more often as being a better partner and leader than the obese figure (Counts, Jones, Frame, Jarvie, & Strauss, 1986). Finally, high scores on the Eating Attitudes Test for children were associated with thinking that friends would like them better if they were thinner (Maloney et al., 1989). Therefore, if the ectomorph body image is currently viewed as positive by girls, then girls may want to look thin to attain popularity or acceptance by their peers.

Family Factors

Retrospective research indicated that at least 40% or more of bulimic individuals had a history of obesity (Fairburn & Cooper, 1984; Johnson, Stuckey, Lewis, & Schwartz, 1983; Pyle, Mitchell, Eckert, Halvorson, Neuman, & Goff, 1983). Although there may be a genetic predisposition among bulimic individuals toward obesity, no research exists to support this supposition. If the child is overweight, this may result in pressure from parents to lose weight or an increased sensitivity to the weight issue. A disturbed body image may linger even if the child later loses weight.

In a recent study, data were obtained from the mothers of college-aged bulimics and a comparable control group (Moreno & Thelen, 1990). Compared with the mothers of normals, the mothers of bulimics were significantly more likely to report encouraging their daughters to diet and exercise. They also reported a greater likelihood of perceiving their daughters as being or having been overweight. This particular study failed to provide information, however, as to when the mothers had these perceptions and exerted pressure on their daughters. It is unknown whether these perceptions and suggestions on the part of the mother occurred when the daughter was a child. It is noteworthy that the mothers of bulimics and the mothers of normal-weight children did not differ in frequency of dieting or in their self-perceptions of whether they were or had been overweight. An additional finding is of interest here. Data taken from the fathers of bulimics compared with the fathers of normal subjects showed no significant differences on any of the measures. These data suggest that the mothers of bulimics played a more pivotal role than fathers in their daughters' eating problems. An alternative possibility would be that mothers are more accurate reporters of weight and diet issues than fathers.

Comparison of Factors Associated With Eating Disorders and Factors Associated With Body Dissatisfaction in Children

Data indicate that social biases toward thinness, especially in girls, have been adopted by children. Because by definition anorectic children have an intense fear of becoming obese, we might infer that these children have adopted socio-cultural biases toward thinness. However, no research shows that sociocultural factors, such as the media, play a role in the drive for thinness in anorectic children. Two lines of research that have been conducted in connection with dieting and body-image problems and with anorectic children are peer influences and family factors.

Research showed that children adopted negative attitudes toward obesity and that teasing was related to negative body image. This would be a factor in eating disorders only to the extent that anorectic girls had been obese. Research suggested that some anorectic girls had been obese, but most had been of normal weight. Negative peer reactions to obese girls may be a factor in anorexia nervosa in some children, but apparently many were not obese and therefore they probably were not teased about their weight.

Retrospective research suggested that the mothers of college-age bulimics had seen their daughters as overweight and had encouraged them to diet. These mothers did not report that they dieted more than did the mothers of nonbulimics. Research with the mothers of anorectic children showed inconsistent results. Some studies found greater body-image concern and more dieting among the parents of anorectic children than in a control group, whereas other research found no differences between parents of anorectic and control children. Similarly, some research showed that mothers of anorectic children are more likely to be anorexic than mothers of normal controls. Other research failed to find differences.

The research allows us to make no definitive statements about whether the factors critical to the development of eating disorders in children are also important to the development of dieting behavior and body-image concerns. This is an important question and one that deserves the attention of researchers.

METHODOLOGICAL ISSUES AND FUTURE RESEARCH

Because problem-eating behaviors in children received relatively little attention from researchers, numerous problems need to be addressed. Some of the major areas are discussed, and relevant research questions are put forth.

Before pursuing various facets of this area of research, the nature, frequency, and scope of eating problems in children should be determined. The prevalence of bulimia nervosa and other eating disorders in prepubertal children should also be assessed. However, before embarking on large-scale epidemiological research, the question of whether the diagnostic criteria used for adolescents and adults are suitable for children needs to be addressed. Obviously, cessation of menses as a criteria for anorexia nervosa is not applicable with prepubertal children. Perhaps the absence of reports of bulimia nervosa in children indicate that anorexia nervosa is more common than bulimia nervosa in children. Why might bulimia nervosa be uncommon in children? Is there something about bulimic behaviors that requires that the children be older? Perhaps children do not have the freedom to binge and purge even if they wanted to because of their inability to access large amounts of food and the lack of privacy for bingeing. Restricting food intake, as is found in anorexia, is a more innocuous behavior that bingeing and purging and, therefore, less likely to alarm parents initially.

With respect to the frequency of significant eating problems in children, we examined dieting and body image, but these and other variables need to be studied further. Do eating-related problems in perceptions, attitudes, and behavior put a child at risk for eating disorders? For example, are children who have a poor body image and diet at risk of developing anorexia nervosa or bulimia nervosa in adolescence or adulthood? There is some evidence that a poor body image precedes eating disorders in an adolescent population (Attie & Brooks-Gunn, 1989).

To address these questions, we need to develop valid and reliable measures to assess dieting and body image in children. Although some preliminary initiatives have been taken (Mahoney, McGuire, & Daniels, 1988; Thelen et al., in press), we need more effort in developing sound measures. We must try to ensure that the children understand the terms that are used. For example, what do children have in mind when they say they have dieted or binged? We need to define these terms in concrete language. When studying developmental changes, results might stem from age differences in the children's interpretation of the material presented to them. Also, the secrecy that is part of bulimia (the binge–purge cycle) makes assessment especially difficult. Because children have little power and independence, they might be even less likely than older females to acknowledge such behavior.

Often a new area of research starts with several case histories. Research on eating problems among children should move beyond that stage. We now need methodologies that include adequate sample sizes, but this may be difficult because of the scarcity of cases of eating disorders in children. Also future research should often include not only a normal control group but a group that shows other forms of psychopathology. With the exception of one study (Jacobs & Isaacs, 1986), this has not been done. A group that controls for other types of psychopathology allows for a determination of specific factors related to eating difficulties.

An important feature of our thinking and of this chapter is that eating-related problems, even eating disorders, can and do begin before puberty. Some of the research that we reviewed supports our assumption, but more and better research is needed. One problem in this area is that there is little agreement among researchers concerning an adequate measure of pubertal status. Some researchers use breast development as an indictor. Others use the presence of pubic hair, and still others assess menses. The use of different measures creates "noise" as we attempt to draw comparisons across studies. Also research on the importance of pubertal status should control for age so that differences cannot be attributed solely to age.

Future research should be directed toward determining from whom and where children learn eating attitudes, perceptions of body image, and dieting behaviors. The role of specific male and female family members, peers, and the media warrant attention. Also, what is the critical age at which the attitudes, perceptions, and behaviors are influenced?

Although the data are inconsistent, some research suggested that younger children with eating disorders, specifically anorexia nervosa, have a better prognosis than other children. This is an intriguing question that needs further research. Are younger girls with eating disorders different than older girls? Is the problem behavior in younger children simply a developmental stage that often is resolved by time and development? Is the prognosis better with younger children because their behaviors are less entrenched and therefore more readily remediated? Alternatively, is the prognosis poorer with younger children perhaps because eating-disordered behavior signals deep problems that are manifested early? These and other ideas should be pursued to examine the influence of age on prognosis in eating disorders.

CONCLUSION

One of the potential values of studying problem-eating behaviors in children relates to the issue of cause and effect. Research with adolescents and adults who have already developed clear symptoms of disordered eating almost always allows for the possible interpretation that the disorder in some way is an antecedent to the other variables under study. By conducting research with children, one can examine possible associated and etiological variables before the onset of eating problems. A natural outgrowth of this line of thinking is longitudinal research. In such research, certain associated and possible etiological variables could be identified and assessed before the onset of significant eating disorders. The children would then be followed to determine who developed eating difficulties. In the only known prospective study, Marchi and Cohen (1989) reported that pica and problem meals in childhood predicted symptoms of bulimia nervosa in adolescence.

A natural outgrowth of research on children, especially longitudinal research, is the notion that information will be obtained to be used for the development of prevention programs. If we can reach the children who are at risk before the development of eating problems, we can attempt to initiate programs that remediate those difficulties and reduce the likelihood that such children will develop a significant eating disorder.

REFERENCES

Alessi, N. E., Krahn, D., Brehm, D., & Wittekindt, J. (1989). Case study: Prepubertal anorexia nervosa and major depressive disorder. *Journal of the American Academy of Child and Adolescent Psychiatry, 28*, 380–384.

American Psychiatric Association. (1980). *Diagnostic and statistical manual of mental disorders* (3rd ed.). Washington, DC: Author.

American Psychiatric Association. (1987). *Diagnostic and statistical manual of mental disorders* (3rd ed., rev.). Washington, DC: Author.

Attie, L., & Brooks-Gunn, J. (1989). Development of eating problems in adolescent girls: A longitudinal study. *Developmental Psychology, 25*, 70–79.

Blitzer, J. R., Rollins, N., & Blackwell, A. (1961). Children who starve themselves: Anorexia nervosa. *Psychosomatic Medicine, 23*, 369–383.

Bryant-Waugh, R., Knibbs, J., Fosson, A., Kaminski, Z., & Lask, B. (1988). Long term follow up of patients with early onset anorexia nervosa. *Archives of Diseases of Childhood, 63*, 5–9.

Casper, R. C., Eckert, E. D., Halmi, K. A., Goldberg, S. C., & Davis, J. M. (1980). Bulimia: Its incidence and clinical importance in patients with anorexia nervosa. *Archives of General Psychiatry, 37*, 1030–1035.

Cavior, J., & Lombardi, D. A. (1973). Developmental aspects of judgment of physical attractiveness in children. *Developmental Psychology, 8*, 67–71.

Counts, C. R., Jones, C., Frame, C. L., Jarvie, S. J., & Strauss, C. C. (1986). The perception of obesity of normal-weight versus obese school-age children. *Child Psychiatry and Human Development, 17*, 113–120.

Crisp, A. H., Hsu, L. K. G., & Harding, B. (1980). Clinical features of anorexia nervosa: A study of consecutive series of 102 female patients. *Journal of Psychosomatic Research, 24,* 179–191.

Fabian, L. J., & Thompson, J. K. (1989). Body image and eating disturbance in young females. *International Journal of Eating Disorders, 8,* 63–74.

Fairburn, C. G., & Cooper P. J. (1984). The clinical features of bulimia nervosa. *British Journal of Psychiatry, 144,* 238–246.

Fosson, A., Knibbs, J., Bryant-Waugh, R., & Lask, B. (1987). Early onset anorexia nervosa. *Archives of Disease in Childhood, 62,* 114–118.

Furnham, A., & Alibhai, N. (1983). Cross-cultural differences in the perception of female body shapes. *Psychological Medicine, 13,* 829–837.

Garner, D. M., Garfinkel, P. E., Schwartz, D., & Thompson, M. (1980). Cultural expectations of thinness in women. *Psychological Reports, 47,* 483–491.

Goetz, P. L., Succop, R. A., Reinhart, J. B., & Miller, A. (1977). Anorexia nervosa in children: A follow-up study. *American Journal of Orthopsychiatry, 47,* 597–603.

Halmi, K. A. (1974). Anorexia nervosa: Demographic and clinical features in 94 cases. *Psychosomatic Medicine, 36,* 18–26.

Hart, K. J., & Ollendick, T. H. (1985). Prevalence of bulimia in working and university women. *American Journal of Psychiatry, 142,* 851–854.

Hawley, R. M. (1985). The outcome of anorexia nervosa in younger subjects. *British Journal of Psychiatry, 146,* 657–660.

Irwin, M. (1981). Diagnosis of anorexia nervosa in children and the validity of DSM-III. *American Journal of Psychiatry, 138*(10), 1382–1383.

Jacobs, B. W., & Isaacs, S. (1986). Pre-pubertal anorexia nervosa: A retrospective controlled study. *Journal of Child Psychology and Psychiatry, 27,* 237–250.

Jaffe, A. C., & Singer, L. T. (1989). Atypical eating disorders in young children. *International Journal of Eating Disorders, 8,* 575–582.

Johnson, C. L., Stuckey, M. K., Lewis, L. D., & Schwartz, D. M. (1983). Bulimia: A descriptive survey of 316 cases. *International Journal of Eating Disorders, 2,* 3–16.

Lawrence, C. (1990). *Body image, dieting, and self-concept—their relation in young children.* Unpublished master's thesis, University of Missouri-Columbia.

Lawrence, C., Thelen, M. H., & Powell, A. (1990, November). *Eating and body image concerns among children.* Paper presented at the meetings of the Association for Advancement of Behavior Therapy, San Francisco, CA.

Leon, G. R., Bemis, K. M., Meland, M., & Nussbaum, D. (1978). Aspects of body image perception in obese and normal-weight youngsters. *Journal of Abnormal Child Psychology, 6,* 361–371.

Lerner, R. M., & Gellert, E. (1969). Body build identification, preference, and aversion in children. *Developmental Psychology, 1,* 456–462.

Lerner, R. M., Karabenick, S. A., & Meisels, M. (1975). Effects of age and sex on the development of personal space schemata towards body build. *Journal of Genetic Psychology, 127*, 91–101.

Lerner, R. M., & Korn, S. J. (1972). The development of body-build stereotypes in males. *Child Development, 43*, 908–920.

Lerner, R. M., & Schroeder, C. (1971). Body build identification, preference, and aversion in kindergarten children. *Developmental Psychology, 5*, 538.

Lesser, L. I., Ashender, B. J., Debuskey, M., & Eisenberg, L. (1960). Anorexia nervosa in children. *American Journal of Orthopsychiatry, 30*, 572–580.

Maloney, M. J., McGuire, J. B., & Daniels, S. R. (1988). Reliability testing of a children's version of the Eating Attitudes Test. *Journal of American Academy of Child and Adolescent Psychiatry, 27*, 541–543.

Maloney, M. J., McGuire, J., Daniels, S. R., & Specker, B. (1989). Dieting behavior and eating attitudes in children. *Pediatrics, 84*, 482–489.

Marchi, M., & Cohen, P. (1989). Early childhood eating behaviors and adolescent eating disorders. *Journal of American Academy of Child and Adolescent Psychiatry, 29*, 112–117.

Mazur, A. (1986). U.S. trends in feminine beauty and overadaptation. *Journal of Sex Research, 22*, 281–303.

Mendelson, B. K., & White, D. R. (1985). Development of self body-esteem in overweight youngsters. *Developmental Psychology, 21*, 90–96.

Mitchell, J. E., Hatsukami, D., Pyle, R. L., & Eckert, E. D. (1986). The bulimia syndrome: Course of the illness and associated problems. *Comprehensive Psychiatry, 27*, 165–170.

Moreno, A., & Thelen, M. H. (1990, August). *Familial factors related to bulimia nervosa.* Paper presented at the annual meeting of the American Psychological Association, Boston, MA.

Moreno, A. B., & Thelen, M. H. (in press). Eating behavior in junior high school females. *Adolescence.*

Morris, A., Cooper, T., & Cooper, P. J. (1989). The changing shape of female fashion models. *International Journal of Eating Disorders, 8*, 593–596.

Nemiah, J. C. (1950). Anorexia nervosa: A clinical psychiatric study. *Medicine, 29*, 225.

Pertschuk, M., Collins, M., Kreisberg, J., & Fager, S. S. (1986). Psychiatric symptoms associated with eating disorder in a college population. *International Journal of Eating Disorders, 5*, 563–568.

Pope, H. G., Hudson, J. I., & Yurgelun-Todd, D. (1984). Anorexia nervosa and bulimia among 300 suburban women shoppers. *American Journal of Psychiatry, 141*, 292–294.

Pyle, R. L., Mitchell, J. E., Eckert, E. D., Halvorson, P. A., Neuman, P. A., & Goff, G. M. (1983). The incidence of bulimia in freshman college students. *International Journal of Eating Disorders, 2*, 75–85.

Reinhart, J. B., Kenna, M. D., & Succop, R. A. (1972). Anorexia nervosa in children: Outpatient management. *Journal of the American Academy of Child Psychiatry, 11,* 114–131.

Rosen, J. C., & Gross, J. (1987). Prevalence of weight reducing and weight gaining in adolescent girls and boys. *Health Psychology, 6,* 131–147.

Russell, G. F. M. (1979). Bulimia nervosa: An ominous variant of anorexia nervosa. *Psychological Medicine, 9,* 429–448.

Schwartz, D. M., Thompson, M. G., & Johnson, C. L. (1982). Anorexia nervosa and bulimia: The socio-cultural context. *International Journal of Eating Disorders, 1,* 20–36.

Silverman, J. A. (1974). Anorexia nervosa: Clinical observations in a successful treatment plan. *Journal of Pediatrics, 84,* 68–73.

Simmons, R. G., & Rosenberg, F. (1975). Sex, sex roles, and self-image. *Journal of Youth and Adolescence, 4,* 229–258.

Staffieri, J. R. (1967). A study of social stereotype of body image in children. *Journal of Personality and Social Psychology, 7,* 101–104.

Striegel-Moore, R. H., Silberstein, L. R., & Rodin, J. (1986). Toward an understanding of risk factors for bulimia. *American Psychologist, 41,* 246–263.

Theander, S. (1970). Anorexia nervosa. *Acta Psychiatry Scandinavian Supplement, 214,* 5–190.

Thelen, M. H., McLaughlin-Mann, L., Pruitt, J., & Smith, M. (1987). Bulimia: Prevalence and component factors in college women. *Journal of Psychosomatic Research, 31,* 73–78.

Thelen, M. H., Powell, A. L., Lawrence, C., & Kuhnert, M. E. (in press). Eating and body image concerns among children. *Journal of Clinical Child Psychology.*

Tobin-Richards, M. H., Boxer, A. M., & Peterson, A. C. (1983). The psychological significance of pubertal change: Sex differences in perceptions of self during early adolescence. In J. Brooks-Gunn & A. C. Peterson (Eds.), *Girls at puberty: Biological, social, and psychological perspectives* (pp. 127–154). New York: Plenum Press.

Warren, M. (1968). A study of anorexia nervosa in young girls. *Journal of Child Psychology and Psychiatry, 9,* 27–40.

6

RELATIONSHIP OF FAMILY AND PERSONALITY FACTORS IN BULIMIA

Stephen Wonderlich
University of North Dakota
School of Medicine

It is generally accepted that the cause of eating disorders is a complex phenomenon involving the intricate interplay of biological, psychological, and social factors (Johnson & Connors, 1987; Strober & Humphrey, 1987). Within this etiological framework, family relationships have received considerable theoretical attention as risk factors for the onset and maintenance of anorexia nervosa (Minuchin, Rosman, & Baker, 1978; Palazzoli, 1978) and more recently for bulimia nervosa (Johnson & Connors, 1987; Humphrey & Stern, 1988). Although numerous empirical studies examined this association, it remains unclear if specific family-interaction patterns exist that are causally related to the onset of an eating disorder (Strober & Humphrey, 1987). Much of the research on family factors in eating disorders examined what might be called the main effect of family factors. That is, eating-disordered individuals and their families are studied in an effort to find a type of family interaction that is generally associated with bulimia or anorexia nervosa. One drawback of this approach is that it minimizes the variability among families of eating-disordered individuals in spite of a growing appreciation of the heterogeneity of family environments within the population of anorectic and bulimic persons (e.g., Kog, Vandereycken, & Vertommen, 1989; Yager & Strober, 1985). Strober and Humphrey (1987) noted that such variability among the various eating disorders will need to be considered "if pathogenic familial influences are to be identified more precisely" (p. 655).

One means of understanding such heterogeneity in family functioning is through examination of the covariation of eating-disordered individuals' personality types and their family transactions. Benjamin (in press) hypothesized that each of the various personality disorders listed in *Diagnostic and Statistical Manual of Mental Disorders* (third edition, revised) (*DSM–III–R*; American Psychiatric Association, 1987) has specific backgrounds of family interaction that are etiologically significant. For example, the individual with borderline personality disorder is thought to have been raised in a very chaotic family; the borderline individual specifically experienced frequent threats of attack or abandonment, especially when pursuing personal autonomy or happiness. Alternatively, the obsessive–compulsive personality is thought to have lived in a highly controlled family with relentless pressure to perform, minimal warmth, minimal reward for success, and a constant threat of punishment for failure. When one considers Benjamin's ideas together with the reported variability in the type and extent of personality disorders among eating-disordered individuals (Wonderlich & Mitchell, in press), it is reasonable to believe that various family environments may be identified within specific eating disorders based at least in part on associated personality traits and disorders.

The present chapter examines the evidence for an association between bulimia nervosa and specific familial relationships with particular emphasis on the possible mediating role of personality in this association. Because of space limitations, I do not review literature pertaining to family demographics or family history studies of associated psychopathology or obesity in bulimia (see Vandereycken, Kog, & Vanderlinden, 1989, for a review of this literature). Also because the focus of this chapter is on bulimia nervosa, my discussion of familial interaction in anorexia nervosa is limited, and the reader is referred to several excellent reviews of this topic (e.g., Strober & Humphrey, 1987; Vandereycken et al., 1989). After reviewing the available family literature on bulimia, I briefly review and summarize theoretical and empirical data regarding personality factors associated with bulimia. Finally, recent preliminary data addressing variability in family functioning among eating-disordered individuals based on differences in personality disturbance are examined along with possible theoretical explanations of such variability.

THEORETICAL PERSPECTIVES ON THE ASSOCIATION OF FAMILIAL RELATIONSHIPS AND BULIMIA NERVOSA

Although family theorists have been interested in the study of anorexia nervosa for some time (e.g., Minuchin et al., 1978; Palazzoli, 1978), family-based conceptualizations of bulimia nervosa have, until recently, been scarce. Clinically oriented systems theorists developed a few typologies of families with a bulimic member. For example, Schwartz, Barrett, and Saba (1985) organized bulimic families along a dimension characterizing the degree to which the family has retained its ethnic heritage versus having adopted an Americanized identity. This categorization results in three theoretical types of families: Americanized, ethnic, and mixed. The authors suggested that in the Americanized family, the daughters are pushed to compete and excel socially and financially, whereas daughters from the ethnic families are encouraged to submerge personal ambitions in favor of conforming to traditional cultural or family roles (i.e., marriage, personal security, family acceptability). The mixed type is described as torn by the pull of ethnic tradition versus Americanization; the bulimic daughter is often interpersonally trapped between parents who are themselves divided on their level of traditional values. In all three types, the bulimic child is thought to become enmeshed in a family that is relatively isolated, lacking in intimacy, and child centered.

Similarly, Root, Fallon, and Friedrich (1986) delineated three types of bulimic families: perfect, overprotective, and chaotic. They suggested that all three types of bulimic families have boundary problems, attach unusual significance to weight and appearance, and are characterized by extreme levels of paternal (versus maternal) power. However, these three types are thought to differ in the nature of their family conflicts, rules, family of origin issues, and the interpersonal function of the bulimic symptoms. For example, bulimic symptoms in the demanding and often critical "perfect" family type may symbolize hostile individuation efforts, whereas the same behaviors in the disengaged and abusive "chaotic" family may represent self-abuse, a search for nurturance, or dissociation from a problematic environment. In all types, however, the bulimic symptoms are thought to reflect the difficulty that the family experiences negotiating the affected child's transition from adolescence to young adulthood.

Giat-Roberto's (1986) transgenerational family perspective on bulimia places particular emphasis on the idea of the child's extreme loyalty to the family, which is thought to disrupt the child's burgeoning self-development. She suggested that in bulimia such familial loyalty is transmitted through transgenerational family legacies, which are considered the experiential portion of the family belief systems. These multigenerational belief systems are deeply imbued with food and weight symbolism, which are thought to have pertinence to the development of bulimic symptoms.

On the basis of developmental psychodynamic theory, Johnson and Connors (1987) differentiated restricting anorexics from bulimics in terms of the degree of maternal involvement with the affected child. The restrictor's self-starvation is thought to reflect an effort to assert and separate from a highly overinvolved mother, whereas the bulimic's bingeing represents an attempt to avoid the emptiness and dysphoria associated with maternal unavailability. The authors noted that the mothers of bulimic individuals typically are not blatantly neglectful; rather, they display a subtle emotional unavailability and may struggle with their own intrapsychic deficits in the realm of affect regulation. Within this perspective, the mother's unavailability is considered a critical factor in the development of self-regulatory problems that predispose the individual to develop bulimia.

Humphrey and Stern (1988) attempted to integrate systems theory and object relations theory in a family-based conceptualization of bulimia. Relying heavily on Winnicott's (1965) concept of a deficient holding environment, they suggested that the entire bulimic family system is characterized by deficits in nurturance, soothing and tension regulation, empathy, and affirmation of separate identities. Furthermore, this inadequate holding function of the family is thought to be transmitted transgenerationally so that parents and children all display difficulty in establishing a self-contained personality and must rely on each other to complete a cohesive sense of a self. It is thought that the family defensively maintains an image of itself as all good or perfect through the defensive operation of idealization (Klein, 1975) but that the bulimic individual is split off from this ideal image through projective identification (Klein, 1975) and becomes the family's repository of unwanted or bad aspects of its individual members. Thus, the bulimic member accepts and protects the family from its own pervasive sense of inadequacy and becomes their vulnerable "sick" member, which is thought to predispose the child to the development of bulimia. Humphrey and Stern suggested that the bulimic's binge–purge cycle serves as a metaphor for the family's pattern of deficits and difficulties. The bulimic's food cravings are thought to parallel the family's pervasive longing for nurturance, soothing, and empathy, whereas bingeing reflects the family's periodic loss of control over their strivings for affection and acceptance. Similarly, the purging behavior symbolizes the unfocused hostility that the family endures.

Overall, the development of theories describing the relationship of familial factors and bulimia is in its infancy. The family typologies and systemic models of Schwartz et al. (1985), Root et al. (1986), and Giat-Roberto (1986) highlight both the variability among families with a bulimic member and the cognitive and affective processes within such families but are based almost totally on clinical observation and are clearly in need of empirical examination. The psychodynamic models of Johnson and Connors (1987) and Humphrey and Stern (1988) are also clinically interesting but rest in part on posited mechanisms and concepts (e.g., projective identification, part–object) that are difficult to operationalize and incorporate into hypotheses that can be empirically tested. However, other more testable interpersonal themes and hypotheses based on these psychodynamic theories have, to a limited degree, been tested in empirical studies that are reviewed in the next section.

Perhaps the greatest limitation of all of these family conceptualizations of bulimia is that they do not thoroughly account for how the affected individual chooses dieting, bingeing, and purging as symptoms rather than depression, drug use, or some other breakdown in personal functioning that may be related to problematic family transactions. Indeed, Johnson and Connors (1987) embedded their family conceptualization in a larger biopsychosocial model to account for bulimic symptom choice better. Although family theories may then help account for vulnerability to and maintenance of bulimia, they currently must incorporate other factors (biological, psychological, sociocultural) to help account for the specific symptoms and features of bulimia.

EMPIRICAL STUDIES OF THE ASSOCIATION OF FAMILIAL RELATIONSHIPS AND BULIMIA NERVOSA

Research on familial relationships in bulimic disorders can generally be grouped into two methodologically distinct categories: self-report and observation. Although some believed that self-report measures of family functioning are limited in value (Haley, 1964; Jacob, 1974), others argued that they serve important functions in terms of the validation of the constructs in family theories (Kog, Vertommen, & Vandereycken, 1987; Skinner, 1987). Kog et al. (1987) suggested that self-report measures provide an "insider's perspective" on the ideational world of the family, whereas observational techniques allow an "outsider's view" of how the family behaves. Because these approaches differ in terms of the nature of the data they provide, each is reviewed separately.

Self-Report Studies

Several self-report family-assessment instruments have been used in the study of families with a bulimic member. Perhaps the most widely used is the Family Environment Scale (FES; Moos & Moos, 1981), which yields 10 subscales of family functioning. Results of the studies using the FES generally converge to suggest that normal-weight bulimics perceive their families as less expressive and cohesive (Johnson & Flach, 1985; Ordman & Kirschenbaum, 1986; Stern et al., 1989) but more conflicted (Humphrey, 1986a; Johnson & Flach, 1985; Ordman & Kirschenbaum, 1986) and achievement oriented (Johnson & Flach, 1985; Stern et al., 1989) than do controls, although one study failed to find any relationship between subjects' scores on the FES and a self-report measure of bulimia (Kent & Clopton, 1988). The ratings of bulimics' parents on the FES generally indicate that they see their families more positively than do their daughters (Humphrey, 1986a; Stern et al., 1989), although they acknowledge less involvement and intellectual emphasis in their families than do control parents. Comparisons of bulimic and bulimic anorectic families on the FES reveal minimal eating-disorder subtype differences in the family perceptions of both the bulimic daughters and their parents (Humphrey, 1986a; Stern et al., 1989).

Measures based on circumplex models of social or family behavior have also been commonly used in studies of bulimic families. Circumplex models involve the circular ordering of interpersonal behaviors around two latent orthogonal dimensions (e.g., adaptability and cohesion or affiliation and interdependence; Wiggins, 1982). The Family Adaptability and Cohesion Evaluation Scale (FACES; Olson, Bell, & Portner, 1978) is a self-report measure of the two dimensions that underly the circumplex model of Olsen, Russell, and Sprenkle (1983): adaptability and cohesion. Some evidence exists that cohesion scores on the FACES are low for individuals scoring high on a self-report measure of bulimia (Coburn & Ganong, 1989) and for subjects meeting *DSM-III* criteria for bulimia (Ordman & Kirschenbaum, 1986), whereas the adaptability scale has generally not been associated with bulimic behavior in these studies. Humphrey (1986a) factor analyzed the FACES and produced eight factors, five of which differentiated the families of normal-weight bulimics and bulimic–anorexics from control families. Mothers, fathers, and daughters in the bulimic and bulimic–anorectic groups rated their families as less involved with each other than did control families. Similarly, in bulimic–anorectic families, all family members reported more detachment and isolation than controls. However, in normal-weight bulimia, only bulimic daughters and their fathers (not their mothers) converged in their perception of detachment and isolation in the family. Humphrey speculated that, in normal-weight bulimia, there may be a father–daughter link and that the mother's lack of reported detachment and isolation in the family is a product of her meeting her emotional needs primarily through her family. Finally, there was evidence that bulimic anorexics, but not bulimics, display problems with interpersonal boundaries in the family.

Intrex is a self-report measure based on Benjamin's Structural Analysis of Social Behavior (SASB; Benjamin, 1974, 1984). SASB is a model of interpersonal and intrapsychic behavior consisting of three circumplex surfaces, each of which corresponds to a different interpersonal focus: (1) focus on other (transitive behaviors), (2) focus on self (intransitive behaviors), and (3) intrapsychic (introject). Each of the three surfaces is based on the same two dimensions: affiliation (love–hate) and interdependence (freedom–enmeshment). Each surface consists of 36 behaviors that can be collapsed into 8 behavioral clusters per surface. Thus, in its cluster form, SASB theory posits that any behavior can be categorized into at least one of the 24 behavioral clusters in the model. Along with Intrex, there is a behavioral coding system that parallels the model, thus providing multiple measures for the constructs in the theory.

Humphrey (1986c, 1987, 1988) used Intrex in several studies to test her previously described hypotheses about family-wide nurturance deficits in bulimic families. She reported data suggesting that bulimic and bulimic anorectic patients view their parents as more blaming, rejecting, and neglectful but less nurturing and comforting than do control subjects. Importantly, restricting anorexics also reported high levels of parental blaming, rejecting, and neglect but not a lack of parental nurturance, supporting Humphrey's contention that nurturance deficits are specific to bulimia in the eating disorders. However,

Wonderlich and Swift (1990b) failed to find any differences between restricting anorexics, bulimic anorexics, and bulimics on Intrex ratings of parents. This may have been due in part to differences between the studies in the restricting anorectic samples. Humphrey relied on younger, classic restrictors, whereas Wonderlich and Swift included older restrictors whose age and possible comorbid personality disturbance may have been associated with a greater perception of parental nurturance deficits than younger anorexics (Wonderlich & Swift, 1990a).

The Belgian group reported findings with the Leuven Family Questionnaire (LFQ; Kog, Vertommen, & Vandereycken, 1989), which consists of three scales of family functioning: Conflict, Cohesion, and Disorganization. They reported that bulimics see their families as more conflicted and disorganized than do controls (Kog & Vandereycken, 1989; Kog, Vertommen, & Vandereycken, 1989). Kog, Vertommen, and Vandereycken (1989) also reported a tendency for bulimics and bulimic anorexics to perceive more conflict and disorganization in their families than restricting anorexics, but direct statistical tests of this relationship were not conducted, thereby limiting any conclusions about subtype differences. Interestingly, and contrary to many other findings, the bulimic and anorectic subtypes in this study failed to differ from controls on the Cohesion subscale of the LFQ. In another study, these authors do report, however, that normal-weight bulimics perceived less cohesion than anorexics (Kog & Vandereycken, 1989), but their own multitrait–multimethod validity study indicated that the LFQ Cohesion scale lacked discriminant validity. Clearly, further studies of the validity of the Cohesion scale of the LFQ are indicated, particularly with eating-disordered samples.

Kog, Vertommen, and Vandereycken (1989) also pointed out the possible effect of confounding factors such as social status and the family's life-cycle phase on family ratings. For example, they noted that differences between controls and eating-disordered groups in conflict and disorganization diminish as social status increases (Kog, Vertommen, & Vandereycken, 1989), but the statistical test supporting this inference is not clear. They also reported some interesting data indicating that mothers and fathers of eating-disordered individuals report more family cohesion as the child approaches emancipation from the family, whereas the parents of normal control children report less cohesion as the child approaches departure from the home (Kog, Vertommen, & Vandereycken, 1989). Although this invites interesting speculation on the significance of staging of family transactions, a later study failed to find a significant effect for the eating-disordered subject's age on any subscale of the LFQ (Kog & Vandereycken, 1989). More research is needed, however, to address the possible effects of factors such as social status and the family's life-cycle stage.

Various other self-report assessment instruments have also been administered to bulimic individuals to gain an understanding of their perception of their family functioning. In general, these findings converge with many of the previously described studies to depict the bulimic family as conflicted, disorganized, and lacking in cohesion. For example, studies using the Parental Bonding Instrument (PBI; Parker, Tupling, & Brown, 1979) suggested that bulimics perceive their parents (particularly mothers) as less caring than do controls (Palmer, Oppenheimer, & Marshall, 1988) and that, when they do perceive high levels of caring, there is an accompanying perception that their parents are overprotective (Pole, Waller, Stewart, & Parkin-Feigenbaum, 1988). Pole et al. (1988) also reported that low maternal care scores and high paternal protectiveness scores were the two best PBI predictors of bulimic symptomatology.

Other studies using multiscale family measures such as the Family Assessment Device (FAD; Epstein, Bishop, & Levin, 1983) or the Family Assessment Measure (FAM; Skinner, Steinhauer & Santa Barbara, 1983) also suggest that bulimics perceive pervasive disturbances in family functioning. Waller, Calam, and Slade (1989) found bulimics with a history of anorexia nervosa and restricting anorexics to be quite similar in their FAD profiles, which generally were less unhealthy than those of bulimics without a history of anorexia, although a direct statistical post hoc comparison was not conducted. Garner, Garfinkel, and O'Shaughnessy (1985) reported that bulimics and bulimic anorexics failed to differ on any scale of the FAM but that both groups differed from restricting anorexics on all scales. Woodside et al. (1990) also used the FAM in the only available longitudinal study of family factors in bulimia. They found that at index evaluation bulimics perceived more pervasive family disturbance than their parents, who acknowledged distress in their relationship with their bulimic daughter but denied personal or marital dysfunction. Furthermore, ratings after treatment indicated that the bulimics and their mothers viewed substantial improvement in their relationships but that paternal relationships remained unchanged.

In summary, the self-report studies of bulimics' families tend to suggest that bulimics view their families as hostile, inexpressive, noncohesive, and lacking in nurturance or caring. Although bulimics' parents also report similar perceptions, they tend to be less extreme than their daughters. There is some indication that bulimics and bulimic anorexics differ from restricting anorexics in their perceptions of their family, but there are notable contradictions in the literature. Similarly, and perhaps most important, it is unclear if these perceptions are specific to eating disorders or simply are associated with psychopathology in general. Studies with appropriate clinical control groups (e.g., affective disorder, anxiety disorder) are clearly needed. Another problem in this research is that the family perceptions may be largely influenced by the state effect of the bulimic condition and any associated mood disturbance. Lewinsohn and Rosenbaum (1987) indicated that individuals who are in a depressed state recall more negative family experiences than remitted depressives, suggesting that these recollections are significantly influenced by mood. Studies examining the effects of mood on self-report family measures in eating-disordered persons have been contradictory; one report found no depression effect on the PBI (Pole et al., 1988), and two found significant effects of mood on family ratings (Blouin, Zuro & Blouin, 1990; Wonderlich & Swift, 1990b). Furthermore, the family measures used in many of these studies also have uncertain or limited demonstrated validity (see Skinner, 1987, for a review), which limits the strength of the findings. Finally, the lack of prospective longitudinal data fails to address the issue of temporal precedence; it remains unclear whether perceived family disturbance predisposes to bulimia or is a consequence of it.

Observational Studies

Observational studies of bulimic families, although considered essential in testing family models of the eating disorders (Kog & Vandereycken, 1985; Strober & Humphrey, 1987), are less common than self-report studies. Sights and Richards (1984) conducted a modified observational study in which parents of both bulimic and nonbulimic daughters were interviewed about their marriages and their relationship to their daughters. Raters blind to subjects' diagnostic status listened to audiotapes of the interviews and completed the Parental Characteristics Rating Scales, an instrument designed for the study that assesses 11 categories of parental and family characteristics. On the basis of these ratings, bulimics' mothers were judged to be more domineering and controlling and holding higher expectations for their daughters than were control mothers. Fathers of bulimic daughters were described as being close to their daughters in early childhood but distant during adolescence, a pattern not characteristic of control fathers. This study, although intriguing, was based on very small sample sizes, and direct observation of parents and children was not conducted, which limits any conclusions it offers.

Kog and Vandereycken (1989), in their previously described self-report study, also gathered behavioral and observational data on the families of restricting and bulimic anorexics and normal-weight bulimics. Three family-related constructs were assessed in the study: boundaries, stability, and disagreement. The concept of boundaries was operationalized as the degree of conformity or agreement between family members on a written task, whereas stability was defined as the extent to which the family members consistently reported the same family members as their choice for various activities. Disagreement was assessed as the degree of avoidance versus escalation of conflict on a negotiation task. The eating-disorder subtype comparisons failed to differ on measures of boundaries or stability, but anorexics' families (both subtypes) displayed less disagreement than controls. Although the authors concluded that families of bulimics display more marked boundaries (disengagement) than did those of controls and anorexics, this does not seem warranted by the data because post hoc tests on this measure were not significant between eating-disordered groups. Overall, in fact, families of the bulimics in the study displayed very minimal evidence of dysfunction and failed to differ from controls on any observational measure and only one self-report measure (disorganization).

Humphrey (1986, 1987, 1989) reported three observational studies in which she used Benjamin's SASB (Benjamin, 1974) to code role plays of eating-disordered families' discussions of their daughters' separation from home. This observational coding system places behaviors in a geometric circumplex space based on the dimensions underlying the SASB model: interpersonal focus, affiliation, and interdependence. Coding can be focused on the process (the manner in which something is discussed) or the content (the literal meaning of the words) of a transaction. Consider, for example, a mother saying to her daughter, "You never eat what I cook for you." If this was coded in terms of process, it would be considered transitive (mother is focused on daughter), moderately hostile (low affiliation), and moderately controlling (enmeshed), resulting in a code of "belittling and blaming" in the model.

Humphrey's observational studies converge to depict bulimic families as hostilely enmeshed. Mothers of bulimics were more belittling and blaming than were mothers of restricting anorexics, bulimic anorexics, and controls, and also more ignoring, neglecting, sulking, and appeasing than were the mothers of controls. Similarly, bulimics were more belittling and blaming toward their mothers than were controls. Observed transactions between daughters and their fathers revealed that fathers of bulimics displayed more watching and managing as well as belittling and blaming than did control fathers, but this was also characteristic of fathers of restricting and bulimic anorexics. Bulimic daughters were less likely to help and protect or trust and rely but more likely to sulk and appease in relation to their fathers than were controls. Interestingly, although the parents of restricting anorexics shared many of these patterns with the parents of bulimics, they distinguished themselves with their unique combination of nurturing and comforting as well as ignoring and neglecting their anorectic daughters. Restricting anorexics similarly distinguished themselves from the other clinical groups by their submissiveness to their parents. The families of bulimic anorexics consistently differed from controls but were not distinctly different from the other eating-disorder subtypes on any measure. Humphrey hypothesized that this may be a product of the bulimic anorexics' symptomatic similarity to both restrictors (in weight) and bulimics (in behaviors). Finally, Humphrey, Apple, and Kirschenbaum (1986) also coded the family transactions of bulimic anorectic families with Robin and Weiss's (1980) cognitive behavioral marital interaction coding system (modified MICS). Although the MICS differentiated bulimic anorexics from controls, it did so largely on the basis of its interpersonal codes (e.g., put down, laugh at, and humor) rather than its principal construct related to problem solving. The authors concluded that social problem solving may be less related to bulimic anorexia than interpersonal transactions among family members.

Overall, observational studies of bulimics' families are notably conspicuous by their absence. The limited data, which primarily come from two research centers, suggest that there is greater correspondence between the self-reports of bulimic individuals and observation of their families than for restricting anorexics. Observers tend to see bulimics' parents as hostile and neglectful and bulimic daughters as angrily submissive. As Humphrey (1989) postulated, this may indeed disturb and compromise the daughters' developing autonomy. The finding suggesting a specific relationship between daughters and fathers in bulimia (e.g., Sights & Richards, 1984) is interesting but clearly in need of further study. As with the self-report studies, issues of specificity, temporal precedence of family interaction and bulimia, and the uncertain validity of some observational constructs remain methodologically and conceptually limiting.

Finally, although the self-report and observational studies reviewed to this point shed light on average family patterns or processes in bulimia or anorexia nervosa, clinical evidence highlights the considerable variability in family functioning within the broad categories of bulimia and anorexia (e.g., Root et al., 1986; Schwartz et al., 1985). A recent cluster analytic study supports these impressions. Kog, Vandereycken, and Vertommen (1989) cluster analyzed three behavioral measures of family functioning (intrafamilial boundaries, adaptability, and conflict) in a sample of 55 families with a member meeting *DSM-III* criteria for anorexia nervosa (restricting and bulimic subtypes), bulimia nervosa, or atypical eating disorder. The analysis resulted in seven clusters of families with each of the various eating-disorder subtypes spread throughout the clusters. Kog et al. concluded that the type of eating disturbance does not appear connected to any particular type of family functioning. Similarly, Grigg, Friesen, and Sheppy (1989) found considerable variability in their cluster analysis of Intrex ratings completed by anorectic individuals and their parents. Strober and Humphrey (1987) acknowledged this variability among families and suggested that researchers must appreciate how individual differences between eating-disordered patients may covary with familial measures. One area of individual differences that they acknowledge as potentially significant is the degree or type of comorbid psychopathology associated with the eating disturbance. Recent theoretical conceptualizations and empirical data suggest that personality disturbance displays significant comorbidity with the eating disorders and, furthermore, that there is considerable variability in the type of personality disturbance among bulimic individuals. In the next section, I briefly review the literature on personality disturbance in the eating disorders with the intention of examining how it may clarify our understanding of the variability of family functioning among eating-disordered people.

PERSONALITY AND BULIMIA NERVOSA

Personality trait studies converge to depict bulimics as impulsive, interpersonally sensitive, and low in self-esteem (Swift & Wonderlich, 1988). Although there have been empirical cluster analyses attempting to identify personality subtypes of anorexics (e.g., Strober, 1983), similar efforts are absent for normal-weight bulimics. Johnson and Connors (1987), however, did offer a theoretical scheme that delineates different types of character disturbance among bulimic individuals. They posited that bulimic individuals can be broadly classified into four categories of ego disturbance: psychotic, borderline, false self/narcissistic, and neurotic. Psychotic bulimics are quite rare and do not display the typical cognitive organization seen in bulimia (e.g., drive for thinness, body dissatisfaction). Their bulimic behavior may be best characterized as a symptom in a large psychotic organization. Parents of these individuals are described as highly disorganized themselves (possibly psychotic) and provide the child with an extremely chaotic and ungratifying environment. The two character-disordered groups (borderline and false self/narcissistic) are considered the most prevalent type of personality functioning in bulimia.

Borderline bulimics are thought to have experienced their parental relationships as malevolently underinvolved and use impulsive hysterical defenses to promote attachment and gain nurturance from others. They are thought to internalize the emotional unavailability of their caretakers as evidence that they are unlovable, worthless, and deserving of punishment, which they often inflict on themselves. The false self/narcissistic bulimic is also thought to have experienced parental underinvolvement but not as a malevolent action. Although quite impaired, these patients seem to possess greater ego resources than the borderline bulimic. They adapt to their parental relationships through pseudomature behavior that is thought to provide them with a sense of control. Because they fear that their pseudomaturity will be discovered, they adopt a rather avoidant interpersonal posture that is described as a "distant closeness." Finally, the neurotic group of bulimics is not thought to present the severe ego impairments associated with the other groups. Their bulimic behavior often has clear precipitants and may represent a developmental adjustment reaction. They can think quite abstractly and have well-differentiated and appropriate interpersonal relationships. Unfortunately, Johnson and Connors (1987) did not outline the nature of the family relationships characteristic of the neurotic group, although it is implied that they are more stable and involved than in the other groups.

Although there have been no explicit empirical tests of Johnson and Connor's (1987) model, several studies suggested a prominent comorbidity of eating disorders and personality disorders (e.g., Gartner, Marcus, Halmi, & Loranger, 1989; Powers, Coovert, Brightwell, & Stevens, 1988; Wonderlich, Swift, Slotnick, & Goodman, 1990). These reports suggested that 53% to 93% of eating-disordered individuals display at least one *DSM–III–R* personality disorder and 37% to 56% meet criteria for two or more personality disorders. Although there has been considerable variability across studies, several personality disorders have shown moderate prevalence rates in the eating disorders. For example, borderline personality disorder generally displays a moderate prevalence across all eating-disorder subtypes, whereas histrionic personality disorder appears more specifically prominent in normal-weight bulimics (Wonderlich & Mitchell, in press). Although the *DSM–III–R* anxious-fearful personality disorders have generally been most prominent in anorectic conditions, certain studies noted an association between bulimia and avoidant and, possibly, obsessive–compulsive personality disorders (Gartner et al., 1989; Powers et al., 1988). Thus, studies of the prevalence of personality disorders in bulimia suggest that several personality types, differing markedly in style (e.g., histrionic vs. avoidant), may be prominent in bulimia nervosa.

DIFFERENCES IN FAMILY FUNCTIONING BASED ON PERSONALITY DISTURBANCE

Two studies attempted to compare eating-disordered individuals with and without borderline personality disorder on family environment variables. Johnson, Tobin, and Enright (1989) divided their sample of eating-disordered patients into either a borderline or nonborderline group based on their scores on the Borderline Syndrome Index. Although there were minimal differences between the groups in terms of eating disturbance, the groups did differ on several of the FES subscales. The borderline subjects perceived their families as being less supportive of independence (enmeshment), less cohesive, and less expressive but more controlling and conflicted than did the nonborderline subjects. Interestingly, the nonborderline eating-disordered subjects differed minimally from the FES results typically found in normal controls. These data imply that the FES profile commonly associated with the bulimic family (disengaged, conflicted, and so on) is most characteristic of those bulimics displaying personality disturbance.

In an effort to identify family factors that are specific to borderline personality disorder, Wonderlich and Swift (1990a) controlled for the simple presence of any personality disorder. They compared eating-disordered subjects with either borderline personality disorder (BPD), other personality disorders (OPD), or no personality disorder (NPD) to normal controls on Intrex ratings of mother and father. All personality disorder diagnoses were based on interviews using the Structured Clinical Interview for *DSM–III–R:*Axis II. The BPD subjects distinguished themselves from all other groups in their perceptions of their relationship to their mother as mutually attacking and hostilely withdrawn. Their ratings of their relationship to their fathers distinguished them much less specifically from the other eating-disordered groups than the ratings of mother. Also, as in the Johnson et al. (1989) study, the NPD group generally did not differ from normal controls in their family ratings. Finally, Wonderlich and Swift also reported that there was more sexual abuse associated with the BPD (72%) than with the OPD (27%) or NPD groups (0%).

These studies together indicate that eating-disordered persons' perceptions of their family environment differed considerably depending on the amount and type of personality disturbance that accompanied the eating disorder. However, both studies are methodologically limited by either inadequate assessment of personality disorder (e.g., Johnson et al., 1989) or small sample sizes (e.g., Wonderlich & Swift, 1990a) or, in both studies, the sole reliance on self-report measures of family functioning. Furthermore, both studies relied on mixed samples of restricting anorexics and bulimics, making it impossible to determine if the findings generalize specifically to bulimia. Nonetheless, they provide preliminary data suggesting that the search for the "bulimic" family is a complex matter. Those with borderline personality disorder reported extreme family disturbance that is consistent with other reports of family environments associated with severe personality disorders (Carrol, Schaffer, Spensley & Abramowitz, 1982; Paris & Frank, 1989). However, those with other personality disorders reported less severe family problems, and those without personality disorder denied marked family problems.

Interestingly, although these studies indicated that the presence of personality disorder may be associated with specific family environments, there was minimal evidence that the personality subtypes differed in eating-disorder symptoms. This suggests that specific family environments may be related to personality features associated with eating disorders but not the eating disorder specifically. Head and Williamson (1990) addressed this issue in a study examining the interrelationship of personality variables, family environment variables, and eating-related attitudes and traits in a sample of bulimic women. The results of their canonical correlation analysis supported the idea that particular personality types were associated with specific family environments. For example, a conflicted family environment was associated with neuroticism and introversion, whereas a stimulating and achievement-oriented family environment was associated with extroversion, perfectionism, and paranoia. Neither of these family patterns, however, was specifically associated with eating behaviors and symptoms, suggesting that family environment had more of an influence on the comorbid personality pathology than the bulimia itself.

Although these findings are highly preliminary and in need of replication, they suggest that personality variables may serve as valuable descriptive indicators for subtyping various family patterns in the eating disorders, although it appears that these subtypes do not differ in eating behavior. Beyond description and diagnostic subtyping of families, however, lies the explanatory issue of how personality factors, eating disturbance, and family variables may interrelate, which is discussed next.

RELATIONSHIP OF PERSONALITY AND FAMILIAL PROCESSES IN BULIMIA

Understanding of the relationship of personality disturbance and family functioning in bulimia is quite limited, and empirical study of this idea is in its infancy. Yet several recent conceptual advances could begin to clarify our understanding of possible differences among bulimic families based on personality variables. For example, Scarr (1987; Scarr & McCartney, 1983) suggested that highly heritable personality factors that drive and restrain individual experience may have a substantial influence on the structure and process of the family transactions:

> We have not yet begun to explore how differences in family environments, measured by an observer, relate to personality differences. Nor have we considered seriously the possibility (in my mind the probability) that differences in parental treatment are instead largely caused by differences in children's personalities or by the match or mismatch between parental and child characteristics. (Scarr, 1987, p. 56).

From such a theoretical perspective, it may be predicted that variability in family functioning among bulimics may be due in part to variability between families in heritable personality traits that have a profound influence on family interactions.

Recent behavior-genetic findings indicate that a variety of personality traits are indeed substantially influenced by genetic factors (e.g., Bouchard, Lykken, McGue, Segal, & Tellegen, 1990; Tellegen et al., 1988). Cloninger (1986, 1987, 1988) theorized that there are three genetically independent and highly heritable dimensions of personality: novelty seeking, harm avoidance, and reward dependence. Novelty seeking is hypothesized to be a tendency toward exhilaration and excitement in response to novel stimuli or cues for potential reward or avoidance of punishment. Harm avoidance is posited as a tendency to respond to signals of aversive stimuli, which helps the organism to inhibit behavior. Reward dependence is thought to be a tendency to respond intensely to possible signals for reward and to maintain behavior or resist extinction of behaviors that have been associated with rewards. Harm avoidance is also thought to be influenced by environmental events that exert a modulatory effect on novelty seeking and reward dependency, allowing for environmental influence throughout the model.

Strober (Strober, in press; Strober, Lampert, Morrell, Burroughs, & Jacobs, 1990) discussed how Cloninger's dimensions may clarify our understanding of the personality functioning of prototypic restricting anorexics. He posited that restrictors often display low novelty seeking, high harm avoidance, and high reward dependence, a pattern Cloninger suggested depicts the passive-dependent personality. Casper's (1990) study of recovered anorexics supports Strober's prediction that anorexics would be characterized by high harm avoidance and low novelty seeking, but there are no available studies of bulimics using this model. Personality variability in bulimia may be greater than in anorexia, and although some bulimics might display such a passive-dependent style, others might be better viewed as high in novelty seeking and reward dependence but low in harm avoidance (histrionic). Still others may be low in novelty seeking and harm avoidance but high in reward dependence (cyclothymic).

If such personality traits or others are to some degree heritable, the question of how family experiences might interact with these traits to increase the risk of bulimia becomes critical to the topic of this chapter. Plomin, DeFries, and McClearn (1980) suggested that genes and environment may correlate in three different ways. Passive gene–environment correlation refers specifically to the correlation of the children's genotype with the family–environment that they passively receive. For example, highly intelligent parents often give their children their genes and a stimulating environment, both of which contribute to intelligence. Reactive gene–environment correlation refers to the influence that the genotype may have on reactions that others have to the individual. For example, highly sociable children may invite affection and interaction from adults and peers. Active gene–environment correlation occurs when individuals are not passive recipients of their environment but actively seek and create one that is correlated with their genotype. For example, shy children may seek more solitary play rather than peer activities.

Although gene–environment correlations can be either positive (direct relationship between genetic and environmental differences) or negative (inverse relationship between genetic and environmental differences), negative correlations may be particularly significant in the development of personality (Plomin, 1986). Negative gene–environment correlations reflect mismatches of the children's innate proclivities and the environment. It is possible to envision numerous examples of gene–environment correlations that may occur in bulimic families. For example, negative, passive gene–environment correlation would occur if a child high in reward dependence feels particularly neglected by a family that has problems with cohesion and expressiveness, whereas a child who is less reward dependent may feel less neglected. Similarly, high levels of family conflict may be generated when the anger of a quick-tempered child is not well tolerated by genetically similar parents who are unaccepting of their child's hostility. We can then begin to see how the personality traits of the bulimic individual might elicit and shape specific types of family interactions and also that responses to family interaction may vary substantially based on the personality of the bulimic individual.

Currently, we know very little, however, about what degree of influence such heritable aspects of personality would have in extremely abusive or deprived environments. In families in which there is long-standing and deeply entrenched abuse or neglect, the personality features of the individual may have minimal influence on structuring such patterns. However, personality may play a prominent role in determining the type of abusive environment that children experience and their personal reaction to such abuse. Thus, from such a behavior-genetic perspective, no particular family type would be posited to "cause" bulimia; instead, the nature or degree of mismatch between the bulimic individual's personality traits and specific family experiences, coupled with accompanying sociocultural pressures for thinness, would serve as the best predictors of bulimia.

Although the effects of genes and gene–environment correlations on personality may be substantial, it should not be concluded that behavior genetic research has found that environmental effects on personality are insignificant. That identical twins differ fairly substantially in personality can be accounted for only by environmental effects (Plomin & Daniels, 1987). In fact, Plomin and Daniels (1987) suggested that environmental factors have a profound influence on personality development but that it is environmental effects that produce differences between children in the same family (i.e., nonshared environment) that account for most of the environmental variance in personality. For example, environmental differences between two sisters, such as in the quality of their relationships to their parents, a history of sexual abuse, or teasing by siblings or peers about weight, would be more likely to influence personality than global constructs like family cohesion or parenting style, which are thought to be relatively consistent and to create similarities between family members. Indeed, some evidence suggests that siblings in the same family experience very different family environments (Daniels & Plomin, 1985; Plomin & Daniels, 1987).

Taken together, these findings imply that unique "nonshared" family experiences may be extremely significant in shaping personality. This is consistent with personality theories that suggest that specific types of environmental (possibly familial) experiences influence and shape the development of specific types of personality disturbance, which may in turn increase the chance of developing a clinical syndrome, such as bulimia. Theories of this type, which I describe as family predispositional theories, generally acknowledge some organismic vulnerability factor such as temperament (e.g., Benjamin, in press) or affective instability (e.g., Johnson & Connors, 1987), but the emphasis is more clearly on the role of interpersonal (family) relationships in the development of significant personality disturbance. Thus, from such a family predispositional perspective, it would be predicted that the bulimic with borderline personality would have had specific family experiences that are believed to be associated with the development of borderline personality such as physical and sexual abuse, neglect, and hostility (Benjamin, in press; Carrol et al., 1980; Paris & Frank, 1989). Alternatively, the histrionic bulimic may have experienced family transactions posited to be associated with histrionic or hysterical personality (e.g., attention and affection for physical beauty, the provision of nurturance primarily when unhappy or needy, as well as an overromanticized relationship with her father; Benjamin, in press; Slipp, 1977). These family processes would be considered etiologically critical and conceptually before the development of both personality disorder and any associated eating disturbance; furthermore, the personality disturbance would be considered a reasonable and expected adaptation to the family environment.

Finally, in spite of these theoretical speculations about families predisposing to eating disorder or interacting with heritable personality features to increase liability for eating disorder, it is theoretically possible that family-interaction patterns and personality disturbance are simply a consequence of the bulimic disorder, which arises independent of family factors. Of course, from such a perspective, family factors may be thought to complicate the course and treatment of the disorder but are not granted etiologic significance. Until prospective longitudinal studies have been conducted, it remains unclear whether bulimia or family factors have temporal precedence.

SUMMARY AND FUTURE DIRECTIONS

Our understanding of the relationship of bulimia and family factors is in the early stages of development, with the expected conceptual and methodological limitations. However, the preliminary speculations and findings in this area of study are exciting and invite further consideration of how familial relationships may be involved in the cause and maintenance of bulimia. Available self-report and observational studies suggested that bulimic individuals and, to a lesser degree, their parents perceive their families as disengaged, hostile, disorganized, and conflictual. However, this research has several methodological limitations. First, the absence of psychopathological control groups raises issues about the specificity of these findings. Whether descriptors such as disengaged, hostile, and conflicted specifically characterize bulimic families or are characteristic of other families with depressed, anxious, or simply distraught adolescent or young adult children is unclear. Second, there are very few observational studies of bulimic families, and the available observational findings come almost exclusively from two data sets (e.g., Humphrey, 1989; Kog, Vandereycken, & Vertommen, 1989) that have relatively small numbers of bulimic families. Third, the ubiquitous problem of cross-sectional studies leaves open the questions of causality. Longitudinal studies are needed to clarify the direction of association between family factors and bulimic symptomatology. High-risk designs relying on risk factors such as adolescent dieting, bingeing, or body-image disturbance may prove useful in identifying individuals for longitudinal family studies.

Several other specific issues deserve greater attention in future research on family factors associated with bulimia. Generally, a finer grained approach to studying relationships within the family is needed. For example, although there is some evidence indicating that bulimics perceive their maternal and paternal relationships differently, this needs further examination. Also the role of siblings has been generally ignored in family studies of bulimia. Whether or not bulimic individuals experience unusual or unique sibling relationships is unclear and in need of further examination.

Future research efforts also need to be directed toward understanding the considerable variability in family functioning among bulimics. I have proposed in this chapter that bulimic families may differ in accord with the personality traits or disorders of the affected individual. However, numerous characteristics of the bulimic individual such as comorbid depression, alcohol abuse, and anxiety disorders may also be useful in elucidating family subtypes among bulimics.

Finally, the possibility that bulimic families may vary in accord with personality variables raises immensely complex theoretical issues about the interplay of genetic and family factors. Available evidence suggests that certain personality dimensions are quite heritable and that the environmental factors that influence personality, and perhaps bulimia itself, are unique to each child in a family. This indicates that future family studies of bulimia may benefit from research designs that carefully consider the unique environments that bulimic individuals encounter within their families and also how their constitutional propensities may influence their experience of these families.

REFERENCES

American Psychiatric Association. (1987). *Diagnostic and statistical manual of mental disorders* (3rd ed., rev.). Washington, DC: Author.

Benjamin, L. S. (1974). Structural analysis of social behavior. *Psychological Review, 81,* 392–425.

Benjamin, L. S. (1984). Principles of prediction using structural analysis of social behavior (SASB). In R. A. Zucker, J. Aronoff, & A. J. Rabin (Eds.), *Personality and prediction of behavior* (pp. 121–174). New York: Academic Press.

Benjamin, L. S. (in press). *Structural analysis of interactional patterns in personality disorders.* New York: Guilford Press.

Blouin, A. G., Zuro, C., & Blouin, J. H. (1990). Family environment in bulimia nervosa: The role of depression. *International Journal of Eating Disorders, 9,* 649–658.

Bouchard, T. J., Lykken, D. T., McGue, M., Segal, N. L., & Tellegen, A. (1990). Sources of human psychological difference: The Minnesota study of twins reared apart. *Science, 250,* 223–228.

Carrol, J., Schaffer, C., Spensley, J., & Abramowitz, S. (1980). Family experiences of self-mutilating patients. *American Journal of Psychiatry, 137,* 852–853.

Casper, R. C. (1990). Personality features of women with good outcome from restricting anorexia. *Psychosomatic Medicine, 52,* 156–170.

Cloninger, C. R. (1986). A unified biosocial theory of personality and its role in the development of anxiety states. *Psychiatric Developments, 4,* 167–226.

Cloninger, C. R. (1987). A systematic method for clinical description and classification of personality variants. *Archives of General Psychiatry, 44,* 573–588.

Cloninger, C. R. (1988). A reply to commentaries. *Psychiatric Developments, 6,* 83–120.

Coburn, J., & Ganong, L. (1989). Bulimic and non-bulimic college females' perceptions of family adaptability and family cohesion. *Journal of Advanced Nursing, 14,* 27–33.

Daniels, D., & Plomin, R. (1985). Differential experience of siblings in the same family. *Developmental Psychology, 21,* 747–760.

Epstein, N. B., Bishop, D. S., & Levin, S. (1983). The McMaster family assessment device. *Journal of Marital and Family Therapy, 9,* 171–180.

Garner, D. M., Garfinkel, P. E., & O'Shaughnessy, M. (1985). The validity of the distinction between bulimia with and without anorexia nervosa. *American Journal of Psychiatry, 142,* 581–587.

Gartner, A. F., Marcus, R. N., Halmi, K., & Loranger, A. W. (1989). DSM-III-R personality disorders in patients with eating disorders. *American Journal of Psychiatry, 146,* 1585–1591.

Giat-Roberto, L. (1986). Bulimia: The transgenerational view. *Journal of Marital and Family Therapy, 12,* 231–240.

Grigg, D., Friesen, J. D., & Sheppy, M. I. (1989). Family patterns associated with anorexia nervosa. *Journal of Marital and Family Therapy, 15,* 29–42.

Haley, J. (1964). Research on family patterns: An instrument measurement. *Family Process, 3,* 41–65.

Head, S. B., & Williamson, D. A. (1990). Association of family environment and personality disturbance in bulimia nervosa. *International Journal of Eating Disorders, 9,* 667–674.

Humphrey, L. L. (1986a). Family dynamics in bulimia. In S. C. Feinstein, A. H. Esman, J. G. Looney, A. Z. Schwartzberg, A. D. Sorosky, & M. Sugar (Eds.), *Annals of adolescent psychiatry: Developmental and clinical studies.* (Vol. 13, pp. 315–332). Chicago: University of Chicago Press.

Humphrey, L. L. (1986b). Family relations in bulimic anorexic and nondistressed families. *International Journal of Eating Disorders, 5,* 223–232.

Humphrey, L. L. (1986c). Structural analysis of parent-child relationships in eating disorders. *Journal of Abnormal Psychology, 95,* 395–402.

Humphrey, L. L. (1987). A comparison of bulimic-anorexic and non-distressed families using structural analysis of social behavior. *Journal of the American Academy of Child and Adolescent Psychiatry, 26,* 248–255.

Humphrey, L. L. (1988). Relationships within subtypes of anorexic, bulimic, and normal families. *Journal of the American Academy of Child and Adolescent Psychiatry, 27,* 544–551.

Humphrey, L. L. (1989). Observed family interactions among subtypes of eating disorders using structural analysis of social behavior. *Journal of Consulting and Clinical Psychology, 57,* 206–214.

Humphrey, L. L. Apple, R. F., & Kirschenbaum, D. S. (1986). Differentiating bulimic-anorexic from normal families using interpersonal and behavioral observational systems. *Journal of Consulting and Clinical Psychology, 54,* 190–195.

Humphrey, L. L., & Stern, S. (1988). Object relations and the family system in bulimia: A theoretical integration. *Journal of Marital and Family Therapy, 14,* 337–350.

Jacob, T. (1975). Family interaction in disturbed and normal families. A methodological and substantive review. *Psychological Bulletin, 82,* 33–65.

Johnson, C., & Connors, M. E. (1987). *The etiology and treatment of bulimia nervosa.* New York: Basic Books.

Johnson, C., & Flach, A. (1985). Family characteristics of 105 patients with bulimia. *American Journal of Psychiatry, 142,* 1321–1324.

Johnson, C., Tobin, D., & Enright, A. (1989). Prevalence and clinical characteristics of borderline patients in a eating-disordered population. *Journal of Clinical Psychiatry, 50,* 9–15.

Kent, J. S., & Clopton, J. R. (1988). Bulimia: A comparison of psychological adjustment and familial characteristics in a non-clinical sample. *Journal of Clinical Psychology, 44,* 964–971.

Klein, M. (1975). *Envy and gratitude and other works, 1946–1963.* London: Hogarth Press and the Institute of Psycho-Analysis.

Kog, E., & Vandereycken, W. (1985). Family characteristics of anorexia nervosa and bulimia: A review of the research literature. *Clinical Psychology Review, 5,* 159–180.

Kog, E., & Vandereycken, W. (1989). Family interaction in eating disorder patients and normal controls. *International Journal of Eating Disorders, 8,* 11–23.

Kog, E., Vandereycken, W., & Vertommen, H. (1989). Multimethod investigation of eating disorder families. In W. Vandereycken, E. Kog, & J. Vanderlinden, (Eds.), *The family approach to eating disorders* (pp. 81–106). New York: PMA.

Kog, E., Vertommen, H., & Vandereycken, W. (1987). Minuchin's psychosomatic family model revised: A concept validation study using a multitrait-multimethod approach. *Family Process, 26,* 235–253.

Kog, E., Vertommen, H., & Vandereycken, W. (1989). Self-report study of family interaction in eating disorder families compared to normals. In W. Vandereycken, E. Kog, & J. Vanderlinden (Eds.), *The family approach to eating disorders* (pp. 107-118). New York: PMA.

Lewinsohn, P. M., & Rosenbaum, M. (1987). Recall of parental behavior by acute depressives, remitted depressives, and nondepressives. *Journal of Personality and Social Psychology, 52,* 611-619.

Minuchin, S., Rosman, B. L., & Baker, L. (1978). *Psychosomatic families: Anorexia nervosa in context.* Cambridge, MA: Harvard University Press.

Moos, R., & Moos, B. (1981). *Family environment scale manual.* Palo Alto, CA: Consulting Psychologists Press.

Olson, D. H., Bell, R., & Portner, J. (1978). *Family adaptability and cohesion evaluation scale.* St. Paul: University of Minnesota Press.

Olson, D. H., Russell, C. S., & Sprenkle, D. H. (1983). Circumplex model of marital and family systems: 4. Theoretical update. *Family Process, 22,* 69-83.

Ordman, A. M., & Kirschenbaum, D. S. (1986). Bulimia: Assessment of eating, psychological adjustment and familial characteristics. *International Journal of Eating Disorders, 5,* 865-878.

Palazzoli, M. (1978). *Self-starvation: From individual to family therapy in the treatment of anorexia nervosa.* New York: Jason Aronson.

Palmer, R. L., Oppenheimer, R., & Marshall, P. D. (1988). Eating-disordered patients remember their parents: A study using the parental bonding instrument. *International Journal of Eating Disorders, 7,* 101-106.

Paris, J., & Frank, H. (1989). Perceptions of parental bonding in borderline patients. *American Journal of Psychiatry, 146,* 1498-1499.

Parker, G., Tupling, H., & Brown, L. B. (1979). A parental bonding instrument. *British Journal of Medical Psychology, 52,* 1-10.

Plomin, R. (1986). *Development, genetics and psychology.* Hillsdale, NJ: Erlbaum.

Plomin, R., & Daniels, D. (1987). Why are children in the same family so different from one another. *Behavior and Brain Sciences, 10,* 1-60.

Plomin, R., DeFries, J. C., & McClearn, G. E. (1980). *Behavioral genetics: A primer.* San Francisco: W.H. Freeman.

Pole, R., Waller, D. A., Stewart, S. M., & Parkin-Feigenbaum, L. (1988). Parental caring versus overprotection in bulimia. *International Journal of Eating Disorders, 7,* 601-606.

Powers, P. S., Coovert, D. L., Brightwell, D. R., & Stevens, B. A. (1988). Other psychiatric disorders among bulimic patients. *Comprehensive Psychiatry, 29,* 503-508.

Robin, A. L., & Weiss, J. G. (1980). Criterion related validity of behavioral and self-report measures of problem-solving communication skills in distressed and non-distressed parent adolescent dyads. *Behavioral Assessment, 2,* 339-352.

Root, M. P. P., Fallon, P., & Friedrich, W. N. (1986). *Bulimia: A systems approach to treatment.* New York: W.W. Norton.

Scarr, S. (1987). Personality and experience: Individual encounters with the world. In J. Arnoff, A. I. Rabin, & R. Zucker (Eds.), *The emergence of personality* (pp. 49-78). New York: Springer.

Scarr, S., & McCartney, K. (1983). How people make their own environment: A theory of genotype environmental effects. *Child Development, 54,* 424-435.

Schwartz, R. C., Barrett, M. J., & Saba, G. (1985). Family therapy for bulimia. In D. M. Garner & P. E. Garfinkel (Eds.), *Handbook of psychotherapy for anorexic nervosa and bulimia* (pp. 280-307). New York: Guilford Press.

Sights, J. R., & Richards, H. C. (1984). Parents of bulimic women. *International Journal of Eating Disorders, 3,* 3-13.

Skinner, H. A. (1987). Self-report instruments for family assessment. In T. Jacob (Ed.), *Family interaction and psychopathology* (pp. 427-452). New York: Plenum Press.

Skinner, H. A., Steinhauer, P. D., & Santa Barbara, J. (1983). The family assessment measure. *Canadian Journal of Community Mental Health, 2,* 91-105.

Slipp, S. (1977). Interpersonal factors in hysteria: Freud's reduction theory and the case of Dora. *Journal of the American Academy of Psychoanalysis, 5,* 359-376.

Stern, S. L., Dixon, K. N., Jones, D., Lake, M., Nemzer, E., & Sansone, R. (1989). Family environment in anorexia nervosa and bulimia. *International Journal of Eating Disorders, 8,* 25-31.

Strober, M. (1983). An empirically derived typology of anorexia nervosa. In P. Darby, P. Garfinkel, D. Garner, & D. Coscina (Eds.), *Anorexia nervosa: Recent developments in research* (pp. 185-198). New York: Alan R. Liss.

Strober, M. (1991). Disorders of the self in anorexia nervosa. An organismic-developmental paradigm. In C. Johnson (Ed.), *Psychoanalytic theory and treatment for eating disorders* (pp. 354-373). New York: Guilford Press.

Strober, M., & Humphrey, L. L. (1987). Familial contributions to the etiology and course of anorexia nervosa and bulimia. *Journal of Consulting and Clinical Psychology, 55,* 654-659.

Strober, M., Lampert, C., Morrell, W., Burroughs, J., & Jacobs, C. (1990). A controlled family study of anorexia nervosa: Evidence of familial aggregation and lack of shared transmission with affective disorders. *International Journal of Eating Disorders, 9,* 239-253.

Swift, W. J., & Wonderlich, S. A. (1988). Personality factors and diagnosis in eating disorders. In D. M. Garner & P. E. Garfinkel (Eds.), *Diagnostic issues in anorexia nervosa and bulimia nervosa* (pp. 121–165). New York: Bruner/Mazel.

Tellegen, A., Lykken, D. T., Bouchard, T. J., Wilcox, K. J., Seval, N. L., & Rich, S. (1988). Personality similarity in twins reared apart and together. *Journal of Personality and Social Psychology, 54,* 1031–1039.

Vandereycken, W., Kog, E., & Vanderlinden, J. (1989). *The family approach to eating disorders.* New York: PMA.

Waller, G., Calam, R., & Slade, P. (1989). Eating disorders and family interaction. *British Journal of Clinical Psychology, 28,* 285–286.

Wiggins, J. S. (1982). Circumplex models of interpersonal behavior in clinical psychology. In P. C. Kendall & J. N. Butcher (Eds.), *Handbook of research methods in clinical psychology* (pp. 183–221). New York: Wiley.

Winnicott, D. W. (1965). *The maturational processes and the facilitating environment.* New York: International Universities Press.

Wonderlich, S. A., & Mitchell, J. E. (in press). The comorbidity of personality disorders and the eating disorders. In J. Yager (Ed.), *Special problems in managing eating disorders.* Washington, DC: American Psychiatric Association Press.

Wonderlich, S. A., & Swift, W. J. (1990a). Borderline versus other personality disorders in the eating disorders. *International Journal of Eating Disorders, 9,* 629–638.

Wonderlich, S. A., & Swift, W. J. (1990b). Perceptions of parental relationships in eating disorder subtypes. *Journal of Abnormal Psychology, 99,* 353–360.

Wonderlich, S. A., Swift, W. J., Slotnick, H. B., & Goodman, S. (1990). DSM-III-R personality disorders in eating disorder subtypes. *International Journal of Eating Disorders, 9,* 607–617.

Woodside, D. B., Shekter-Wolfson, L. F., Garfinkel, P. E., Olmsted, M. P., Kaplan, A. S., & Maddocks, S. E. (1990). *Family interaction in bulimia nervosa. 1. Study design comparisons to establish population norms and changes over the course of an intensive day hospital treatment.* Unpublished manuscript, University of Toronto.

Yager, J., & Strober, M. (1985). Family aspects of eating disorders. In A. Frances & R. Hales (Eds.), *Annual review—psychiatry update* (pp. 481–502). Washington, DC: American Psychiatric Association Press.

II

INDIVIDUAL FACTORS

7

OVERVIEW

Deborah S. Rosch
Kristen L. Shepherd
Kent State University

The cause of bulimia nervosa has been discussed and investigated by researchers from a variety of perspectives. Part I of this book addressed the developmental and familial influences on the cause of bulimia nervosa as dieting, maladaptive eating and weight-related attitudes, and eating problems and disorders that emerge during childhood and adolescence at the time of developmental transitions and in individuals who have certain familial characteristics. Although these systemic influences are important to our understanding of the development of bulimia nervosa, characteristics of the individual that increase her vulnerability to bulimia nervosa must also be considered. The focus of the chapters in this section is on the role of individual factors in the origin and maintenance of bulimia nervosa.

Focusing at the level of the individual is important because, although it can be argued that all young women in Western culture are exposed to sociocultural messages that promote a desire for extreme, almost unnatural thinness, only a small proportion of women develop bulimia nervosa. Indeed, the pervasive environment of thinness (especially for women) widely encourages maladaptive eating and weight-related attitudes and dieting behaviors, attitudes and behaviors that have almost become normative in our society. Furthermore, focusing at the level of the individual is important because the developmental tasks and particular family characteristics associated with bulimia nervosa also are not unique to young women who develop this disorder. Thus, the following questions can be raised. Why do only certain individuals develop bulimia nervosa? What are the predisposing factors involved in the development of bulimia nervosa? Are there different subtypes or manifestations of bulimia nervosa? If so, what do they suggest about the cause of this disorder? The authors of the chapters in this section attempt to address such questions.

One factor that has been identified in the literature and discussed in earlier chapters of this volume (Attie & Brooks-Gunn, this volume, ch. 3; Levine & Smolak, this volume, ch. 4; Thelen, Lawrence, & Powell, this volume, ch. 5) as channeling some individuals into eating disorders is dieting. The major contribution of Heatherton and Polivy (ch. 8) is their introduction of the "spiral model." This model addresses the initiation and maintenance of dieting behavior and the psychological and behavioral consequences of dieting that may play a role in the development of bulimia nervosa and anorexia nervosa. Heatherton and Polivy point out that dieting is widespread in this culture and that although overweight individuals are prone to dieting, normal-weight and underweight individuals diet as well. They propose that body-image dissatisfaction, regardless of weight status, may serve as the trigger for dieting.

For individuals who do not diet successfully, Heatherton and Polivy argue that a spiral may be established whereby successive dieting failures lead to diminished self-esteem and increased negative affect, which in turn increase the likelihood of overeating and increase the need to diet. Because low self-esteem and negative affect make dieting failures more likely, the spiral perpetuates itself. According to Heatherton and Polivy, increased psychopathology is associated with movement down the spiral toward bulimia nervosa and anorexia nervosa. Clearly, the spiral model is valuable as an explanatory model for why dieting begins, how dieting is maintained, and how dieting may lead to eating disorders. The model also has implications for the prevention of eating disorders in high-risk individuals and the treatment of established eating disorders.

Given that Heatherton and Polivy argue that body dissatisfaction triggers dieting, examining the role of body image in the cause of bulimia nervosa is vital. In chapter 9, Rosen discusses the construct of body-image disorder, creatively compares and contrasts body-image disorder with body dysmorphic disorder, and proposes new ways of considering body-image disorder and its association with bulimia nervosa. Rosen describes body-image disorder as the fundamental core underlying eating disorders and persuasively argues that eating pathology is secondary to basic body-image disturbance. His multidimensional conceptualization of body-image disorder consists not only of disorders of perception (inaccurate perceptions of body size) and disorders of cognition (excessive salience of body size in evaluating self-worth and distorted negative evaluation of appearance) but also disorders of behavior. Indeed, one of the major contributions of his chapter is his addition of disorders of behavior, such as weight- or size-checking behaviors and avoidance behaviors, to a conceptualization of body-image disorder.

Rosen suggests that the fundamental body-image disorder that underlies eating disorders develops as a result of an interaction of unrealistic sociocultural pressures for thinness, disturbances in the development of self-identity and self-esteem, and social feedback about physical appearance. He suggests that socio-cultural pressures for thinness may be a predisposing factor for body-image disorders. However, individuals who hold dysfunctional assumptions about physical appearance and who are subjected to negative social feedback, such as familial criticism or teasing by peers, will be more vulnerable to the development of body-image disorders and, ultimately, eating disorders. Rosen introduces the notion of "critical incidents"—specific incidents that may or may not be related to physical appearance—that validate the young woman's dysfunctional assumptions about her own physical appearance relative to societal standards. His chapter provides a new perspective on the etiological role of body-image disorder that has implications for increasing the emphasis on body-image issues in the treatment of eating disorders.

Although body dissatisfaction and dieting also play a role in the biopsychosocial model that Johnson and his associates have proposed, Johnson and Wonderlich (ch. 10) focus on personality characteristics and personality disorders as risk factors for eating disorders. Johnson and Wonderlich provide an integrative review of the literature documenting the relatively high comorbidity of Axis II personality disorders and eating disorders. On the basis of the relationships between personality disorders and eating disorders, they suggest that the presence of certain personality characteristics may increase a young woman's vulnerability to psychopathology. The selection of eating-related symptoms as an expression of this vulnerability may be largely socioculturally determined. Indeed, they note that bulimia nervosa and anorexia nervosa may be "culture-bound" syndromes. In addition to their literature review on the cormobidity of personality disorders and eating disorders, one of the major contributions of their chapter is the discussion of potential relationships between temperament, personality traits and disorders, and restricting and bulimic subtypes of eating disorders. Further investigation of the development of these eating-disorder subtypes may help us better understand the role of individual differences in the development of bulimia nervosa.

Clearly, these chapters differ in their focus. Heatherton and Polivy discuss the role of chronic dieting; Rosen discusses body-image disorder; and Johnson and Wonderlich discuss personality disorders. However, across all three chapters is a recognition that, within our current sociocultural climate, psychological maladjustment also may play an important etiological role in eating disorders. For example, Heatherton and Polivy note that dieters have lower self-esteem and greater maladjustment than nondieters. Within their spiral model, dietary failures lead to lower self-esteem and greater negative affect and maladjustment. They note that as one moves from chronic dieting to clinical eating disorders, their spiral model predicts greater psychopathology. Rosen also discusses the role of self-esteem and effectiveness within the context of the development of body-image disorder. He notes that during adolescence girls may develop dysfunctional assumptions about their physical appearance that may become central to their self-identity and self-esteem. He suggests that once these dysfunctional assumptions are established, they may be maintained by selective attention, avoidance behavior, checking behavior, and reassurance seeking. Finally, in a more traditional vein, Johnson and Wonderlich emphasize the roles of temperament, personality characteristics, and comorbid psychopathology in the cause of eating disorders.

All of these chapters present new perspectives from which clinicians and researchers can begin to view the roles of chronic dieting, body image, and personality factors in the etiology of eating disorders. The models and conceptualizations presented in this section should stimulate additional thought regarding future research directions in this area.

8

CHRONIC DIETING AND EATING DISORDERS: A SPIRAL MODEL

Todd F. Heatherton
Harvard University

Janet Polivy
University of Toronto

Many researchers agree that dieting plays an important role in the onset and maintenance of anorexia nervosa and bulimia nervosa (Abraham & Beumont, 1982; Agras & Kirkley, 1986; Davis, Freeman, & Garner, 1988; Garfinkel & Garner, 1982; Johnson & Connors, 1987; Polivy & Herman, 1985, 1987; Polivy, Herman, Olmsted, & Jazwinski, 1984; Rosen, Tacy, & Howell, 1990; Russell, 1979; Vanderheyden, Fekken, & Boland, 1988; Williamson, 1990). Yet not all dieters become bulimics or anorexics, and there are important differences between simple dieters and those with more serious eating disorders (Herman & Polivy, 1988; Polivy, 1989; Polivy & Herman, 1985, 1987; Ruderman & Grace, 1987, 1988). This chapter examines the possible progression from dieting to binge eating and clinical eating disorders.

In the first section, we examine the determinants of dieting. That is, what steps are involved in the conscious decision to undertake dieting? In the second section, the causes and consequences of decisions to undertake chronic dieting are discussed. The third section examines mechanisms that may promote disinhibited eating. In this regard, we propose a spiral model that integrates what is known about the initiation and consequences of dietary restraint. In the final section, the possible pathway from dieting to clinical eating disorders is studied.

DECIDING TO DIET

There is an unfortunate paucity of developmental research investigating the initiation of dieting in preadolescent and adolescent girls. Rosen and colleagues recently investigated the incidence of weight-reduction efforts in high school students (Rosen & Gross, 1987). They surveyed 1,373 high school students and found that on the day of the study 63% of the girls and 16.2% of the boys were dieting to lose weight despite the fact that most of these adolescents were already at a normal weight level. Earlier studies in the 1960s and 1970s reported dieting in about one third of adolescent girls and in substantially fewer boys (e.g., Dwyer, Feldman, & Mayer, 1967, 1970; Dwyer, Feldman, Seltzer, & Meyer, 1969; Huenemann, Shapiro, Hampton, & Mitchell, 1966; Nylander, 1971). Many more of these female high school students reported wanting to weigh less (80% of Dwyer et al.'s subjects, e.g.), and the percentage of college women dieting to lose weight or maintain a lowered weight was as high as 82% (Jakobovits, Halstead, Kelley, Roe, & Young, 1977).

These data on incidence of dieting indicate that women are significantly more likely to feel a pressure to be thinner (or at least are more likely to report wanting to be thinner) and to attempt to lose weight by dieting. They do not tell us, however, what leads these women to desire a thinner physique or to decide that this is a goal worth pursuing. We know remarkably little about the factors that contribute to the decision to try to change one's appearance by losing weight. We can deduce, however, that body-image dissatisfaction is important to the decision to undertake dieting.

Body-Image Dissatisfaction

Whatever a woman's body weight, at some point she compares herself to societal ideals and decides how her appearance and, in this case, her physique measure up to this ideal. Given the incidence of dieting in the studies we have just reviewed, it is clear that many women feel fatter than their perception of the ideal. One obvious question, then, is to what extent are these women actually overweight?

We do have some information about the physiques as well as social class characteristics of dieting compared with nondieting women. For example, Rosen and Gross (1987) found that dieters were more likely to be white and upper class than black or lower class. Also almost all of the overweight girls surveyed and two thirds of the normal-weight girls were trying to lose weight. Even 18% of the underweight girls were actually trying to lose weight. Miller, Coffman, and Linke (1980) found that 61% of the college women and 32% of the men (52% of the total sample) they surveyed were dieting to lose weight on the day of the study. Only 35% of the students in the survey were classified as overweight, however, although all of those were dieting. Similarly, Dwyer et al. (1967, 1970, 1969) found that only half of the girls in their sample who were dieting on the day of the study were actually overweight. It seems, then, that although body weight per se may contribute to the decision to diet, many young women who are not relatively overweight also diet.

Herman and Polivy (1980) pointed out that among normal-weight dieters, there can be substantial overlap in physique; the only way to distinguish which of two young women is the dieter is through a questionnaire about their dieting and eating behaviors and attitudes (such as the Restraint Scale, which measures chronic dieting; Herman & Polivy, 1980). One factor consistently related to such questionnaires assessing dieting is the presence of body-image dissatisfaction (e.g., Hawkins, Turell, & Jackson, 1983; Polivy, Herman, & Pliner, 1990; Rosen, Gross, & Vara, 1987; Ruderman & Grace, 1988). Miller et al. (1980) found that 81% of those who reported being dissatisfied with their weights were dieting. Moreover, 63% of the women surveyed saw themselves as belonging to a higher weight category than was actually the case. It seems, then, that although physique alone, especially for normal-weight individuals, may not predict who diets, body-image dissatisfaction (or desiring to be thinner, which is actually what most of these studies have measured) does. Not surprisingly, wanting a thinner body is strongly related to a decision to diet to lose weight. (Although, again, we cannot be certain of the direction of a correlation, we can be reasonably confident in this case that it is wanting to be thin that leads to dieting!)

Heatherton (1990) examined aspects of body-image dissatisfaction and low self-esteem among dieters and nondieters (as assessed by the Restraint Scale). Restrained and unrestrained eaters completed a version of the Fallon and Rozin (1985) figures task. Dieters and nondieters chose similar ideal body shapes, suggesting that dieters are not striving to be thinner than the average nondieting women finds attractive. However, because they were actually heavier than nondieters, dieters had a greater discrepancy between their current body shape and their ideal body shape. This discrepancy was related to greater body dissatisfaction and lower appearance self-esteem. Thus, dieting and body dissatisfaction are closely related. Moreover, actual overweight does not appear to be a prerequisite for body dissatisfaction, although women who are overweight may be especially likely to feel dissatisfied with their bodies and therefore be dieting.

Personality and Adjustment Factors

Given a comparison to an ideal, a perception that one has not achieved this ideal, and dissatisfaction with this state, what else might contribute to a decision to change one's weight and appearance through dieting? One form of information available concerning how to distinguish those who decide to diet from those who do not pertains to personality and adjustment. We have found repeatedly in our laboratory that chronic dieters (restrained eaters) have lower self-esteem than do nondieters (Heatherton, 1986, 1990; Heatherton, Herman, & Polivy, 1991; Heatherton & Polivy, 1991; Polivy, Heatherton, & Herman, 1988). Other studies also concur with this (e.g., Dykens & Gerrard, 1986; Eldredge, Wilson, & Whaley, 1990; Hawkins et al., 1983; Kagan & Squires,

1984; Rosen et al., 1987; Ruderman & Grace, 1988). Unfortunately, we cannot ascertain whether this lowered self-esteem precedes dieting or occurs as a result of it. That is, low self-esteem may predispose individuals to be less satisfied with their physical appearance and therefore make them more likely to attempt to improve themselves or, alternatively, continued failures to lose weight could lead to deficits in self-esteem.

Investigations of restrained eaters have also found correlations between restraint and measures of neuroticism (Herman & Polivy, 1980; Ruderman & Grace, 1988), depression (Edwards & Nagelberg, 1986; Eldredge et al., 1990; Rosen et al., 1987), and maladjustment (Edwards & Nagelberg, 1986; Ruderman, 1985b; Ruderman & Grace, 1987, 1988). Such cross-sectional data do not tell us, however, whether dieters become more maladjusted as a result of dieting or whether maladjusted people are more likely to decide to diet. Either way, chronic dieters seem to be more maladjusted than nondieters.

Evidence indicates that heightened distress may be linked to a worsening of eating disorders over time. Striegel-Moore, Silberstein, Frensch, and Rodin (1989) examined changes in affect and in disordered-eating patterns for 947 college students over their freshman year at college. They found that high perceived stress was associated with a worsening of disordered eating among women but not men. A worsening of eating disorders was also related to increased feelings of dysphoria about weight, decreased ratings of attractiveness, and decreased feelings of self-efficacy. However, it is still unclear whether initial stress promoted dieting (and disordered eating) or whether such stress resulted from attempts to diet.

Rosen et al's. (1990) prospective study of dieting and nondieting teenage girls tried to answer the question of causality. They attempted to determine whether stress and poor psychological functioning contribute to increased dieting behavior or whether dieting leads to increased stress and poorer psychological adjustment. As in their earlier study (Rosen & Gross, 1987), the authors found that close to two thirds of the girls were dieting both initially and after 4 months, although it was not necessarily the same individuals each time. Dieting was significantly correlated with psychological symptoms and degree of stress at the initial phase of the study. More important, the authors found that although dieting predicted the degree of stress 4 months later, neither degree of stress nor level of symptomatology at any point predicted dieting. Thus, the relation between dieting and stress seems to be caused by the impact of dieting on stress levels rather than the reverse. The influence of psychological maladjustment and dieting on each other was not able to be established conclusively in the 4-month period of this study.

We may conclude, then, that although definitive causal evidence remains to be collected, numerous women in our society, whatever their weight or shape, perceive that they are not as thin as the current ideal, however defined. Many of them, possibly more of those with somewhat lower self-esteem and certainly most of those who actually are heavier than average, are dissatisfied with their weight or shape and decide to become thinner by dieting. Some, however, either do not perceive themselves to be deviant from the ideal or are not dissatisfied with this; these women remain unrestrained eaters or nondieters. However, what happens to these putative first-time dieters?

Responses to Dieting Efforts

According to Rosen et al.'s (1990) prospective study, dieting increases girls' stress levels. This may not always be true, however. If the dieter attains her weight-loss goals successfully, she may quickly end her dietary restriction, feel better about herself, and stop dieting or merely restrict her intake slightly to maintain the loss. Indeed, there are people who successfully lose weight and maintain their new physiques (Schachter, 1982). It seems, however, that these successful dieters are actually a small minority of those who attempt to change their weight (Stunkard & Pennick, 1979; Wilson & Brownell, 1980). What seems to happen more typically is that the dieter initially loses some weight but not as much as was desired. Even if she loses as much as intended, the dieter finds that the lost weight quickly returns and often with a few extra pounds (Polivy & Herman, 1983).

We recently examined whether dieters lose weight outside of the lab (Heatherton, Polivy, & Herman, 1991). Restrained and unrestrained subjects were weighed daily for a 6-week period and 6 months later to determine whether restrained people are actually successful dieters. Neither restrained nor unrestrained subjects lost a significant amount of weight during the 6-month period. We also found that restrained subjects had greater weight fluctuations than unrestrained subjects. These fluctuations were attributable to dietary restraint rather than body weight because partial correlations between fluctuations and restraint remained significant when percentage overweight was partialed out, whereas the correlation between percentage overweight and fluctuations was not significant when restraint was partialed out. We concluded that exaggerated weight fluctuations were not a natural concomitant of higher body weight but rather a consequence of dieting and overeating behavior. The typical cycle of strict dieting and overeating appears to preclude successful weight loss.

Moreover, recent physiological work supports the notion that repeated dieting is counterproductive to successful weight loss. That is, weight loss and weight gain become progressively more difficult because of metabolic changes that lead to more or less efficient processing of food intake (see Bennett, 1984). The high relapse rates associated with treatment for obesity are testament to the extraordinary difficulty that people have in maintaining weight loss (Bennett, 1984; Marcus, Wing, & Hopkins, 1988; Stunkard & Pennick, 1979; Wilson & Brownell, 1980). Likewise, there is considerable animal evidence showing that weight gain occurs much faster in previously starved animals than would be expected by caloric intake alone (Levitsky, Faust, & Glassman, 1976). Repeated alterations between caloric deprivation and overfeeding have also been shown to have cumulative metabolic effects so that weight loss and metabolic functioning are slowed progressively more each time the animal is placed on caloric deprivation, and weight gain occurs more rapidly with each occurrence of refeeding (Brownell, Greenwood, Stellar, & Shrager, 1986). This pattern has implications for the observation that so-called yo-yo dieting in humans can lead to less efficient weight loss and increased weight gain (Brownell et al., 1986).

After failure to lose weight, the dieter is faced with the question of continuing to diet (i.e., to go on with an unsuccessful or even counterproductive course of action) or discarding the enterprise of losing weight and accepting herself as she is. At this point, the dieter could decide that it is not worth the effort to try to change her body weight or that she is unlikely ever to succeed. She could abandon her weight-loss efforts and become an unrestrained or normal eater again. Unfortunately, given the pressures on women to be thin, which mark our culture (e.g., Polivy, Garner, & Garfinkel, 1986; Striegel-Moore, Silberstein, & Rodin, 1986), the usual response seems to be to choose to continue to diet. The dieter may feel that she did not try hard enough initially, that she used the wrong technique to lose weight, or that circumstances somehow intervened and prevented her from succeeding. She may fail repeatedly using various rationales, and over time failure may become even more likely for each episode of dieting. Thus, the dieting becomes more and more habitual or persistent, and the dieter soon becomes what we call a restrained eater, or chronic dieter.

CAUSES AND CONSEQUENCES
OF DIETARY FAILURE

Self-Esteem

Common sense dictates that we feel better about ourselves when we succeed at important tasks. Conversely, when we fail, we feel worse about ourselves, especially if we fail at something that is important to us. For the dieter, failing to lose weight or failing to maintain successful weight suppression will undoubtedly lead to a worsened sense of self. To create the motivation to diet, the dieter must feel convinced that she is inadequate in her present form. Cognitions to the effect that one is unattractive, incompetent, and unworthy may be used to motivate dieting. The dieter hopes that losing weight will transform her into someone who is more attractive, competent, and worthy. Much is invested in the decision to diet, and dietary success or failure is likely to have important effects on subsequent self-esteem. In fact, as mentioned earlier, restrained eaters are well known for having low self-esteem (cf. Heatherton, 1990; Polivy et al., 1988). This low self-esteem may be important in determining not only which individuals undertake dieting but also how successful they are at dieting.

Low self-esteem dieters are more susceptible to dietary disinhibitors than are high self-esteem dieters (who are relatively few in number). Polivy et al. (1988) compared low with high self-esteem restrained eaters in a preload paradigm. In the absence of a preload, low self-esteem restrained subjects ate very little, but they ate a great deal after a disinhibiting preload. In contrast, high self-esteem restrained subjects ate at an intermediate level and were unaffected by the preload manipulation (they ate the same amount whether preloaded or not). Unrestrained subjects, whether high or low in self-esteem, showed appropriate regulation to the preload by eating less when preloaded than when not preloaded. Similarly, Heatherton, Herman, and Polivy (1991) recently showed that low self-esteem restrained subjects are more likely to become disinhibited by ego threats than are high self-esteem restrained subjects. Once again, high self-esteem restrained subjects were less affected by the ego threats.

Although there is currently no evidence demonstrating that dieters experience lowered self-esteem after dietary failures, there is evidence that therapeutic interventions designed to stop dieting behaviors lead to increased self-esteem (Ciliska, 1990). For example, a 10-week program that stressed the importance of accepting one's body produced increases in self-esteem among a group of obese women (see also Heatherton & Polivy, 1991).

Clearly, more research is needed to examine the interaction between dieting and self-esteem. Because each dietary failure may produce lower self-esteem and because lower self-esteem may, in turn, make dietary failure more likely, individuals who undertake chronic dieting may enter a spiral in which each failure at dieting produces greater negative affect and precludes either successful acceptance or successful alteration of their bodies.

Depression and Other Negative Affect

The spiral pattern just described suggests that continual dietary failures diminish self-esteem. Over time, such attacks on self-esteem are likely to generalize to negative affect, such as chronically depressed or anxious mood. As mentioned earlier, restrained eaters have been shown to be more depressed (Edwards & Nadelberg, 1986; Rosen et al., 1987) and anxious (Herman & Polivy, 1975; Rosen et al., 1987) than nondieters.

Consistent with this thinking, negative emotion, or emotionality, has also been implicated in triggering overeating by dieters (Baucom & Aiken, 1981; Grilo, Shiffman, & Wing, 1989; Heatherton, Herman, & Polivy, 1991; Herman, Polivy, & Heatherton, 1990; Ruderman, 1985a) and binge eating by bulimics (Abraham & Beumont, 1982; Crowther, Lingswiler, & Stephens, 1984; Davis et al., 1988; Johnson & Larson, 1982; Larson & Johnson, 1985; Lingswiler, Crowther, & Stephens, 1989a, 1989b). Similarly, Greenberg and

Harvey (1986) found that the interaction of restraint and depression was a better predictor of binge eating than either scale alone.

Not all forms of emotional distress, however, are equally likely to trigger overeating (Herman et al., 1990). Experimental manipulations of physical fear (such as threat of electrical shock or blood sampling) fail to increase the eating of obese or dieting individuals, although these manipulations do reduce the eating of control subjects (Herman & Polivy, 1975; McKenna, 1972; Schachter, Goldman, & Gordon, 1968). In contrast, manipulations that involve ego threat (i.e., threats to an individual's sense of self-esteem or identity) or negative mood inductions do significantly increase the eating by obese or dieting subjects, whereas controls are unaffected (Baucom & Aiken, 1981; Frost, Goolkasian, Ely, & Blanchard, 1982; Herman, Polivy, Lank, & Heatherton, 1987; Ruderman, 1985a; Schotte, Cools, & McNally, 1990; Slochower, 1976, 1983; Slochower & Kaplan, 1980, 1983; Slochower, Kaplan, & Mann, 1981).

A direct test of the hypothesis that different types of stressors have different effects on eating was recently conducted by Heatherton, Herman, and Polivy (1991). Restrained and unrestrained eaters were subjected to either a physical fear-inducing stress (i.e., threat of shock) or one of two forms of ego threat (i.e., failure at an easy task or speaking in front of an evaluative audience) before an ad-lib taste task. The dieters increased their eating in response to the ego threat, but they showed no significant change in response to the fear manipulation. Nondieters showed no eating changes in response to either of the ego threats but ate less in the fear condition (presumably because the autonomic correlates of distress mimic satiety).

Thus, self-relevant forms of emotional distress interfere with dietary restraint as evidenced by disinhibited eating. Because dieting and dietary failure may promote affect instability, restrained eaters may be especially responsive to external threats to self-esteem. Such threats may undermine the dieter's resolve to restrict intake and thereby promote overeating.

External Responsiveness

To be successful at dieting, individuals have to ignore the internal sensations of hunger that might otherwise promote (over)eating. Over time, cognitive cues may take on greater importance than internal cues, and the eating of the chronic dieter may be especially vulnerable to external and cognitive influences.

To our knowledge, Polivy (1976) was the first to demonstrate that cognitive factors may play an important role in dieter's food intake. Polivy gave dieters and nondieters pudding that was described as high or low in calories. Moreover, some subjects who were told their pudding was high in calories were actually given pudding low in calories and vice versa. This balanced design revealed that dieters were disinhibited only when they believed that they had consumed a high-calorie preload. The actual caloric content of the food did not influence eating. This same pattern was later replicated by Spencer and Fremouw (1979); restrained eaters became disinhibited only when they believed that they had surpassed some dietary quota.

A series of recent studies expanded on Polivy's (1976) finding. Knight and Boland (1989) found that it was the type of food rather than the perception of calories that disinhibited eating. That is, they found that the type of food (milkshake vs. cottage cheese) was more important than perceived caloric content in disinhibiting eating among dieters such that milkshakes were more likely than cottage cheese to disinhibit dieters. Similarly, dieters became disinhibited when they expected to consume a forbidden food whether it was high or low in calories. The anticipation of nonforbidden foods did not disinhibit dieters. Thus, the subjective perception of food types is important to the maintenance of dietary restraints (see King, Herman, & Polivy, 1987).

Heatherton, Polivy, and Herman (1989) reasoned that if cognitive cues were important to restrained eating largely because of relative insensitivity (or nonresponsiveness) to internal sensations, then a cognitive manipulation of hunger state should have a particularly strong effect on dieter's eating. Heatherton et al. (1989) gave restrained and unrestrained eaters a vitamin (actually a placebo) that was supposed to produce side effects that were similar to the sensations typically associated with hunger or satiety. Compared with a control group that was not led to expect any side effects, restrained subjects—in two separate studies—ate more when they were led to expect sensations of hunger and ate less when they expected sensations of satiety. Unrestrained eaters showed the opposite pattern; they ate less when given hunger expectations than when given satiety expectations. This reversal of standard placebo effects in unrestrained eaters supports the notion that nondieters are sensitive to internal state, because such reversals occur as a result of a discrepancy between actual and expected internal state (Ross & Olson, 1981). Because dieters are unresponsive (or insensitive) to internal state, there was no actual–expected discrepancy, and a placebo effect was observed on amount eaten. Again restrained eaters rely on the cognitive control of food intake, which may be disrupted by preloading or emotional distress (see Heatherton, Polivy, & Herman, 1990). Thus, external food cues are important to the disinhibition of dietary restraints.

In summary, disinhibited eating is promoted by dieting, low self-esteem, negative affect, and susceptibility to external and cognitive influences. Disinhibited eating makes successful weight loss unlikely, which in turn exacerbates feelings of low self-esteem and promotes affect instability and increases the reliance on external cues to guide eating.

MECHANISMS OF DISINHIBITED EATING

The preceding section identified the circumstances in which disinhibited eating was likely; however, it did not specify the process by which bingeing occurs. In fact, relatively little is known about the mechanisms of disinhibited eating (see Heatherton et al., 1990). How does overeating occur among restrained subjects?

Theories of Disinhibited Eating

Although a number of theories exist as to how dieters become disinhibited, little research has directly investigated the mechanics of disinhibition. Herman and Polivy (1975) originally proposed that emotional distress or preloading interfered with the cognitive control of food intake because there is only so much that a person can worry about at any one time. When other concerns become paramount, dieting is relegated to secondary importance and restrained eating is released. There is currently little evidence that such an explanation is complete. It certainly does not explain why only certain types of circumstances (such as only certain types of distress) disinhibit eating.

Herman and Polivy (1988) more recently suggested that eating may serve a masking function for the dieter. That is, when dieters feel badly about any aspect of their lives, they can sabotage their diets and then blame their negative affect on breaking their diet rather than on potentially more threatening life events. Although this explanation may explain distress-related eating, it may be less relevant to overeating that follows preloading because eating to mask the distress associated with eating seems an implausible strategy to minimize emotional upset.

A more general theory of overeating has been proposed by Heatherton and Baumeister (1991). Drawing on the bulimia and restraint literatures, Heatherton and Baumeister outlined a process by which binge eating may occur. This model specifies that dieters (and others with more serious eating disorders) have an aversive sense of self-awareness from which they desire to escape (e.g., Duval & Wicklund, 1972). That is, there are large discrepancies between the person's current and ideal standards for attractiveness that lead to increased negative affect and a desire to escape from that negative affect. Central to this theory is the notion of multiple levels of meaning, which are linked to multiple ways of being aware of one's self (see Carver, 1979; Carver & Scheier, 1981; Pennebaker, 1989; Vallacher & Wegner, 1985, 1987). That is, individuals can be operating at either high or low levels of awareness and meaning. Low-level meaning involves thinking of the self in narrow, concrete, and temporally limited ways, such as self-awareness only of movement and sensation in the immediate present. In contrast, high-level meanings incorporate broad implications and the comparison of self against relevant and important standards. The negative affect that arises from comparison of self against standards (see Higgins, 1987) is relevant only to high levels of awareness because a relatively high degree of self-awareness is necessary to make such comparisons. Operating at low levels of awareness strips away meaning (and therefore affect) and thereby removes threatening implications and long-lasting concerns. Thus, one method of reducing the threatening implications of ideal–self discrepancies is to shift to low levels of awareness. Unfortunately, because inhibitions (including those associated with food intake) exist at high levels of meaning, a shift to low levels of awareness has the consequence of removing inhibitions, which, for the dieter, means an increased chance of overeating. A variety of evidence implicates such low levels of awareness in a number of disinhibited behaviors, such as suicide (Baumeister, 1990), masochism (Baumeister, 1988, 1989), and excessive alcohol consumption (Hull & Young, 1983; Steele & Josephs, 1988, in press; Steele & Southwick, 1985). Thus, overeating that results from distress or preloading is assumed to occur as a function of diminished self-awareness (see Herman, Polivy, & Silver, 1979; Polivy, Herman, Hackett, & Kuleshnyk, 1986).

Heatherton, Polivy, Herman, and Baumeister (in press) recently demonstrated that self-awareness is an important determinant of disinhibited eating among restrained eaters. In this study, the eating of restrained subjects was disinhibited by emotional distress only when self-awareness was low; when high self-awareness was enforced, inhibitions against eating were heightened and dieters ate very little. Nondieters were less affected by the self-awareness manipulation. Thus, conditions that promote self-awareness inhibit eating among dieters, and escape from self-awareness is associated with increased eating.

Currently, little direct evidence supports any particular theory of disinhibited or binge eating, and it seems particularly important to examine the mental states associated with such eating in greater detail. We propose that such research should be regarded as the highest priority for future restraint studies. We now know many of the circumstances that promote overeating, but we are as yet ignorant about how these events lead to dietary failure.

Spiral Model

The preceding sections outlined some of the determinants and consequences of dieting. We now outline a more formal model of dieting behavior. Beginning in early adolescence, individuals (especially women) begin comparing their body weights and shapes to their perceptions of cultural or peer-related ideals. A perception of no deviance from the ideal, or an acceptance of any deviation that does exist, produces a normal, unrestrained eater. However, many adolescents, whether overweight or not, are dissatisfied with their bodies and begin attempts at dieting. Adolescents with low self-esteem may be especially vulnerable to societal and peer influences and therefore may be more likely to undertake dieting than their high self-esteem peers. If the first-time dieter is successful (i.e., obtains a body weight considered ideal), she is likely to resume an unrestrained eating style. However, dieting seldom results in significant or lasting weight loss, and most individuals who begin dieting will experience dietary failure.

An initial failure at dieting forces individuals to reconsider the viability of their chosen course of action, and some will give up trying to achieve weight loss. Unfortunately, many more individuals will attribute failure to internal deficits (i.e., a lack of willpower or effort) and will increase their efforts to be successful dieters. Dieting exerts a psychological as well as a physiological toll on those who restrict intake. Increased organic stress and heightened emotionality make diet failure increasingly likely to occur. Likewise, an increased efficiency in metabolic response makes weight loss more difficult both to achieve and to sustain. Thus, most dieters fail to achieve or maintain weight loss.

Over time, successive dietary failures lead to diminished self-esteem and increased negative affect. Moreover, an increasing reliance on cognitive guides for eating renders the dieter vulnerable to external eating cues. When individuals begin this cycle of dieting and overeating, they have entered the diet spiral in which each dietary failure increases the need for additional dieting but reduces the likelihood of future success. That is, negative affect and low self-esteem make diet failure more likely, and each failure increases negative affect and lowers self-esteem. The deeper into the diet spiral that individuals are, the more likely they are to experience severe dysphoria and low self-esteem as a result of dietary failure. Thus, over time, dieting produces greater psychopathology and forces the dieter to engage in more extreme efforts to lose weight, such as by increasing restriction, increasing exercise, or beginning some form of purging.

PATH TO EATING DISORDERS

Our spiral model proposes a causal pathway leading from dietary restraint to anorexia nervosa and bulimia nervosa. According to our model, chronic dieters enter a spiral in which self-esteem is battered with each diet failure, leading to dysphoria and other negative affect. Over time, self-esteem may become so damaged and negative affect and maladjustment so ingrained that clinical eating disorders may result.

We are not trying to suggest that bulimics and anorexics are simply "superrestrained" individuals, nor are we arguing for a continuum between dieting and eating disorders. There are many important differences between bulimics and restrained eaters (see Garner, Olmsted, Polivy, and Garfinkel, 1984; Herman & Polivy, 1988; Polivy, 1989); the essential differences between those with genuine eating disorders and simple dieters appear to be related to levels of psychopathology that are independent of eating. That is, bulimics and anorexics exhibit a number of psychological deficits that dieters do not, such as clinical affective disorders, increased levels of interpersonal distrust, and the presence of ego deficits (see Garner et al., 1984; Polivy, 1989; Polivy & Herman, 1987).

However, a number of similarities between dieters and eating-disordered individuals cannot (and should not) be ignored. For example, both dieters and bulimics experience low self-esteem and negative affect, and both groups engage in apparent binge eating (see Heatherton & Baumeister, 1991, for a review of these similarities). According to a strict interpretation of our spiral model, bulimics have become this way because they are much further down the spiral. The spiral is primarily an affective spiral and may be largely unrelated to eating per se. Thus, our model predicts increased psychopathology (and perhaps more severe bingeing and purging) the longer one remains in the diet spiral. This may explain, in part, why so many bulimics have affective disorders (see Hinz & Williamson, 1989) and why such affective disorders are more serious among bulimics than among those with subclinical eating disorders and among other dieters.

The pathway from restraint to anorexia nervosa is less clear. For these individuals, bingeing is rare and so it is not bingeing that is the dietary failure. Rather, it is the inability to attain extreme goals that may be viewed as the failure. The anorexic who weighs 80 pounds may view herself as a dismal dieter because she really wants to lose an additional 10 pounds but is unable to do so. Thus, anorexics may go down the spiral without binge eating. They too become more depressed, have lower self-esteem, and are prone to irrational cognitions (Garfinkel & Garner, 1982), but they do not experience the same sorts of dietary failure as do bulimics at least on the face of it. Although they may appear to be successful to the objective observer, they may still feel as if they have failed.

Once caught in the diet spiral, it may be very difficult for the dieter to escape. One possibility is that successful weight loss may help offset low self-esteem and negative affect. For those few individuals who diet to suppress weight gain rather than to lose weight, the negative concomitants of dieting may not be as severe. The notion of weight suppression has been most clearly articulated by Lowe and his colleagues (see Lowe, 1987; Lowe & Kleifield, 1988). Contrary to unsuccessful dieters (i.e., typical restrained eaters), those who score high on a measure of weight suppression are actually less likely to show disinhibited eating after the standard preload procedure (Lowe & Kleifield, 1988). Thus, these individuals may have different underlying motivations for dieting. That is, they may not be dissatisfied with their current appearance, but they may fear what they would look like if they gained weight. These individuals also differ from those who have lost significant amounts of weight but who continue to try to lose more. For example, it is often observed that bulimics have a history of obesity even though they might have a current weight that is normal. Bulimics, however, are not satisfied with their current reduced weight and would, in fact, like to be thinner. Successful weight suppressors are probably more satisfied with themselves than are chronic dieters or bulimics. Again, it appears that the self-perception of overweight and concurrent dissatisfaction are important characteristics of those trapped within our spiral model.

An additional way to break out of the spiral is to give up dieting (or to have treatment for more serious eating disorders). In this way, the individual no longer experiences the constant consequences of dietary failure. Obviously, however, these individuals will still experience the other sorts of negative affect and low self-esteem proposed by our model (unless these deficits are also addressed). Consider findings by Yager, Landsverk, Edelstein, and Jarvik (1988), who found that the alleviation of eating problems among binge eaters and bulimics was often coupled with increased substance-abuse problems. That is, these individuals were still very unhappy, but rather than using food to shut out painful awareness of self these individuals turned to substance abuse. The only true solution or exit from the spiral thus seems to be self-acceptance.

RESEARCH IMPLICATIONS

The current model has many research implications, and many aspects of dieting behavior have received little empirical attention. For example, we know little about why adolescents undertake dieting, and we know even less about the mechanisms of dietary failure. Such basic work has been ignored for far too long, and much work needs to be done.

Our model proposes a pattern of dieting and disinhibited eating that can adversely affect self-esteem and psychological adjustment and that may spiral into bulimia nervosa or anorexia nervosa in susceptible individuals. We need more research on the relation between clinical eating disorders and dieting. For example, what role do familial factors play in the initiation of dieting behaviors? We know that the families of bulimics have increased incidence of alcoholism and clinical affective disorders (Schlesier-Stropp, 1984), but we know very little about the families of chronic dieters. Because familial factors may promote the initiation of dieting and hence entry into a possible dietary spiral, we need more research that addresses the developmental and situational determinants of dieting behavior.

Our model also proposes that there are important differences in what is being measured by the various dietary restraint scales. This point was made explicitly by Heatherton, Herman, Polivy, King, and McGree (1988) but is often ignored by other researchers. The Stunkard and Messick Three Factor Eating Questionnaire (TFEQ; Stunkard & Messick, 1985) and the Dutch Eating Behavior Questionnaire (DEBQ; Van Strien, 1986) are not interchangeable substitutes for the Herman and Polivy scale, and they likely measure something altogether different. For example, the cognitive restraint factor of the TFEQ has been found to be unrelated to feeling fat (Striegel-Moore, McAvay, & Rodin, 1986) even though body dissatisfaction has been shown to be related to the original restraint scale (Heatherton, 1990; Polivy et al., 1990). Furthermore, there is a well-established link between emotional distress and eating binges so that dieters, restrained eaters, and bulimics have been shown (in both lab studies and through self-report) to become disinhibited by distress. However, the TFEQ scales do not seem to predict distress-induced eating (e.g., Cooper & Bowskill, 1986). A recent examination of the three best known measures of dietary restraint concluded that, in fact, the TFEQ and the DEBQ measured successful restriction of food intake, whereas the Restraint Scale was related to various body-dissatisfaction, bulimia, and drive for thinness measures (Laessle, Tuschl, Kotthaus, & Pirke, 1989). We therefore strongly encourage researchers to consider carefully which scales they use. Although a restrained eater (as measured by the original scale) is not a bulimic, a successful restrained eater (as measured by the TFEQ or DEBQ) is even less so.

Individuals undertake dieting for a wide variety of reasons. Recent trends in fitness and nutrition have led to a promotion of healthful eating styles, which include components of restriction (certain foods and amounts). The motivations that underlie such healthy restriction are likely to differ in many significant ways from dieting motivated by fears of social rejection, distorted or disgruntled body image, low self-esteem, and susceptibility to cultural messages that one must be "starved to perfection." The problematic eating that is the focus of this volume is more likely related to the latter than the former. Researchers attempting to draw parallels between dieting and more serious eating disorders should use the Restraint Scale rather than scales that measure successful food restriction.

CLINICAL IMPLICATIONS

Although giving up dieting may have important implications for self-esteem (Ciliska, 1990), the dynamic structure of the spiral model is as yet unclear. For example, raising one's level of self-esteem or decreasing one's level of depression may have the property of lifting one higher in the spiral where individuals may be less vulnerable to disinhibiting situations. Accordingly, antidepressants might be effective in the treatment of bulimia in part because they raise bulimics out of the deepest point of the spiral to a point at which crises and temptations are dealt with more easily (in addition, of course, to any physiological effects of antidepressant mediations, which we do not mean to discount). Similarly, trying to encourage individuals to accept themselves and their bodies and concurrently discouraging dieting may prevent the onset of more serious eating disorders (see Polivy & Herman, 1987). Moreover, teaching individuals to cope effectively with emotional upsets and distress may lessen their aversive sense of self-awareness and promote increased self-esteem. An important aspect of this emphasis is to encourage individuals to pay greater attention to their internal hunger and satiety signals so that they place less reliance on unpredictable external cues (see Polivy & Herman, 1983). In summary, more emphasis must be placed on the underlying self-esteem and emotional deficits that may lead dieters down the spiral to more serious eating disorders.

SUMMARY AND CONCLUSION

Our spiral model was developed as a framework in which to understand the initiation of dieting, the causes and consequences of diet failure, and the development of more serious eating disorders. Individuals undertake dieting as a result of discrepancies between what they believe they look like and what they wish to look like (i.e., body dissatisfaction). Although low self-esteem, emotional instability, and maladjustment may predispose individuals to undertake dieting, the current evidence indicates that dieting may cause these psychological deficits or at least exacerbate existing deficits in some individuals.

Because diets are seldom successful, individuals who choose to continue dieting may have increasingly diminished self-esteem, heightened negative affect, and greater vulnerability to situational and cognitive disinhibitors. The process by which overeating occurs is not yet known, although it is possible that such eating occurs in an attempt to escape aversive self-awareness or as a strategy to mask general emotional distress. These factors interact so that dieting increases overall negative affect, and negative affect sabotages dietary success so that the individual must diet even harder. This spiral may exact a serious toll on psychological functioning, which may eventually promote the onset of more serious eating disorders.

REFERENCES

Abraham, S. F., & Beumont, P. J. V. (1982). How patients describe bulimia or binge eating. *Psychological Medicine, 12,* 625–635.

Agras, W. S., & Kirkley, B. G. (1986). Bulimia: Theories of etiology. In K. D. Brownell & J. P. Foreyt (Eds.), *Handbook of eating disorders* (pp. 367–378). New York: Basic Books.

Baucom, D. H., & Aiken, P. A. (1981). Effect of depressed mood on eating among obese and nonobese dieting persons. *Journal of Personality and Social Psychology, 41,* 577–585.

Baumeister, R. F. (1988). Masochism as escape from self. *Journal of Sex Research, 25,* 28–59.

Baumeister, R. F. (1989). *Masochism and the self.* Hillsdale, NJ: Erlbaum.

Baumeister, R. F. (1990). Suicide as escape from self. *Psychological Review, 97,* 90–113.

Bennett, W. I. (1984). Dieting: Ideology versus physiology. *Psychiatric Clinics of North America, 7,* 321–334.

Brownell, K. D., Greenwood, M. R. C., Stellar, E., & Shrager, E. E. (1986).

The effects of repeated cycles of weight loss and regain in rats. *Physiology and Behavior, 38,* 459–464.

Carver, C. S. (1979). A cybernetic model of self-attention processes. *Journal of Personality and Social Psychology, 37,* 1251–1281.

Carver, C. S., & Scheier, M. F. (1981). *Attention and self-regulation: A control theory approach to human behavior.* New York: Springer-Verlag.

Ciliska, D. (1990). *Beyond dieting—psychoeducational interventions for chronically obese women: A non-dieting approach.* New York: Brunner/Mazel.

Cooper, P. J., & Bowskill, R. (1986). Dysphoric mood and overeating. *British Journal of Clinical Psychology, 25,* 155–156.

Crowther, J. H., Lingswiler, V. M., & Stephens, M. A. (1984). The topography of binge eating. *Addictive Behaviors, 9,* 299–303.

Davis, R., Freeman, R. J., & Garner, D. M. (1988). A naturalistic investigation of eating behavior in bulimia nervosa. *Journal of Consulting and Clinical Psychology, 56,* 273–279.

Duval, S., & Wicklund, R. A. (1972). *A theory of objective self-awareness.* New York: Academic Press.

Dwyer, J. T., Feldman, J. I., & Mayer, J. (1967). Adolescent dieters: Who are they? *American Journal of Clinical Nutrition, 20,* 1045–1056.

Dwyer, J. T., Feldman, J. I., & Mayer, J. (1970). The social psychology of dieting. *Journal of Health and Social Behavior, 11,* 269–287.

Dwyer, J. T., Feldman, J. I., Seltzer, C. C., & Mayer, J. (1969). Adolescent attitudes toward weight and appearance. *Journal of Nutrition Education, 1,* 14–19.

Dykens, E. M., & Gerrard, M. (1986). Psychological profiles of purging bulimics, repeat dieters, and controls. *Journal of Consulting and Clinical Psychology, 54,* 283–288.

Edwards, F. E., & Nagelberg, D. B. (1986). Personality characteristics of restrained/binge eaters versus unrestrained/nonbinge eaters. *Addictive Behaviors, 11,* 207–211.

Eldredge, K., Wilson, G. T., & Whaley, A. (1990). Failure, self-evaluation, and feeling fat in women. *International Journal of Eating Disorders, 9,* 37–50.

Fallon, A. E., & Rozin, P. (1985). Sex differences in perceptions of desirable body shape. *Journal of Abnormal Psychology, 94,* 102–105.

Frost, R. O., Goolkasian, G. A., Ely, R. J., & Blanchard, F. A. (1982). Depression, restraint and eating behavior. *Behavior Research and Therapy, 20,* 113–121.

Garfinkel, P. E., & Garner, D. M. (1982). *Anorexia nervosa: A multidimensional perspective.* New York: Brunner/Mazel.

Garner, D. M., Olmsted, M. P., Polivy, J., & Garfinkel, P. E. (1984). Comparison between weight preoccupied women and anorexia nervosa. *Psychosomatic Medicine, 46,* 255–266.

Greenberg, B. R., & Harvey, P. D. (1986). The prediction of binge eating over time. *Addictive Behaviors, 11,* 383–388.

Grilo, C. M., Shiffman, S., & Wing, R. R. (1989). Relapse crises and coping among dieters. *Journal of Consulting and Clinical Psychology, 57,* 488–495.

Hawkins, R. C., Turell, S., & Jackson, L. J. (1983). Desirable and undesirable masculine and feminine traits in relation to students' dietary tendencies and body image dissatisfaction. *Sex Roles, 9,* 705–724.

Heatherton, T. F. (1986). *Restraint and misattribution: An analysis of cognitive control mechanisms.* Unpublished master's thesis, University of Toronto.

Heatherton, T. F. (1990). *Aspects of dissatisfaction among dieters.* Manuscript submitted for publication.

Heatherton, T. F., & Baumeister, R. F. (1991). Binge eating as escape from self-awareness. *Psychological Bulletin, 110,* 86–108.

Heatherton, T. F., Herman, C. P., & Polivy, J. (1991). Effects of physical threat and ego threat on eating behavior. *Journal of Personality and Social Psychology, 60,* 138–143.

Heatherton, T. F., Herman, C. P., Polivy, J., King, G. A., & McGree, S. T. (1988). The (mis)measurement of restraint: An analysis of conceptual and psychometric issues. *Journal of Abnormal Psychology, 97,* 19–28.

Heatherton, T. F., & Polivy, J. (1991). The measurement of state self-esteem. *Journal of Personality and Social Psychology, 60,* 895–910.

Heatherton, T. F., Polivy, J., & Herman, C. P. (1989). Restraint and internal responsiveness: Effects of placebo manipulations of hunger state on eating. *Journal of Abnormal Psychology, 98,* 89–92.

Heatherton, T. F., Polivy, J., & Herman, C. P. (1990). Restrained eating: Some current findings and speculations. *Psychology of Addictive Behaviors, 4,* 100–106.

Heatherton, T. F., Polivy, J., & Herman, C. P. (1991). Restraint, body weight, and weight variability. *Journal of Abnormal Psychology, 100,* 78–83.

Heatherton, T. F., Polivy, J., Herman, C. P., & Baumeister, R. F. (in press). Self-awareness, task failure and disinhibition: How attentional focus affects eating. *Journal of Personality.*

Herman, C. P., & Polivy, J. (1975). Anxiety, restraint and eating behavior. *Journal of Abnormal Psychology, 84,* 666–672.

Herman, C. P., & Polivy, J. (1980). Restrained eating. In A. J. Stunkard (Ed.), *Obesity* (pp. 208–225). Philadelphia: Saunders.

Herman, C. P., & Polivy, J. (1988). Restraint and excess in dieters and bulimics. In K. M. Pirke, D. Ploog, & W. Vandereycken (Eds.), *The psychobiology of anorexia nervosa* (pp. 33–41). Heidelberg, Germany: Springer.

Herman, C. P., Polivy, J., & Heatherton, T. F. (1990). *The effects of distress on eating: A review of the experimental literature.* Manuscript submitted for publication.

Herman, C. P., Polivy, J., Lank, C. L., & Heatherton, T. F. (1987). Anxiety, hunger and eating. *Journal of Abnormal Psychology, 96,* 264–269.

Herman, C. P., Polivy, J., & Silver, R. (1979). The effects of an observer on eating behavior: The induction of sensible eating. *Journal of Personality, 47,* 85–99.

Higgins, E. T. (1987). Self-discrepancy: A theory relating self to affect. *Psychological Review, 94,* 319–340.

Hinz, L. D., & Williamson, D. A. (1987). Bulimia and depression: A review of the affective variant hypothesis. *Psychological Bulletin, 102,* 150–158.

Huenemann, R. L., Shapiro, L. R., Hampton, M. C., & Mitchell, B. W. (1966). A longitudinal study of gross body composition and body confirmation and their association with food and activity in a teenage population. *American Journal of Clinical Nutrition, 18,* 325–338.

Hull, J. G., & Young, R. D. (1983). The self-awareness-reducing effects of alcohol: Evidence and implications. In J. Suls & A. G. Greenwald (Eds.), *Psychological perspectives on the self* (Vol. 2, pp. 159–190). Hillsdale, NJ: Erlbaum.

Jakobovits, C., Halstead, P., Kelly, L., Roe, D., & Young, C. (1977). Eating habits and nutrient intake of college women over a thirty year period. *Journal of the American Dietetic Association, 71,* 405–411.

Johnson, C., & Connors, M. E. (1987). *The etiology and treatment of bulimia nervosa.* New York: Basic Books.

Johnson, C., & Larson, R. (1982). Bulimia: An analysis of moods and behavior. *Psychosomatic Medicine, 44,* 341–351.

Kagan, D. M., & Squires, R. L. (1984). Eating disorders among adolescents: Patterns and prevalence. *Adolescence, 19,* 207–211.

King, G. A., Herman, C. P., & Polivy, J. (1987). Food perception in dieters and non-dieters. *Appetite, 8,* 147–158.

Knight, L., & Boland, F. (1989). Restrained eating: An experimental disentanglement of the disinhibiting variables of calories and food type. *Journal of Abnormal Psychology, 98,* 412–420.

Laessle, R. G., Tuschl, R. J., Kotthaus, B. C., & Pirke, K. M. (1989). A comparison of the validity of the three scales for the assessment of dietary restraint. *Journal of Abnormal Psychology, 98,* 504–507.

Larson, R., & Johnson, C. (1985). Bulimia: Disturbed patterns of solitude. *Addictive Behaviors, 10,* 281–290.

Levitsky, D. A., Faust, I., & Glassman, M. (1976). The ingestion of food and the recovery of body weight following fasting in the naive rat. *Physiology and Behavior, 17,* 575–580.

Lingswiler, V. M., Crowther, J. H., & Stephens, M. A. P. (1989a). Affective and cognitive antecedents to eating episodes in bulimia and binge eating. *International Journal of Eating Disorders, 8,* 533–539.

Lingswiler, V. M., Crowther, J. H., & Stephens, M. A. P. (1989b). Emotional and somatic consequences of binge episodes. *Addictive Behaviors, 14,* 503–511.

Lowe, M. R. (1987). Set point, restraint, and the limits of weight loss: A critical analysis. *Advances in Eating Disorders, 1,* 1–37.

Lowe, M. R., & Kleifield, E. I. (1988). Cognitive restraint, weight suppression, and the regulation of eating. *Appetite, 10,* 159–168.

Marcus, M. D., Wing, R. R., & Hopkins, J. (1988). Obese binge eaters: Affect, cognitions, and response to behavioral weight control. *Journal of Consulting and Clinical Psychology, 56,* 433–439.

McKenna, R. J. (1972). Some effects of anxiety level and food cues on the eating behavior of obese and normal subjects: A comparison of the Schachterian and psychosomatic conceptions. *Journal of Personality and Social Psychology, 22,* 311–319.

Miller, T. M., Coffman, J. G., & Linke, R. A. (1980). Survey of body image, weight, and diet of college students. *Journal of the American Dietetic Association, 77,* 561–566.

Nylander, I. (1971). The feeling of being fat and dieting in a school population. *Acta Socio-Medica Scandinavica, 1,* 17–26.

Pennebaker, J. W. (1989). Stream of consciousness and stress: Levels of thinking. In J. S. Uleman & J. A. Bargh (Eds.), *The direction of thought: Limits of awareness, intention and control* (pp. 327–350). New York: Guilford Press.

Polivy, J. (1976). Perception of calories and regulation of intake in restrained and unrestrained subjects. *Addictive Behaviors, 1,* 237–243.

Polivy, J. (1989). Is dieting itself an eating disorder? *BASH Magazine, 8,* 186–190.

Polivy, J., Garner, D. M., & Garfinkel, P. E. (1986). Causes and consequences of the current preference for thin female physiques. In C. P. Herman, M. P. Zana, & E. T. Higgins (Eds.), *Physical appearance, stigma and social behavior: The Ontario symposium* (Vol. 3, pp. 89–112). Hillsdale, NJ: Erlbaum.

Polivy, J., Heatherton, T. F., & Herman, C. P. (1988). Self-esteem, restraint, and eating behavior. *Journal of Abnormal Psychology, 97,* 354–356.

Polivy, J., & Herman, C. P. (1983). *Breaking the diet habit: The natural weight alternative.* New York: Basic Books.

Polivy, J., & Herman, C. P. (1985). Dieting and bingeing: A causal analysis. *American Psychologist, 40,* 193–201.

Polivy, J., & Herman, C. P. (1987). Diagnosis and treatment of normal eating. *Journal of Consulting and Clinical Psychology, 55,* 635–644.

Polivy, J., Herman, C. P., Hackett, R., & Kuleshnyk, I. (1986). The effects of self-attention and public attention on eating in restrained and unrestrained subjects. *Journal of Personality and Social Psychology, 50,* 1253–1260.

Polivy, J., Herman, C. P., Olmsted, M. P., & Jazwinski, C. (1984). Restraint and binge eating. In R. C. Hawkins, W. J. Fremouw, & P. F. Clement (Eds.), *The binge purge syndrome: Diagnosis, treatment and research* (pp. 104–122). New York: Pergamon Press.

Polivy, J., Herman, C. P., & Pliner, P. (1990). Perception and evaluation of body image: The meaning of body shape and size. In J. Olson (Ed.), *Ontario symposium on personality 1988*, 87–114. Hillsdale, NJ: Erlbaum.

Rosen, J. C., & Gross, J. (1987). Prevalence of weight reducing and weight gaining in adolescent girls and boys. *Health Psychology, 6*, 131–147.

Rosen, J. C., Gross, J., & Vara, L. (1987). Psychological adjustment of adolescents attempting to lose or gain weight. *Journal of Consulting and Clinical Psychology, 55*, 742–747.

Rosen, J. C., Tacy, B., & Howell, D. (1990). Life stress, psychological symptoms and weight reducing behavior in adolescent girls: A prospective study. *International Journal of Eating Disorders, 9*, 17–26.

Ross, M., & Olson, J. (1981). An expectancy-attribution model of the effects of placebos. *Psychological Review, 88*, 408–437.

Ruderman, A. J. (1985a). Dysphoric mood and overeating: A test of restraint theory's disinhibition hypothesis. *Journal of Abnormal Psychology, 94*, 78–85.

Ruderman, A. J. (1985b). Restraint and irrational cognitions. *Behavior Research and Therapy, 23*, 557–561.

Ruderman, A. J., & Grace, P. S. (1987). Restraint, bulimia, and psychopathology. *Addictive Behaviors, 12*, 249–255.

Ruderman, A. J., & Grace, P. S. (1988). Bulimics and restrained eaters: A personality comparison. *Addictive Behaviors, 13*, 359–368.

Russell, G. F. M. (1979). Bulimia nervosa: An ominous variant of anorexia nervosa. *Psychological Medicine, 9*, 429–448.

Schachter, S. (1982). Recidivism and self-cure of smoking and obesity. *American Psychologist, 37*, 436–444.

Schachter, S., Goldman, R., & Gordon, A. (1968). Effects of fear, food deprivation, and obesity on eating. *Journal of Personality and Social Psychology, 10*, 91–97.

Schlesier-Strop, B. (1984). Bulimia: A review of the literature. *Psychological Bulletin, 95*, 247–257.

Schotte, D. E., Cools, J., & McNally, R. J. (1990). Induced anxiety triggers overeating in restrained eaters. *Journal of Abnormal Psychology, 99*, 317–320.

Slochower, J. (1976). Emotional labelling and overeating in obese and normal weight individuals. *Psychosomatic Medicine, 38*, 131–139.

Slochower, J. (1983). Life stress, weight, and cue salience. In J. Slochower (Ed.), *Excessive eating* (pp. 75–87). New York: Human Sciences Press.

Slochower, J., & Kaplan, S. P. (1980). Anxiety, perceived control and eating in obese and normal weight persons. *Appetite, 1*, 75–83.

Slochower, J., & Kaplan, S. P. (1983). Effects of cue salience and weight on responsiveness to uncontrollable anxiety. In J. Slochower (Ed.), *Excessive eating* (pp. 68–74). New York: Human Sciences Press.

Slochower, J., Kaplan, S. P., & Mann, L. (1981). The effects of life stress and weight on mood and eating. *Appetite, 2,* 115–125.

Spencer, J. A., & Fremouw, W. J. (1979). Binge eating as a function of restraint and weight classification. *Journal of Abnormal Psychology, 88,* 262–267.

Steele, C. M., & Josephs, R. A. (1988). Drinking your troubles away. II: An attention-allocation model of alcohol's effect on psychological stress. *Journal of Abnormal Psychology, 97,* 196–205.

Steele, C. M., & Josephs, R. A. (1990). Alcoholic myopia: Its prized and dangerous effects. *American Psychologist, 45,* 921–933.

Steele, C. M., & Southwick, L. (1985). Alcohol and social behavior. I: The psychology of drunken excess. *Journal of Personality and Social Psychology, 48,* 18–34.

Striegel-Moore, R., McAvay, G., & Rodin, J. (1986). Psychological and behavioral correlates of feeling fat in women. *International Journal of Eating Disorders, 5,* 935–947.

Striegel-Moore, R. H., Silberstein, L. R., Frensch, P., & Rodin, J. (1989). A prospective study of disordered eating among college students. *International Journal of Eating Disorders, 8,* 499–509.

Striegel-Moore, R. H., Silberstein, L. R., & Rodin, J. (1986). Toward an understanding of risk factors for bulimia. *American Psychologist, 41,* 246–263.

Stunkard, A. J., & Messick, S. (1985). The Three Factor Eating Questionnaire to measure dietary restraint and hunger. *Journal of Psychosomatic Research, 29,* 71–83.

Stunkard, A. J., & Pennick, S. B. (1979). Behavior modification in the treatment of obesity: The problem of maintaining weight loss. *Archives of General Psychiatry, 36,* 801–806.

Vallacher, R. R., & Wegner, D. M. (1985). *A theory of action identification.* Hillsdale, NJ: Erlbaum.

Vallacher, R. R., & Wegner, D. M. (1987). What do people think they are doing? Action identification theory and human behavior. *Psychological Review, 94,* 3–15.

Vanderheyden, D. A., Fekken, G. C., & Boland, F. J. (1988). Critical variables associated with bingeing and bulimia in a university population: A factor analytic study. *International Journal of Eating Disorders, 7,* 321–329.

Van Strien, T. (1986). *Eating behavior, personality traits, and body mass.* Lisse, the Netherlands: Sets & Zeitlinger.

Williamson, D. A. (1990). *Assessment of eating disorders: Obesity, anorexia, and bulimia nervosa.* New York: Pergamon Press.

Wilson, G. T., & Brownell, K. D. (1980). Behavior therapy for obesity: An evaluation of treatment outcome. *Advances in Behavior Research and Therapy, 3,* 49–86.

Yager, J., Landsverk, J., Edelstein, C. K., & Jarvik, M. (1988). A 20-month follow-up study of 628 women with eating disorders: II. Course of associated symptoms and related clinical features. *International Journal of Eating Disorders, 7,* 503–513.

9

BODY-IMAGE DISORDER: DEFINITION, DEVELOPMENT, AND CONTRIBUTION TO EATING DISORDERS

James C. Rosen
University of Vermont

The term *eating disorder* generally refers to psychological disorders involving gross abnormalities in eating. Starvation, rigid dieting, binge eating, and purging are the most dramatic features of eating disorders, and they perhaps provoke the greatest distress among patients and concerned relatives. However, body-image disorder essentially distinguishes eating disorders from other psychological conditions that occasionally involve eating abnormalities and weight loss. Moreover, body-image disorder is the driving force behind the individual's drastic weight-reducing behavior and distress over eating. Were it not for a profound disturbance in the patient's evaluation or perception of her physical appearance, there would be little grounds for the other features related to eating and weight control. (Throughout this chapter, I refer to eating-disordered patients as women because the overwhelming majority are female.) Any definition, theory of cause, or treatment of eating disorders must account for the disorder of body image. The purpose of this chapter is to (1) clarify what is (and is not) a body-image disorder, (2) evaluate the hypothesis that other eating-disorder pathology is secondary to body-image disorder, and (3) propose an explanation for the development of body-image disorder.

DEFINITION OF BODY-IMAGE DISORDER

In trying to achieve some definitional clarity of the problem at hand, I begin by using the term body-image disorder. Body-image distortion, body-size overestimation, and body dissatisfaction are the more commonly used terms. Each refers to one of many manifestations of the eating-disordered patient's body image, but by themselves none represents the entire problem. The problem of body image is multidimensional. By using the term body-image disorder, I emphasize that we are concerned with (1) a constellation of features that as a whole equals more than a single type of disturbance and (2) a degree of distress and disability that is more severe than represented by these other terms or by the idea of a body-image disturbance. Finally, because I argue that other eating-disorder pathology is secondary to body image, I want to consider it as a separate construct, a disorder unto itself. By so doing, I hope that this chapter has relevance not only for our understanding of eating disorders but also for the millions of young women who suffer from a body-image disorder but who do not meet the other criteria for eating disorders.

In defining body-image disorder, a useful starting point is a synopsis of the typical features that are reported in the literature on anorexia nervosa and bulimia nervosa. In addition, I draw on the literature on body dysmorphic disorder to help clarify the boundary of lesser degrees of disturbance and a truly disordered body image. According to the *Diagnostic and Statistical Manual of Mental Disorders* (third edition, revised) (*DSM–III–R;* American Psychiatric Association [APA], 1987), the principal criterion for body dysmorphic disorder is "preoccupation with some imagined defect in appearance in a normal appearing person. If a slight physical anomaly is present, the person's concern is grossly excessive" (p. 256). Before the term body dysmorphic disorder was introduced, it was one of two conditions that were subsumed under the broader category of monosymptomatic hypochrondriasis (Munro & Chmara, 1982; Riding & Munro, 1975). One condition was a somatization disorder of delusional proportion, also known as monosymptomatic hypochondriacal psychosis. This was a single hypochondriacal delusional system accompanied by illusional misperceptions or by poorly defined hallucinations. Common manifestations were belief in being infested (e.g., by insects), emitting a foul odor, or being ugly or misshapen. Presently, this is defined by *DSM–III–R* as delusional disorder, somatic type. In body dysmorphic disorder, as it is known today, the second diagnostic criterion is "the belief is not of delusional intensity (i.e., the person can acknowledge the possibility that he or she may be exaggerating the extent of the defect or that there may be no defect at all)" (APA, 1987) (p. 256). The third diagnostic criterion is that "occurrence is not exclusively during the course of Anorexia Nervosa or Transsexualism" (p. 256). It is debatable as to whether this means that anorexia nervosa should supersede the diagnosis of body dysmorphic disorder when the criteria for both are fulfilled or if the types of body-image disorder in these two conditions are separable constructs. Very little attention has been given to this issue. Some investigators asserted that body dysmorphic disorder complaints are generally restricted to specific body parts or to a defect that is localized such as to the mouth, nose, penis, breasts, and so on. General feelings of fatness are untypical and are related more to eating disorders (Thomas, 1987). Others, however, took the opposite perspective; that is, eating-disordered patients do present with body dysmorphic complaints (Crisp, 1988; Sturmey & Slade,1986). As we see, the phenomenology of body dysmorphic patients is very close indeed to the body image of eating-disordered patients.

Garner and Garfinkel (1981–1982) were the first to present formally a multidimensional perspective on the body-image problem in eating-disordered patients in which they (and others since, e.g., Cash & Brown, 1987) stated that it consists of disturbances in perception (of body size) and disturbances in cognition (negative evaluation of physical appearance). To this conceptualization, I add that there is a third and important feature of body-image disorder: a behavioral disturbance that involves repetitive body-checking behavior and avoidance of body-image anxiety-provoking situations (J. C. Rosen, Srebnik, Saltzberg, & Wendt, 1991).

Disorder of Perception

To my knowledge, Bruch (1962) was the first to postulate that body-image disorder was a pathological feature of anorexia nervosa that she referred to as "the absence of concern about emaciation, even when advanced, and the vigor and stubbornness with which the often gruesome appearance is defended as normal and right" (p. 189). In essence, patients with eating disorders tend to perceive themselves unrealistically as big or fat, grossly out of proportion, or protruding excessively at certain body regions. The distortion of normal size is often evident by the unrealistic standards that the patient attempts to achieve. Eating-disordered patients exhibit a mistrust or disbelief in more conventional standards for comparing their weight to normal. No matter what feedback the patient may receive about her size, she relies on her own perceptions and feelings of being too big. Similarly, patients with body dysmorphic disorder imagine a physical anomaly that is not present or grossly misperceive their appearance. In sum, this disorder does not refer simply to the belief in being overweight but a disturbance in how the patient fundamentally experiences her physique in a visual, tactile-spatial sense.

Although clinicians who work with eating-disordered patients are well aware of this problem, there is some doubt about the importance of size or shape-perception distortion as a fundamental feature of body-image disorder. First, research subjects do not equally distort the size of different body parts (Cash & Brown, 1987). In addition, size distortion of specific body parts correlates poorly with size distortion of the whole body (Cash & Brown, 1987). Some argue that if eating-disordered patients truly possess a perceptual abnormality, they should exhibit consistent or widespread distortion of their appearance. But should they? Because different body parts are more or less salient, depending on the individual, it should not be surprising that size distortion is inconsistent when measured piecemeal. Eating-disordered patients can be quite idiosyncratic in their body preoccupation. As in classic body dysmorphic disorder, negative feelings and distortion may be traced to one perceived defect in appearance (e.g., thick thighs). Thus, inconsistent body-size distortion is not a reason to negate it as a perceptual disturbance.

A greater threat to the validity of perceptual disturbance in body-image disorder is that women without eating disorders also overestimate their size and often by as much as women with eating disorders (Cash & Brown, 1987). Thus, size distortion may not be any more abnormal than dissatisfaction with weight, which also is common among young women. If not discriminatory of eating-disordered patients, some argued, disturbance of body perception should not be an essential feature of an eating disorder (Bowden, Touyz, Rodriguez, Hensley, & Beumont, 1989; Hsu, 1982). There are several reasons not to accept this conclusion at present, if not to reject it completely.

First, more studies, albeit not a strong majority, reported greater size distortion by eating-disordered subjects than by controls (Cash & Brown, 1987; Cooper & Taylor, 1987) especially in the case of bulimia nervosa.

Second, it is not surprising that many normal women overestimate body size given the ubiquitous concern with weight in the current culture. However, body image is a continuous variable, and the difference between abnormality and normality may be more quantitative than qualitative.

Third, control samples are not necessarily free of subjects with body-image disorder. The frequency of body dysmorphic disorder, for example, may be high among these study populations (Fitts, Gibson, Redding, & Deiter, 1989). Other subgroups of noneating disordered patients, such as dietary restrained subjects, exhibit a similar degree of symptoms on many measures of body-image disorder (J. C. Rosen & Srebnik, 1990; Wilson & Smith, 1989).

Fourth, with few exceptions, size distortion has been investigated only under a neutral or resting stimulus condition as if it were a stable trait. A more dynamic approach to assessment has been used with other psychophysical phenomena. In the case of psychosomatic disorders, for example, there is inconsistent support for the idea that chronic sufferers have more pronounced physical arousal than controls while they are in a tonic or resting state. During the phasic period (when the subject is exposed to stress), however, deviations from normal often emerge. In some instances, the differences between the afflicted and control subjects are apparent only during the recovery phase (the period after the stressful stimulus has been removed; Feurstein, Labbe, & Kuczmierczyk, 1986). Taking a more state-dependent approach to the problem of size misperception, a few studies showed that eating-disordered patients increase their size distortion and more so than controls after exposure to threatening situations (Freeman, Thomas, Solyom, & Miles, 1983; Robb & Thompson, 1990; Taylor & Cooper, 1989).

This certainty fits well with clinical experience. For example, after eating frightening foods without vomiting in exposure plus response prevention sessions, bulimia nervosa patients frequently imagine their stomachs protruding dramatically beyond their normal waistline (J. C. Rosen & Leitenberg, 1985). In fact, one purpose of having patients eat in the session is to provoke a variety of perceptual distortions so that the therapist can help patients to correct them. Other daily stressful experiences involving sexuality, social interactions, weight gain, menses, and so on are often associated with changes in appearance perception. In this way, the problem is not being captured by the usual laboratory study of size distortion.

Finally, eating-disordered patients are often hypervigilant to somatic sensations such as feelings of fullness, hunger, digestion, bloatedness, constipation, nausea, pain, and fatigue, which are magnified and exaggerated by selective attention. These somatic stimuli provide the basis for a variety of erroneous beliefs that the patient may have about her metabolic processes, the effect of different foods on her body, what and when she should eat, the effect of purging, her level of physical fitness or disease, and innumerable others related to weight and eating. Like the hypochondriac, the eating-disordered patient interprets these distorted sensations as proof that her body is abnormal. As proposed by Bruch (1962) in her original description of body-image disturbance, eating-disordered patients may be inaccurate in perceiving a variety of somatic characteristics other than body size and weight.

Disorder of Cognition

The most common reference to body-image disorder in terms of its cognitive dimension is the concept of body dissatisfaction. Generally, this refers to the devaluation of physical appearance relative to some ideal, such as thinking that one is too heavy, too big, and too wide and that because of this discrepancy appearance is unattractive or unpleasant. In addition to whole body concerns, body dissatisfaction often can be traced to particular body areas such as the width of the hips or thighs, the protrusion of the abdomen, or the dimpled flesh on the back of the legs. Body dissatisfaction may consist of negative attitudes about physical health and fitness rather than appearance only. Wanting or trying to lose weight, by default, is frequently viewed as an indication of body dissatisfaction.

The most remarkable finding in body-dissatisfaction research is that currently most women and girls report dissatisfaction with their appearance, believe that they weigh too much, and are trying to lose weight. This has been shown repeatedly in survey studies of high school and college students, magazine polls, and communities samples of adults (J. C. Rosen & Gross, 1987; Striegel-Moore, Silberstein, & Rodin, 1986). However, measures of simple body dissatisfaction are poor in discriminating eating-disordered subjects from the larger population of women who are attempting to alter their weight (Wilson & Smith, 1989). If so many women share these concerns, body dissatisfaction simply cannot be a disorder. It may be more accurate to think of these attitudes as being normal given the current culture.

When is weight preoccupation a disorder? Some proposed that body dissatisfaction is significant or pathological only in conjunction with deficits in other areas including belief in personal effectiveness (Johnson & Conners, 1987). This type of two-component model (i.e., eating disorder equals weight preoccupation plus psychopathology) is not helpful in distinguishing between normal and disordered body image. At any rate, this model is based on research with the Body Dissatisfaction Scale of the Eating Disorders Inventory (EDI), which is a superficial measure and does not tap into the more remarkable cognitive features of a body-image disorder.

In body-image disorder, whether talking about body dysmorphic disorder or eating disorder, the person interprets perceived physical defects to mean that she is not only imperfect in appearance or aesthetically unappealing but that she is deficient in other ways. The patient attributes self-worth to her appearance and predicts outcomes in relationships as being dependent on her appearance. Women with eating disorders feel that other people evaluate them mainly on their appearance and that other personal attributes do not mean as much (Fairburn & Garner, 1988). Being thin is the only important aspect of their self-image; if they are not exceedingly thin, it proves they are weak, lazy, unlovable, and incompetent. Other examples of thoughts are as follows: "I gained two pounds this year, so people will think I'm gross." "Because I'm big, people don't like me." "People look at me when I walk across campus—they think I'm gross." "Because I'm big, I'm not feminine." "If I was thinner, I would be more successful." "I am a bad person (weak, selfish, greedy, irresponsible, inadequate, stupid, dull, etc.), but if I lose weight I will be different." "My legs have fat dimples in them (or some other minor imperfection), therefore, men won't like me." Similar dysfunctional assumptions about appearance have been described in cases of body dysmorphic disorder (Bloch & Glue, 1988; Hay, 1970; McKenna, 1984; Munro & Chmara, 1982; Thomas, 1984).

An endless list of maladaptive, erroneous, illogical, distorted beliefs could be made, but this is not the point. The point is that eating-disordered patients process information related to self-worth, especially in times of threat, according to stable appearance-related beliefs (Vitousek & Hollon, 1990). These are the types of overvalued ideas or dysfunctional assumptions that Cooper and Fairburn (1987) argued distinguish women with eating disorders. Indeed, their Eating Disorders Examination (Cooper & Fairburn, 1987), designed in part to measure overvalued ideas, seems to be superior in discriminating truly eating-disordered or body-image disordered women from other weight-preoccupied women (J. C. Rosen, Vara, Wendt, & Leitenberg, 1990; Wilson & Smith, 1989).

Disorder of Behavior

Body-image disorder is accompanied by a life-style that revolves around the individual's physical self-consciousness (J. C. Rosen et al., 1991). Like the phobic patient, the eating-disordered patient may be worried that she will suffer some extreme humiliation in public settings if others were to notice and react to her appearance. To some extent, the patient can completely avoid social situations in which she thinks her body might be scrutinized. For example, she does not go out with friends if it involves eating, talking about weight, or being observed by the opposite sex. The patient avoids physical intimacy or controls it by not letting a mate see or touch certain body parts.

Like the hypochondriac patient whose worries are primarily about threats posed by the body itself, the eating-disordered patient does not always have the option of avoiding anxiety-provoking stimuli, so she resorts instead to behaviors that are designed to minimize body imperfections. For example, she avoids wearing revealing and tight-fitting clothes; rather, she tries to disguise or cover up her appearance by wearing baggy, dark, nonrevealing clothes.

Although this problem among eating-disordered patients has not received much attention, social avoidance has always been regarded as a feature of body dysmorphic disorder. Body dysmorphic disorder patients avoid social or occupational situations because they believe exposure of their physical defect would result in negative reactions by others (American Psychiatric Association, 1987; Giles, 1988; Marks & Mishan, 1988). If they do not avoid these situations altogether, they often go to lengths to disguise their appearance, such as by wearing clothes that mask the problem or maintaining their posture in such a way as to hide or distract one from the defect (Pruzinsky & Edgerton, 1990).

Besides trying to disguise or hide the body, the eating-disordered patient frequently engages in behavior to reassure herself that her appearance has not taken a turn for the worse. The best examples are frequent weigh-ins, inspection in the mirror, and trying on certain clothes to be sure they still fit (J. C. Rosen et al., 1991). This sort of body-checking behavior is also common among body dysmorphic subjects (Marks & Mishan, 1988; Vitiello & de Leon, 1990). A small portion of patients seek reassurance from other people by asking, for example, "Does it look like I gained weight?", "Do my thighs really look too big?", "Is my cellulite noticeable?" Hypochondriacal patients habitually seek reassurance; they want to draw the attention of other people to their physical state in the hopes of detecting and eliminating the problem. They want to say they are abnormal. In contrast, eating-disordered and body dysmorphic disorder patients are less likely to engage in reassurance seeking. They wish to appear normal, and their fear is that other people will notice they are not (Hay, 1970).

BODY-IMAGE DISORDER
IN THE DEVELOPMENT AND MAINTENANCE
OF EATING DISORDERS

The essential features of eating disorders are not completely independent but are linked together and mutually sustaining. The best example is that extreme weight control by dieting or vomiting contributes to the development and maintenance of binge eating in bulimia nervosa (Polivy & Herman, 1985; J. C. Rosen & Leitenberg, 1988). Does body-image disorder also play a role in the development of the other characteristics of eating disorders? Fairburn and Garner (1986, 1988) asserted that it does and that the extreme eating abnormalities and weight control in these disorders are secondary to overconcern with weight and shape. This seems perfectly sensible. Except for those individuals needing to lose weight purely for matters of physical health, why would a young woman begin dieting unless she first was displeased with her appearance? Why would she suffer the consequences of fasting or purging unless she was desperate to lose weight?

Among young women in general, body dissatisfaction was associated with various problematic eating attitudes and habits including a perceived lack of control over food, dietary restraint, binge eating, and purging (Kiemle, Slade, & Dewey, 1987; Striegel-Moore, McAvay, & Rodin, 1986; Wiedel & Dodd, 1983; Wolf & Crowther, 1983; Zakin, 1989). Moreover, body dissatisfaction was a better predictor of bulimic eating attitudes and behaviors in teenage girls than self-esteem, depression, and social anxiety combined, which contributed very little unique variance after body dissatisfaction (Brown, Cash, & Lewis, 1989; Gross & Rosen, 1988). Among women with bulimia nervosa, the severity of eating and dieting symptoms was correlated with body dissatisfaction (Post & Crowther, 1987; Ruderman & Grace, 1988).

In a prospective study, the EDI was administered to ballet students who were evaluated 2 years later for eating disorders. Among the eight scales, only Body Dissatisfaction and Drive for Thinness significantly predicted individuals with eating-disorder symptoms (Garner, Garfinkel, Rockert, & Olmsted, 1987).

Another relevant study used measures of body dissatisfaction, perceived attractiveness, perfectionism, ineffectiveness, stress, competitiveness, and body weight as independent variables to predict increased binge eating, dieting, and purging among female college students from the beginning to the end of their freshman year (Striegel-Moore, Silberstein, Frensch, & Rodin, 1989). The best predictors were changed scores in the pathological direction, from Time 1 to Time 2, on measures of body dissatisfaction and perceived attractiveness. Changes in weight and the other psychological variables added little to the prediction of eating pathology and dieting beyond the measures of body image.

Patton (1988) engaged in a prospective study of eating disorders in high school girls. At Time 1, the best predictor of eating-disorder symptoms was psychopathology. Although he did not include a body-image measure, over a 1-year period increased weight was the best predictor of eating-disorder symptoms at Time 2.

In a prospective longitudinal study of adolescent girls aged 12 to 15 years, the severity of eating disorders over a 2-year period was predicted (Attie & Brooks-Gunn, 1989). Controlling for the level of eating-disorder symptoms at Time 1, symptoms at Time 2 were best predicted by body image at Time 1, albeit modestly. Demographic variables, measures of puberty and weight change, and multiple measures of psychopathology and family relationships did not account for any additional unique variance in the prediction of eating-disorder symptoms. It also is interesting to note the concurrent predictors of eating-disorder symptoms. At both points in time, psychopathology was associated with eating-disorder symptoms. At Time 1, greater physical maturation was positively associated with eating-disorder symptoms. At Time 2, when the subjects had passed puberty, this variable was not predictive. At both points in time, concurrently, body image accounted for more variance in eating-disorder symptoms than any other predictor variable.

In sum, it appears that body-image disorder symptoms contribute to increased eating-disorder symptoms over both short and long periods of time, whereas the contribution of psychopathology and other risk factors is more immediate.

Although the recent appearance of prospective studies suggests that body image plays a causal role in the exacerbation of other eating-disorder pathology, it should be noted that these studies have tackled the problem using a unidirectional model. Because the two types of pathologies are highly interrelated, any prospective study is likely to find that one predicts the other regardless of direction. To date, the prospective relation of eating-disorder symptoms of dieting, binge eating, purging, and so on to subsequent changes in body image has not been examined. (In Thompson's book on body image (1990), he referred to a prospective study in which body-image disturbance was more predictive of eating-disorder symptoms over time than vice versa. However, at present, this study is unpublished; Richards, Thompson, & Coovert, 1990.) It certainly seems possible that women with eating disorders begin to devalue their appearance more severely as they continue to experience failure in controlling their weight. Indeed, prospectively, dieting predicts increases in stress (J. C. Rosen, Tacy, & Howell, 1990). Repeated cycles of weight-loss attempts may actually lead to weight gain over time (Brownell, Steen, & Wilmore, 1987). This paradoxical effect of dieting certainly could alter body image. Thus, the relation between body image and other eating-disorder pathology may be one of reciprocal causation.

DEVELOPMENT OF BODY-IMAGE DISORDER

Body-image disorder in women with eating disorders is attributable to cultural standards for beauty, disturbances in the development of self-identity and self-esteem, and social feedback about physical appearance.

Cultural Standard of Beauty

Certainly a background factor for the development of body-image concerns in women with eating disorders is the prevailing ideal of thinness as a marker of beauty in women. Were it not for this, there would be no epidemic of eating disorders. In non-Western cultures in which plumpness is valued or at least not devalued (e.g., where it is associated with wealth, sexuality, fertility, womanhood, and so on), eating disorders are rare (Nasser, 1988). Also among black women in the United States, who do not seem as concerned about losing weight, the rate of bulimia nervosa is lower (Gross & Rosen, 1988). This finding is not attributable to socioeconomic class differences.

It is not difficult to see how most women today are dissatisfied with their weight given that most are, in fact, overweight relative to the ultraslim ideal. This by itself cannot explain the development of body-image disorder because most women are exposed to the cultural pressure to be thin, yet only a small minority develop true pathology.

Self-Identity, Effectiveness, Self-Esteem

Patients with body-image disorder develop dysfunctional assumptions about issues of physical appearance and their implications for the self that influence their thoughts, emotions, and behaviors. These dysfunctional assumptions are formed as part of early experience usually during adolescence when self-identity and physical development are undergoing rapid transformation.

Young girls with eating disorders are believed to come from families with domineering, intrusive, and overprotective parents who make it difficult for the developing adolescent to become autonomous of parental control and to formulate her own sense of identity (Bruch, 1973). The child's struggle with autonomy is even more difficult during puberty because her body begins to approximate her mother's body at a time that she is seeking differentiation from an overcontrolling parent (Palazzoli, 1974). As a result, the rapid physical development causes the child to feel less rather than more in command of her own life.

According to Bruch (1962, 1973), pursuit of thinness is an adaptive effort for the adolescent to take charge of herself in the midst of this conflict. Although other elements are out of control, weight may be the one issue that remains within self-control. Striving for physical beauty compensates for the lack of an internal point of reference and counters an inner emptiness (Krueger, 1988; Strober, 1991). Losing weight may enhance perceptions of self-effectiveness, which helps the adolescent to separate from parents and to reduce the threat of other developmental stressors (Cattanach & Rodin, 1988; Striegel-Moore, Silberstein, & Rodin, 1986). The emaciation of anorexia nervosa is a regressive defense mechanism that allows the child to preserve the pubertal look, to avoid growing up, and to remain in childhood (Crisp, 1980; Strober, 1991). In any case, the body becomes the focus of attention in the afflicted adolescent as an outward manifestation of a struggle with change in self-image.

Women with eating disorders have extremely low self-esteem, feelings of being a bad person, and dread of rejection or abandonment (Johnson & Conners, 1987). Given the importance placed on appearance in our weight-conscious society, it is not difficult to see how a young woman (with or without an eating disorder) might take the view that her self-worth is dependent on having a perfect body and that if only she were able to lose some weight or look more perfect on the outside, then no one would know just how bad a person she is on the inside. Thus, striving for perfection in appearance may function as a defense or compensation against guilt, low self-esteem, feelings of worthlessness, and defectiveness.

Similar formulations have been proposed for body dysmorphic disorder and hypochondriasis (Barsky & Klerman, 1983; Hay, 1970). The particular bodily part or function that is viewed as defective is meaningfully related to some conflict in the development of self. Overconcern about facial features or sexual organs in the body dysmorphic patient have been interpreted as manifestations of the patient's unresolved autonomy from parents, fears of sexuality, or lack of inner standard for effectiveness (Bloch & Glue, 1988; Hay, 1970). The somatic preoccupation also functions as a defense mechanism because it is more tolerable for patients who lack feelings of effectiveness to believe something is wrong with their body rather than their self.

Although these explanations are widely held by clinicians and researchers, there is little empirical confirmation for the link between self-esteem, self-identity, and body image. The basic idea that negative body image is associated with more negative self-esteem and feelings of ineffectiveness, however, is upheld in studies of simple correlation between the two types of measures (Cash, Winstead, & Janda, 1986; G. M. Rosen & Ross, 1968). At the least, it seems reasonable to conclude that individuals with negative self-esteem are more likely to devalue their appearance just as they do other aspects of their self-image and capabilities. This deficiency in self-image is a necessary but not sufficient ingredient for the formation and maintenance of dysfunctional assumptions about appearance.

Physical Development and Social Feedback about Appearance

The explanations of body-image disorder summarized in the preceding section essentially view the disorder as a consequence of a defect in some other aspect of psychological self-image without regard to the individual's objective physical appearance. According to an important distinction proposed by Cash (1990), this is a thoroughly "inside" view of body image. Viewed from the "outside," body image refers to the patient's outward appearance and attractiveness that she projects to other people. In this section, I propose that physical individuality, or body image from the "outside," may play an important role in the development of body-image disorder. In brief, normal physical changes of puberty such as the development of secondary sexual characteristics can provoke initial concerns about physical appearance. Deviation from the normal course of physical development and imperfections or perfections in appearance elicit feedback from other people. Social feedback ultimately influences the "inside" aspect of body image as well as other psychological variables, such as self-esteem, that are implicated in eating and body-image disorder.

The work of Lerner (Lerner & Jovanovic, 1990) showed that children develop preferences for physical appearance at a very early age and that they make more negative attributions about the psychosocial worth of people with endomorphic physiques. A vast literature on individual differences in appearance shows that people who are rated as more physically attractive are more popular and are rated as more desirable, competent, well-adjusted, and successful in work and school (Dion, Bersheid, & Walster, 1972; Hatfield & Sprecher, 1986). More attractive people also elicit more sex-stereotypic attributions from outside observers and more attentiveness and social reinforcement (Cash, 1990). Thus, physical beauty makes a behavioral difference. By bringing different physical characteristics to a situation, a child or adolescent affects how others react and provide feedback to them. This in turn affects the individual's psychological development (Cash, 1990; Lerner & Jovanovic, 1990).

The question we should ask, then, is: Do eating and body-image disorder patients differ from others in physical appearance? This may seem absurd because, after all, people of all shapes and sizes are afflicted with these disorders. Physical attractiveness has been studied in relation to numerous psychosocial variables; however, no such study has been performed in relation to eating disorder.

The only available data that are relevant to this issue concern the relation between puberty, weight, and eating disorders. In the case of bulimia nervosa, an unusually high proportion of patients had been overweight before the onset of their disorder (Fairburn & Cooper, 1982; Garfinkel, 1981; Striegel-Moore, Silberstein, & Moore, 1986). Two studies of adolescents showed that higher weight or greater weight gain is associated with more eating-disorder symptomatology (Attie & Brooks-Gunn, 1989; Patton, 1988). Also of interest here is that early physical maturation among pubescent girls is associated with less positive body image (Thompson, 1990). Of course, concerns about appearance in eating-disordered patients can be traced to innumerable other physical characteristics that set them apart from some idealized physique. These can include being tall or short, pear shaped, big boned, or large breasted. In our body-conscious society, these real physical differences can provoke social attention. Social feedback does not necessarily have to be critical because the future eating-disordered patient with low self-esteem may be predisposed to interpret any undue attention to her appearance as negative. Moreover, this social interest in one's appearance (e.g., in the adolescent who matures early sexually) may come at a time when she is not equipped socially to handle the physical image she presents.

Critical Incidents

Expanding on the theme of social feedback, there often are critical incidents that trigger or solidify the patient's dysfunctional assumptions about her appearance. These are early incidents of clearly negative feedback that have a lasting impact on the patient's body image. Although the feedback may not be true or no longer is relevant later in life, the low self-esteem patient selectively recalls and believes this information.

In clinical interviews, most eating-disordered patients can recall such specific incidents that ultimately led them to conclude that they were physically defective in some way. Although there is little empirical confirmation of these clinical observations, some relevant data are beginning to emerge. According to a popular woman's magazine survey, those with negative body image were more likely to report having had mothers who were critical of their appearance (Wooley & Kearney-Cooke, 1986). Another large-scale survey (Cash et al., 1986) similarly found a link between reported childhood teasing about appearance and negative body-image attitudes and eating disturbance in adolescence (Brown et al., 1989). Negative body self-esteem and size overestimation in teenage girls were associated with a higher frequency of being teased about their weight or size by other people (Fabian & Thompson, 1989). Finally, in a prospective study, higher weight predicted greater body-image disturbance; a history of being teased for weight emerged as a significant mediating variable (Richards, Thompson, & Coovert, 1990).

In case histories of body dysmorphic disorder, most patients reported that the preoccupation with their appearance "defect" began or worsened as a result of remarks from other people about their appearance. In many instances, patients traced the onset of disorder to an isolated comment that obviously had an enduring impact (Bloch & Glue, 1988; de Leon, Bott, & Simpson, 1989; Giles, 1988; Hay, 1970). This history of being the recipient of attention or being teased for appearance is partly responsible for the body dysmorphic's social avoidance. In fact, one author conceptualized the problem of his body dysmorphic patient as being a social phobia. The feared stimulus was being in public situations in which others might scrutinize or, worse yet, comment on her appearance (Giles, 1988).

Critical incidents are not limited to being teased about appearance. In the case of anorexia nervosa, the drive toward emaciation in young patients at a time when they otherwise would be developing physically clearly raises the possibility of an underlying fear of emerging sexuality. Although women with bulimia nervosa are generally of normal weight and physically mature, they too express strong feelings of disgust toward their bodies and feel that their bodies are out of control. It often seems as if the sexual connotation of body-image disorder in eating-disordered patients was indicative of physical or sexual trauma. Although its rate does not appear to be higher among eating-disordered patients than for other clinical populations (Finn, Hartman, Leon, & Lawson, 1986), physical or sexual trauma certainly could be another type of critical incident in the formation of bodily concerns.

MECHANISMS THAT MAINTAIN PREOCCUPATION WITH APPEARANCE DEFECTS

Several mechanisms operate to maintain the patient's preoccupation with appearance defects.

Selective Attention

Once developed, dysfunctional assumptions lead patients to selectively attend to information that is consistent with their having a physical defect and to selectively ignore or discount evidence that indicates normal appearance. For example, a patient recalls teasing remarks but overlooks compliments about her appearance. She attends closely to variations in appearance such as the rolling of her stomach over the waistline of pants when she is sitting; however, she does not notice that this is normal for others as well.

The patient finds this confirming information in her appearance, bodily sensations, and social feedback about appearance, but she also finds it in experiences related to her nonphysical self-image. That is, she has concerns about her appearance in mind when processing information, especially threatening information, about her self-worth as a person. For example, the patient relates a breakup with her boyfriend to her appearance even if she has no evidence to support this interpretation. Thus, after the original critical incidents, dysfunctional assumptions about appearance and self-worth tend to produce a bias in the patient's interpretation of new information relevant and seemingly irrelevant to appearance such that the dysfunctional assumptions are confirmed. Misinterpretations of physical appearance (i.e., imagined defects or abnormalities) are based on what the patient regards as convincing evidence. Such evidence stems from particularly idiosyncratic beliefs about health and appearance (e.g., the patient believes that a woman who weighs 160 pounds is automatically overweight even if she is 5 feet 10 inches tall). These cognitive processes result in automatic negative thoughts in situations that threaten her physical self-image, subsequently lower self-esteem, and encourage feelings of depression, anxiety, guilt, and shame.

Avoidance Behavior

Anxiety becomes conditioned to various appearance-related stimuli, including the sight or feel of certain bodily characteristics and social situations in which she believes that other people will notice appearance defects. Through avoidance behavior, the patient seeks to control the anxiety associated with her appearance; for example, she avoids revealing clothes, she limits contact with other people, or she does not allow other people or even herself to look at or touch certain body parts. These behaviors terminate exposure to the feared stimuli, thereby preventing habituation from occurring. The patient is prevented from learning that the expected ridicule or rejection from other people does not actually happen. Moreover, by not feeling free to experiment with dress, by inhibiting nonverbal behavior or by suppressing spontaneity in physical activity, the patient may actually reduce her physical attractiveness. Thus, the patient is prevented from receiving some of the positive feedback about her appearance that she otherwise might were it not for these inhibitions. Weight loss and dieting are avoidance behaviors that are reinforced through elimination or anticipated elimination of the defect and other positive consequences such as feelings of self control. Although designed to minimize anxiety states, avoidance can lead to social withdrawal, disruption of relationships, and social anxiety.

Checking Behavior and Reassurance Seeking

Checking behavior and reassurance seeking keep the patients' attention focused on aspects of appearance that elicit the thoughts in the first instance. Behaviors such as looking in mirror, comparing oneself against pictures in magazines, or frequent weigh-ins may provide short-term relief, but in the long run they maintain bodily preoccupation. Patients who seek reassurance from others might enjoy immediate relief. However, ultimately, reassurance is not believed and by having trained other people to show concern and interest in the patients' appearance, their preoccupation is only intensified.

CONCLUSION

Abnormal concerns about physical appearance are extremely distressing and interfere with social functioning. So central are they to other features of eating disorders that it may be more appropriate to think of anorexia and bulimia nervosa as body-image disorders. Although most eating-disordered patients succeed in gaining weight or in eliminating binge eating and vomiting, too much attention in treatment has been focused on achieving these goals relative to altering body image. Patients can improve on these dimensions for many reasons other than coming to terms with their body-image disorder. There are over 100 published reports of psychological or pharmacological treatments for anorexia and bulimia nervosa. In most treatment programs, the patients did not receive any intervention specifically directed at their body image nor was change in body image included as an outcome measure. In approximately one quarter, there was some effort to help patients directly with their body image; however, body image was not measured at the end of treatment. Only about 15% of treatment programs targeted and measured body image in their patients. Many of these programs were not successful in eliminating body-image disturbances (J. C. Rosen, 1990). Even with the most effective treatment for eating disorders, a significant minority of patients do not recover completely. One answer to this problem is a more complete understanding of body-image disorder and its treatment.

REFERENCES

American Psychiatric Association. (1987). *Diagnostic and statistical manual of mental disorders* (3rd ed., rev.). Washington, DC: Author.

Attie, I., & Brooks-Gunn, J. (1989). Development of eating problems in adolescent girls: A longitudinal study. *Developmental Psychology, 25,* 70–79.

Barsky, A. J., & Klerman, G. L. (1983). Overview: Hypochondriasis, bodily complaints, and somatic styles. *American Journal of Psychiatry, 140,* 273–283.

Bloch, S., & Glue, P. (1988). Psychotherapy and dysmorphophobia: A case report. *British Journal of Psychiatry, 152,* 271–274.

Bowden, P. K., Touyz, S. W., Rodriguez, P. J., Hensley, R., & Beumont, P. J. V. (1989). Distorting patient or distorting instrument? Body shape disturbance in patients with anorexia nervosa and bulimia. *British Journal of Psychiatry, 155,* 196–201.

Brown, T. A., Cash, T. F., & Lewis, R. J. (1989). Body-image disturbances in adolescent female binge-purgers: A brief report of the results of a national survey in the U.S.A. *Journal of Child Psychology and Psychiatry, 30,* 605–613.

Brownell, K. D., Steen, S. N., & Wilmore, J. H. (1987). Weight regulation practice in athletes: Analysis of metabolic and health effects. *Medicine and Science in Sports, 19,* 546–556.

Bruch, H. (1962). Perceptual and conceptual disturbances in anorexia nervosa. *Psychosomatic Medicine, 24,* 187–194.

Bruch, H. (1973). *Eating disorders: Obesity, anorexia nervosa, and the person within.* New York: Basic Books.

Cash, T. F. (1990). The psychology of physical appearance: Aesthetics, attributes, and images. In T. F. Cash & T. Pruzinsky (Eds.), *Body images: Development, deviance, and change* (pp. 51–79). New York: Guilford Press.

Cash, T. F., & Brown, T. A. (1987). Body image in anorexia nervosa and bulimia nervosa: A review of the literature. *Behavior Modification, 11,* 487-521.

Cash, T. F., Winstead, B. A., & Janda, L. H. (1986, April). Body image survey report: The great American shape-up. *Psychology Today,* pp. 30-37.

Cattanach, L., & Rodin, J. (1988). Psychosocial components of the stress process in bulimia. *International Journal of Eating Disorders, 7,* 75-88.

Cooper, P. J., & Taylor, M. J. (1987). Body image disturbance in bulimia nervosa. *British Journal of Psychiatry* (Suppl. 2), 34-38.

Cooper, Z., & Fairburn, C. G. (1987). The Eating Disorder Examination: A semi-structured interview for the assessment of the specific psychopathology of eating disorders. *International Journal of Eating Disorders, 6,* 1-8.

Crisp, A. H. (1980). *Anorexia nervosa: Let me be.* London: Academic Press.

Crisp, A. H. (1988). Some possible approaches to prevention of eating and body weight/shape disorders, with particular reference to anorexia nervosa. *International Journal of Eating Disorders, 7,* 1-17.

de Leon, J., Bott, A., & Simpson, G. M. (1989). Dysmorphophobia: Body dysmorphic disorder or delusional disorder, somatic subtype? *Comprehensive Psychiatry, 30,* 457-472.

Dion, K., Berscheid, E., & Walster, E. (1972). What is beautiful is good. *Journal of Personality and Social Psychology, 24,* 285-290.

Fabian, L. J., & Thompson, J. K. (1989). Body image and eating disturbance in young females. *International Journal of Eating Disorders, 8,* 63-74.

Fairburn, C. G., & Cooper, P. J. (1982). Self-induced vomiting and bulimia nervosa: An undetected problem. *British Medical Journal, 284,* 1153-1155.

Fairburn, C. G., & Garner, D. M. (1986). The diagnosis of bulimia nervosa. *International Journal of Eating Disorders, 5,* 403-419.

Fairburn, C. G., & Garner, D. M. (1988). Diagnostic criteria for anorexia nervosa and bulimia nervosa: The importance of attitudes to shape and weight. In D. M. Garner & P. E. Garfinkel (Eds.), *Diagnostic issues in anorexia nervosa and bulimia nervosa* (pp. 36-55). New York: Brunner/Mazel.

Feurstein, M., Labbe, E. E., & Kuczmierczyk, A. R. (1986). *Health psychology: A psychobiological perspective.* New York: Plenum Press.

Finn, S. E., Hartman, M., Leon, G. R., & Lawson, L. (1986). Eating disorders and sexual abuse: Lack of confirmation for a clinical hypothesis. *International Journal of Eating Disorders, 5,* 1051-1060.

Fitts, S. N., Gibson, P., Redding, C. A., & Deiter, P. J. (1989). Body dysmorphic disorder: Implications for its validity as a DSM-III-R clinical syndrome. *Psychological Reports, 64,* 655-658.

Freeman, R. J., Thomas, C. D., Solyom, L., & Miles, J. E. (1983). Body image disturbance in anorexia nervosa: A reexamination and a new technique. In P. L. Darby, P. E. Garfinkel, D. M. Garner, & D. V. Coscona (Eds.), *Anorexia nervosa: Recent developments in research* (pp. 117–127). New York: Alan R. Liss.

Garfinkel, P. E. (1981). Some recent observations on the pathogenesis of anorexia nervosa. *Canadian Journal of Psychiatry, 26,* 218–223.

Garner, D. M., & Garfinkel, P. E. (1981–1982). Body image in anorexia nervosa: Measurement, theory, and clinical implications. *International Journal of Psychiatry in Medicine, 11,* 263–284.

Garner, D. M., Garfinkel, P. E., Rockert, W., & Olmsted, M. P. (1987). A prospective study of eating disturbances in the ballet. *Psychotherapy and Psychosomatics, 48,* 170–175.

Giles, T. R. (1988). Distortion of body image as an effect of conditioned fear. *Journal of Behaviour Therapy and Experimental Psychiatry, 19,* 143–146.

Gross, J., & Rosen, J. C. (1988). Bulimia in adolescents: Prevalence and psychosocial correlates. *International Journal of Eating Disorders, 7,* 51–61.

Hatfield, E., & Sprecher, S. (1986). *Mirror, mirror . . . The importance of looks in everyday life.* Albany, NY: SUNY Press.

Hay, G. G. (1970). Dysmorphophobia. *British Journal of Psychiatry, 116,* 399–406.

Hsu, L. K. G. (1982). Is there a disturbance in body image in anorexia nervosa? *Journal of Nervous and Mental Disease, 82,* 305–306.

Johnson, C., & Conners, M. E. (1987). *The etiology and treatment of bulimia nervosa: A biopsychosocial perspective.* New York: Basic Books.

Kiemle, G., Slade, P. D., & Dewey, M. E. (1987). Factors associated with abnormal eating attitudes and behaviors: Screening individuals at risk of developing an eating disorder. *International Journal of Eating Disorders, 6,* 713–724.

Krueger, D. (1988). Body self, psychological self, and bulimia: Developmental and clinical consideration. In H. Schwartz (Ed.), *Bulimia: Psychoanalytic treatment and theory* (pp. 55–72). New York: International Universities Press.

Lerner, R. M., & Jovanovic, J. (1990). The role of body image in psychosocial development across the life span: A developmental contextual perspective. In T. F. Cash & T. Pruzinsky (Eds.), *Body images: Development, deviance, and change* (pp. 110–127). New York: Guilford Press.

Marks, I., & Mishan, J. (1988). Dysmorphophobic avoidance with disturbed bodily perception: A pilot study of exposure therapy. *British Journal of Psychiatry, 152,* 674–678.

McKenna, P. J. (1984). Disorders with overvalued ideas. *British Journal of Psychiatry, 145,* 579–585.

Munro, A., & Chmara, J. (1982). Monosymptomatic hypochondriacal psychosis: A diagnostic checklist based on 50 cases of the disorder. *Canadian Journal of Psychiatry, 27*, 374-376.

Nasser, M. (1988). Culture and weight consciousness. *Journal of Psychosomatic Research, 32*, 573-577.

Palazzoli, M. S. (1974). *Self-starvation.* London: Chaucer.

Patton, G. C. (1988). The spectrum of eating disorder in adolescence. *Journal of Psychosomatic Research, 32*, 579-584.

Polivy, J., & Herman, C. P. (1985). Dieting and binge eating. *American Psychologist, 40*, 193-201.

Post, G., & Crowther, J. H. (1987). Restricter-purger differences in bulimic adolescent females. *International Journal of Eating Disorders, 6*, 757-761.

Pruzinsky, T., & Edgerton, M. T. (1990). Body-image change in cosmetic plastic surgery. In T. F. Cash & T. Pruzinsky (Eds.), *Body images: Development, deviance, and change* (pp. 217-236). New York: Guilford Press.

Richards, K. J., Thompson, J. K., & Coovert, M. (1990). *Development of body image and eating disturbance.* Unpublished manuscript, University of South Florida.

Riding, J., & Munro, A. (1975). Pimozide in the treatment of monosymptomatic hypochondriacal psychosis. *Acta Psychiatra Scandinavica, 52*, 23-30.

Robb, J., & Thompson, J. K. (1990). *Perceived caloric content, body image, and mood.* Unpublished manuscript, University of South Florida.

Rosen, G. M., & Ross, A. O. (1968). Relationship of body image to self-concept. *Journal of Consulting and Clinical Psychology, 32*, 100.

Rosen, J. C. (1990). Body image disturbances in eating disorders. In T. F. Cash & T. Pruzinsky (Eds.), *Body images: Development, deviance and change* (pp. 190-216). New York: Guilford Press.

Rosen, J. C., & Gross, J. (1987). Prevalence of weight reducing and weight gaining in adolescent girls and boys. *Health Psychology, 6*, 131-147.

Rosen, J. C., & Leitenberg, H. (1985). Exposure plus response prevention treatment of bulimia. In D. M. Garner & P. E. Garfinkel (Eds.), *Handbook of psychotherapy for anorexia nervosa and bulimia* (pp. 193-209). New York: Guilford Press.

Rosen, J. C., & Leitenberg, H. (1988). Eating behavior in bulimia nervosa. In B. T. Walsh (Ed.), *Eating behavior in eating disorders* (pp. 161-174). Washington, DC: American Psychiatric Press.

Rosen, J. C., & Srebnik, D. (1990). Assessment of eating disorders. In P. McReynolds, J. C. Rosen, & G. J. Chelune (Eds.), *Advances in psychological assessment* Vol. 7 (pp. 229-260). New York: Plenum Press.

Rosen, J. C., Srebnik, D., Saltzberg, E., & Wendt, S. (1991). Development of a Body Image Avoidance Questionnaire. *Psychological Assessment: A Journal of Consulting and Clinical Psychology, 3*, 32-37.

Rosen, J. C., Tacy, B., & Howell, D. (1990). Life stress, psychological symptoms and weight reducing behavior in adolescent girls: A prospective analysis. *International Journal of Eating Disorders, 9,* 17-26.

Rosen, J. C., Vara, L., Wendt, S., & Leitenberg, H. (1990). Validity studies of the Eating Disorder Examination. *International Journal of Eating Disorders, 9,* 519-528.

Ruderman, A. J., & Grace, P. S. (1988). Bulimics and restrained eaters: A personality comparison. *Addictive Behaviors, 13,* 359-367.

Striegel-Moore, R. H., McAvay, G., & Rodin, J. (1986). Psychological and behavioral correlates of feeling fat in women. *International Journal of Eating Disorders, 5,* 935-947.

Striegel-Moore, R. H., Silberstein, L. R., Frensch, P., & Rodin, J. (1989). A prospective study of disordered eating among college students. *International Journal of Eating Disorders, 8,* 499-509.

Striegel-Moore, R. H., Silberstein, L. R., & Rodin, J. (1986). Toward an understanding of risk factors for bulimia. *American Psychologist, 41,* 246-263.

Strober, M. (1991). Disorders of the self in anorexia nervosa: An organismic developmental paradigm. In C. Johnson (Ed.), *Psychodynamic treatment for eating disorders* (pp. 354-373). New York: Guilford Press.

Sturmey, P., & Slade, P. D. (1986). Anorexia nervosa and dysmorphophobia. *British Journal of Psychiatry, 149,* 780-782.

Taylor, M. J., & Cooper, P. J. (1989). *Body size perception and depressed mood: A mood induction study.* Unpublished manuscript, Department of Experimental Psychology, Cambridge University, England.

Thomas, C. S. (1984). Dysmorphophobia: A question of definition. *British Journal of Psychiatry, 144,* 513-516.

Thomas, C. S. (1987). Anorexia nervosa and dysmorphophobia. *British Journal of Psychiatry, 150,* 406.

Thompson, J. K. (1990). *Body image disturbance: Assessment and treatment.* New York: Pergamon Press.

Vitiello, B., & de Leon, J. (1990). Dysmorphophobia misdiagnosed as obsessive-compulsive disorder. *Psychosomatics, 31,* 220-221.

Vitousek, K. B., & Hollon, S. D. (1990). The investigation of schematic content and processing in eating disorders. *Cognitive Therapy and Research, 14,* 191-214.

Wiedel, T. C., & Dodd, J. M. (1983). The relationship between dietary restraint, personality measures and weight in college students. *Journal of Obesity and Weight Regulation, 2,* 88-96.

Wilson, G. T., & Smith, D. (1989). Assessment of bulimia nervosa: An evaluation of the Eating Disorders Examination. *International Journal of Eating Disorders, 8,* 173-179.

Wolf, E. M., & Crowther, J. H. (1983). Personality and eating habit variables

as predictors of severity of binge eating and weight. *Addictive Behaviors,*
8, 335–344.

Wooley, S. C., & Kearney-Cooke, A. (1986). Intensive treatment of bulimia
and body-image disturbance. In K. D. Brownell & J. P. Foreyt (Eds.),
Handbook of eating disorders: Physiology, psychology, and treatment of
obesity, anorexia, and bulimia (pp. 476–502). New York: Basic Books.

Zakin, D. F. (1989). Eating disturbance, emotional separation, and body image. *International Journal of Eating Disorders, 8,* 411–416.

10

PERSONALITY CHARACTERISTICS AS A RISK FACTOR IN THE DEVELOPMENT OF EATING DISORDERS

Craig Johnson
Laureate Psychiatric Clinic and Hospital and Northwestern University Medical School

Stephen Wonderlich
University of North Dakota School of Medicine

In our 1987 book (Johnson & Connors, 1987), Connors and I argued that eating disorders are best understood within a biopsychosocial context (Figure 1). Over the last several years, research has continued to clarify how each of these factors might contribute to the onset of anorexia nervosa and bulimia nervosa. The risk factor of particular interest in this chapter is the psychological characteristics of patients with eating disorders.

In previous work (Johnson & Connors, 1987), we reviewed observations that have been made regarding the personality characteristics of eating-disordered patients. These characteristics include low self-esteem, self-regulatory deficits, body-image disturbance, separation and individuation fears, mood disorder, cognitive distortions, boundary disturbance, and a tendency to be perfectionistic, compliant, and distrustful. Since the completion of the 1987 book, increasing attention has been paid to using the descriptive criteria included in *Diagnostic and Statistical Manual of Mental Disorders* (third edition, revised; *[DSM-III-R]* American Psychiatric Association, 1987) to diagnose personality disorders. The specific aim of this chapter is to review what preliminary studies have revealed regarding the type of Axis II personality disorders found among eating-disordered patients. After the review of existing studies, we comment on the importance of personality as a risk factor for the development of an eating disorder.

COMORBIDITY OF EATING DISORDERS AND AXIS II DIAGNOSIS

With refinements in the measurement of personality disturbance, there has been an increase in the number of studies examining the comorbidity of eating disor-

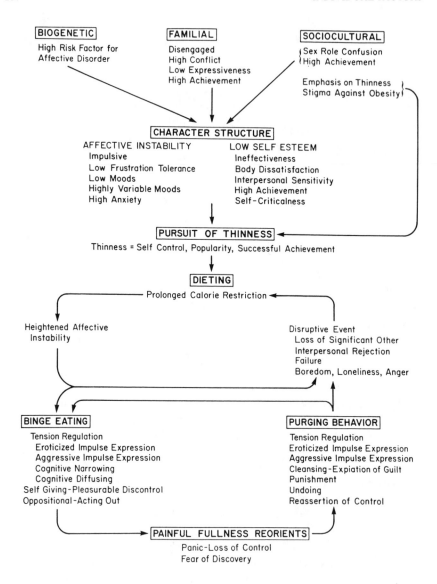

FIGURE 1 Factors that contribute to bulimia (reprinted from *The Etiology and Treatment of Bulimia Nervosa: A Biopsychosocial Perspective* (p. 145) by C. Johnson and M. Conners, 1987, New York: Basic Books. Copyright 1987 by Basic Books. Reprinted by permission).

ders and a full range of *DSM-III-R* personality disorders (e.g., Gartner, Marcus, Halmi, & Loranger, 1989; Kennedy, McVey, & Katz, in press; Levin & Hyler, 1986; Piran, Lerner, Garfinkel, Kennedy, & Brouillette, 1988; Wonderlich, Swift, Slotnick, & Goodman, 1990; Yager, Landsverk, Edelstein, & Hyler, 1989; Yates, Sieleni, Reich, & Brass, 1989). These studies suggest that most (53% to 93%) eating-disordered individuals display at least one personality disorder and that a substantial proportion (37% to 56%) meet criteria for more than one personality disorder (Wonderlich & Mitchell, in press). There is also preliminary evidence suggesting that particular eating-disorder subtypes show specific relationships to individual personality disorders (Wonderlich & Mitchell, in press) and that the presence of a concurrent personality disorder is associated with a greater overall level of psychopathology (Yates, Sieleni, & Bowers, 1989). Evidence for an association between personality disorders and the eating disorders is reviewed for each of the personality disorder clusters outlined in *DSM-III-R*. These three clusters—the odd eccentric (cluster A), dramatic erratic (cluster B), and anxious fearful (cluster C)—were introduced to represent symptomatic similarities between specific disorders, and there has been some preliminary support for their validity with samples of eating-disordered individuals (Yager et al., 1989).

Odd-Eccentric Personality Disorders

Consistent with clinical descriptions, the prevalence of *DSM-III-R* cluster A personality disorders—paranoid, schizoid, and schizotypal—in eating-disordered samples has been quite low (less than 10%; see Table 1). There have been exceptions, however, particularly in studies using self-report instruments such as the Millon Clinical Multiaxial Inventory (MCMI) or the Personality Diagnostic Questionnaire (PDQ) (e.g., Kennedy et al., in press; Yager et al., 1989; & Yates, Sieleni, Reich, & Brass, 1989). These studies indicated that schizoid or schizotypal personalities may be more prominent in eating-disordered samples than was expected. However, Kennedy et al. (in press) reported that reductions over time in schizoid and schizotypal scales on the MCMI are significantly correlated with similar reductions in depression. Thus, as Wonderlich and Mitchell (in press) suggested, the high rates of cluster A personality disorders reported in these studies may reflect the state effects of a comorbid mood disturbance on self-report measures of personality disorder.

However, two studies using semistructured interviews, thought to be more specific than self-report measures of personality, have also revealed high levels of cluster A disorders. Gartner et al. (1989) found that 16% of their restricting anorectic group met criteria for schizotypal personality and 16% also were diagnosed as paranoid personality when using the Personality Disorder Examination (PDE). Similarly, when using the Structured Clinical Interview for *DSM-III-R* Axis II (SCID-II), Powers, Coovert, Brightwell, and Stevens

TABLE 1   Prevalence rates of most common personality disorders in eating-disordered subjects

Study	Criteria for personality disorder	Sample size	ED subtype	Two most prominent PD (%)
Self-report				
Yates et al. (1989)	PDQ	30	BN	Compulsive (37%) Histrionic, dependent Schizotypal (all 33%)
Wonderlich & Swift (1989)	MCMI	10	RA	Dependent (70%) Passive aggressive (60%)
		11	AN/BN	Dependent (64%) Avoidant (60%)
		16	BN	Dependent (63%) Borderline, passive aggressive (both 44%)
		10	BN/A	Passive aggressive (80%) Borderline (60%)
Yager et al. (1989)	PDQ	15	AN/BN	Schizotypal (53%) Dependent (53%)
		300	BN	Schizotypal (55%) Borderline (47%)
		313	Subclinial ED	Schizotypal (34%) Borderline (29%)
Kennedy et al. (in press)	MCMI	44	Mixed (RA, BN, AN/BN)	Dependent (43%) Passive aggressive (41%)
Unstructured interviews				
Levin & Hyler (1986)	PDQ & interview	24	RA	Histrionic (40%) Borderline (25%)
Piran et al. (1988)	Clinical interview DSM-III	30	RA	Avoidant (60%) Compulsive, dependent (both 16%)
		38	AN/BN	Histrionic (18%)
Structured interviews				
Powers et al. (1988)	SCID-II	30	BN	Histrionic (53%) Obsessive–compulsive (33%)
Gartner et al. (1989)	PDE	6	RA	Borderline (33%) Avoidant
		21	AN/BN	Compulsive (38%) Borderline, avoidant (both 33%)
		8	BN	Dependent (38%) Borderline

(*Table continues on next page*)

TABLE 1 Prevalence rates of most common personality disorders in eating disordered subjects (*continued*)

Study	Criteria for personality disorder	Sample size	ED subtype	Two most prominent PD (%)
Structured interviews				
Wonderlich et al. (1990)	SCID-II	10	RA	Obsessive–compulsive (60%) Dependent (40%)
		10	AN/BN	Avoidant (60%) Dependent (40%)
		16	BN	Histrionic (31%) Borderline, avoidant, dependent (all 19%)
		10	BN/A	Borderline (40%) Histrionic (40%)

Reprinted with permission from Wonderlich S, Mitchell J: Eating Disorders and Personality Disorders, in *Special Problems in Managing Eating Disorders.* Edited by Yager J, Gwirtsman HE, Edelstein CK. Washington, DC, American Psychiatric Press, 1992.

Note. ED = eating disorders; RA = restricting anorexics; AN/BN = bulimic anorexics; BN = normal-weight bulimics; BN/A = normal-weight bulimics with a history of anorexia nervosa; subclinical ED = subclinical eating disorder; PDQ = Personality Diagnostic Questionnaire; MCMI = Millon Clinical Multiaxial Inventory; DSM-III = Diagnostic and Statistical Manual of Mental Disorders (3rd edition); SCID-II = Strucured Clinical Interview for DSM-III (revised) Axis II; PDE = Personality Disorder Examination.

(1988) also found a high prevalence (27%) of paranoid personality disorder in a sample of outpatient bulimics. Although further studies are needed to clarify these somewhat unexpected findings, the more generally reported low-prevalence estimates from cluster A are consistent with clinical descriptions of the premorbid personality of eating-disordered individuals as compliant, anxious, dramatic, or labile. It may be, however, that given the polythetic format of *DSM-III-R* Axis II, certain eating-disordered subjects may meet criteria for a cluster A personality disorder without representing the prototype of that diagnostic category. For example, some anorexics display rather paranoid defensive types (Johnson & Connors, 1987) and may meet several of the *DSM-III-R* diagnostic criteria for paranoid personality but still not represent the classic prototype of the paranoid personality. Furthermore, their paranoid style may be intimately intertwined with concerns about body shape and weight associated with the eating disturbance. Further studies reporting high rates of cluster A personality disturbance in eating-disordered individuals may provide important information about possible atypical presentations of such personality disorders but must consider the state effects of the eating disturbance.

Dramatic Erratic Personality Disorders

There has been speculation that the action-oriented personality disorders of *DSM–III–R* cluster B (borderline, histrionic, narcissistic, and antisocial) are likely to be associated with eating disorders, particularly bulimic subtypes (e.g., Swift & Wonderlich, 1988). Borderline personality appears comparably prevalent in both restricting and bulimic eating-disorder subtypes, but some preliminary evidence indicates that histrionic personality disorder shows a greater affinity to bulimia than to restricting anorexia (Wonderlich & Mitchell, in press). A recent review (Wonderlich & Mitchell, in press) suggests that prevalence rates for histrionic personality disorder in normal-weight bulimic samples range from 25% to 53% and that the prevalence of histrionic personality disorder in restricting and bulimic anorectic samples is considerably lower, ranging from 0% to 20%. Even though one study found a low prevalence of histrionic personality disorder across all eating-disorder subtypes (Gartner et al., 1989), there appears to be an association between histrionic personality and normal-weight bulimia.

Although much has been written about the narcissistic vulnerability of eating-disordered individuals, particularly bulimics (e.g., Swift & Wonderlich, 1988), clinical experience does not suggest that the grandiosity, rage reactions, and lack of empathy characteristics of *DSM–III–R* narcissistic personality disorder would be prevalent in eating-disordered samples. In fact, this has been supported in the few studies that examined the prevalence of narcissistic personality disorder in bulimic and anorectic individuals. Both narcissistic and antisocial personality disorders have been relatively uncommon in studies with eating-disordered subjects (see Table 1). Borderline personality disorder diagnoses have been much more common and controversial in the study of eating disorders. Because borderline personality has been studied more extensively in the eating disorders than all other personality disorders, we review this literature in greater depth.

Prevalence of Borderline Personality

Reports of the prevalence of borderline personality disorder in eating-disordered populations have varied widely depending on the research setting, eating-disorder subtype studied, and personality disorder measure used. This seems particularly true of studies using self-report measures of borderline personality disorder. Several self-report instruments have revealed high rates of borderline personality disorder across the full range of eating-disorder subtypes. For example, Wonderlich and Swift (1989) used the MCMI to assess borderline personality disorder in restricting anorexics, bulimic anorexics, and normal-weight bulimics. Over half of the subjects within each eating-disorder subtype met criteria for borderline personality (Table 2). Similarly, Norman,

ABLE 2 Prevalence rates of borderline personality disorder in eating-disordered subjects

Study	Criteria for borderline	Sample size	Eating disorder subtype	Inpatient/ outpatient	Percent
elf-report					
Yates et al. (1989)	PDQ	30	BN	Outpatient	13
Johnson et al. (1989)	BSI	94	Not specified	Outpatient	41
Wonderlich & Swift	MCMI	10	RA	Mixed	50
(1989)		11	AN/BN		63
		16	BN		50
		10	B/AN		60
Yager et al. (1989)	PDQ	15	AN/BN	Not specified	33
		300	BN		47
		313	Subclinial ED		29
Kennedy et al.	MCMI	44	Mixed (RA, BN,	Inpatient	32 (MCMI discharge)
(in press)	BSI		AN/BN)		43 (BSI discharge)
nstructured interviews					
Piran et al. (1988)	*DSM-III*	30	RA	Inpatient	7
		38	AN/BN		55
Levin & Hyler (1986)	*DSM-III*	24	BN	Outpatient	25
emistructured interviews					
Sansone et al. (1989)	DIB	6	RA	Mixed	50
		17	BN		18
		3	Atypical		0
Piran et al. (1988)	DIB	30	RA	Inpatient	37
		38	AN/BN		42
Pope et al. (1987)	DIB–R	52	BN	Outpatient	2
Levendusky & Herring	DIB–R	12	Not specified	Inpatient	75
(1989)					
Wonderlich et al.	SCID-II	10	RA	Mixed	20
(1990)		10	AN/BN		20
		16	BN		19
		10	BN/A		40
Powers et al. (1988)	SCID-II	30	BN	Outpatient	23
Gartner et al. (1989)	PDE	6	RA	Inpatient	33
		21	AN/BN		33
		8	BN		34

Reprinted with permission from Wonderlich S, Mitchell J: Eating Disorders and Personality Disorders, in *ecial Problems in Managing Eating Disorders.* Edited by Yager J, Gwirtsman HE, Edelstein CK. Washing-m, DC, American Psychiatric Press, 1992.

Note. RA = restricting anorexics; AN/BN = bulimic anorexics; BN = normal-weight bulimics; BN/A = rmal-weight bulimics with a history of anorexia nervosa; subclinical ED = subclinical eating disorder; PDQ Personality Diagnostic Questionnaire; BSI = Borderline Syndrome Index; MCMI = Millon Clinical ultiaxial Inventory; *DSM-III* = Diagnostic and Statistical Manual of Mental Disorders (3rd edition); DIB = iagnostic Interview for Borderlines; DIB-R = DIB revised; SCID-II = Strucured Clinical Interview for SM-III (revised) Axis II; PDE = Personality Disorder Examination.

Herzog, and Stasior (1989) found that over half of their sample of eating-disordered individuals showed severe personality deficits on the MCMI and that those subjects with the most extreme personality deficits were particularly elevated on the borderline scale. Johnson, Tobin, and Enright (1989) administered the Borderline Syndrome Index (BSI), another self-report personality measure, to a consecutive series of eating-disordered patients and found that 41% of their sample met BSI criteria for borderline personality disorder. Yager et al. (1989) found similarly high rates in anorexics with bulimic tendencies and normal-weight bulimics when using the PDQ for their borderline personality assessment. However, Yates, Sieleni, Brass, and Reich (1989) found that only 13% of their outpatient bulimic sample met criteria for borderline personality when using the PDQ.

Overall, prevalence rates of borderline personality disorder revealed in studies using self-report measures have been quite high. Although self-report measures of borderline personality disorder are easy to administer and offer the potential research advantage of dimensional scales of measurement, their utility in actually diagnosing personality disorders has been limited by low positive predictive power (Dubro, Wetzler, & Kahn, 1988; Edell, 1984; Widiger & Frances, 1989). Furthermore, the test–retest reliability of the MCMI and the BSI has recently been questioned by Kennedy et al. (in press). They found that the prevalence of borderline personality disorder in a sample of inpatient anorexics and bulimics changed substantially over the course of an inpatient hospitalization. Although 79% of their sample met criteria for borderline personality on the MCMI and BSI at admission, this dropped to 32% at discharge. Thus, it appears that the assessment of personality disorder with these measures may be greatly influenced by state-related eating pathology. At this point in time, therefore, it seems prudent to interpret the prevalence of borderline personality disorder with caution when they are based on self-report instruments.

Other studies relied on *DSM–III* criteria and unstructured clinical interviews to assess the prevalence of borderline personality disorder in eating-disordered individuals. Levin and Hyler (1986) interviewed 24 outpatient bulimic patients and found that 25% of this sample met the *DSM–III* criteria for borderline personality disorder. Piran et al. (1988) also used a *DSM–III*-based clinical interview to obtain discharge personality disorder diagnoses for samples of restricting anorexics and bulimic anorexics. They found that bulimic anorexics were much more likely to obtain a borderline diagnosis than were restricting anorexics. It was suggested that this difference most likely reflects the bulimic anorexics' tendency to use more action-oriented and impulse-dominated defenses than restrictors, which would be more consistent with the *DSM–III* borderline criteria. Taken together, these clinical interview studies suggest that there is a relatively high rate of borderline personality disorder in bulimic subtypes of eating disorders.

Although both of these studies report adequate interrater reliability, it is clear that such clinical interviews may yield quite different findings than more highly structured research-oriented interviews. For example, Powers, Coovert, Brightwell, and Stevens (1988) found substantially different prevalence of personality disorder in eating-disordered subjects depending on whether clinical or semi-structured research interviews were used to assess the prevalence of personality disorder in eating-disordered samples. In the only study to use the PDE, Gartner et al. (1989) examined the prevalence of personality disorders in an inpatient sample of 6 restricting anorexics, 21 bulimic anorexics, and 8 normal-weight bulimics. The authors reported that 2 (33%) of the restricting anorexics, 7 (33%) of the bulimic anorexics, and 3 (38%) of the normal-weight bulimics met criteria for borderline personality disorder.

Two studies used the SCID-II to assess personality disorders in eating-disordered samples. Wonderlich et al. (1990) used the SCID-II to assess personality disorders in a mixed inpatient and outpatient sample of 46 subjects, including restricting anorexics, bulimic anorexics, and bulimics with and without a history of anorexia. They found moderate and comparable rates of borderline personality disorder in all eating-disorder subtypes ranging from 19% in bulimics with no history of anorexia to 40% in bulimics with a history of anorexia. However, there was no significant difference between any of the eating-disordered groups in the prevalence of borderline personality disorder. In a similar study, Powers et al. (1988) found a comparable rate (23%) of SCID-II borderline personality disorder diagnoses in a sample of bulimic volunteers.

Perhaps the most widely used and rigorous measure of borderline personality is the Diagnostic Interview for Borderlines (DIB). The DIB has become the standard of comparison for new measures of borderline personality and has shown reasonable psychometric properties (Reich, 1987). Sansone, Fine, Seuferer, and Bovenzi (1989) found that 6 (21%) of 28 individuals displaying a wide variety of eating symptoms met DIB criteria for borderline personality disorder. In the previously described clinical interview study by Piran et al. (1988), the bulimic and restricting anorexic subjects also received the DIB. Forty-two percent of the bulimic anorexics and 37% of the restricting anorexics met DIB criteria for borderline personality. It is noteworthy that the prevalence of borderline personality is higher for the restricting group when DIB criteria are used than when *DSM-III* borderline criteria are used. The authors suggested that the DIB places less emphasis on active discharge of impulses, which may account for such a discrepancy.

Although most of the studies that addressed the prevalence of borderline personality disorder in eating-disordered individuals found a sizable minority of both bulimic and anorectic patients displaying such features, Pope and his colleagues (Pope et al., 1987; Pope & Hudson, 1989) challenged these findings. They suggested that nearly all of these studies used instruments of questionable specificity, which may lead to overinflated estimates of the prevalence of borderline personality. In support of their contention, they found that only 2% of bulimic outpatients or recovered bulimics met criteria for borderline personality disorder when a revised and more specific version of the DIB was used. Furthermore, they reported that bulimic subjects with current or past major affective disorder displayed significantly higher scores on the DIB than did bulimic subjects without major affective disorder. They concluded that their data provides little support for the relationship of bulimia and borderline personality disorder but does offer some support for the contention that affective disturbance is related to borderline personality.

Although this finding seriously challenges the relationship between bulimia and borderline personality, Wonderlich and Mitchell (in press) suggested that this issue continues to be unresolved and that the setting in which the studies occur may exert a significant influence on the observed relationship between borderline personality and the eating disorders. They noted the study of Levendusky and Herring (1989), who, like Pope et al. (1987), used the DIB–R to study the prevalence of borderline personality disorder in a series of 12 consecutive eating-disordered admissions on an inpatient unit. These authors reported that 75% of the subjects in the study met *DIB–R* criteria for borderline personality. Thus, although the study is limited by a small sample size and an absence of control groups, it stands in stark contrast to the findings of Pope et al. (1987). As Wonderlich and Mitchell (in press) suggested, the most parsimonious explanation seems to be that the Levendusky and Herring study was conducted on inpatients, whereas Pope et al. (1987) relied on outpatients and individuals solicited through newspaper advertisements. It seems critical in future studies to control for inpatient versus outpatient status of the subjects, a factor that is fairly well recognized as influencing personality disorder prevalence rates (Docherty, Fiester, & Shea, 1986).

Clinical Features of Borderline Personality Disorder

Several studies (Cooper et al., 1988; Johnson et al., 1989; Wonderlich & Swift, 1990) suggested that eating-disordered individuals with concurrent borderline personality disorder report more emotional distress, sexual abuse, self-mutilation, suicide gestures, and perceived family dysfunction than other eating-disordered groups. There has also been one study suggesting that eating-disordered individuals with borderline personality disorder display heightened levels of substance abuse (Johnson et al., 1989), although another study found no differences in substance abuse between eating-disordered individuals with and without concurrent borderline personality disorder (Wonderlich & Swift, 1990).

Although borderline personality disorder subjects reported significantly more disturbance in noneating-related behaviors than other eating-disordered individuals, it is interesting that borderline personality disorder subjects differ minimally from other eating-disordered patients in eating-related pathology

(Johnson et al., 1989; Wonderlich & Swift, 1990). The only possible differences seem to be in the area of purging in which there has been some indication that borderline subjects vomit and use laxatives more than nonborderlines, although these findings have been difficult to replicate (Johnson et al., 1989; Wonderlich & Swift, 1989). Borderline subjects may show greater disturbances in eating-related attitudes (Johnson et al., 1989); however, this does not seem specific to borderline personality disorder and may represent a correlate of personality disorder in general (Wonderlich & Swift, 1990).

Treatment Outcome

Johnson, Tobin, and Enright (1990) provided the only study examining the relevance of borderline personality disorder to outcome in the treatment of eating disorders. These authors compared 21 borderline bulimic and 19 nonborderline bulimic subjects at the beginning of treatment and again at 1 year follow-up. Groups did not differ in specific bulimic behaviors at index evaluation, although the borderline group did express greater eating-attitude disturbance and emotional distress than the nonborderline group. At follow-up, only 21% of the nonborderline group continued to meet the *DSM-III-R* criteria for bulimia compared with 62% of the borderlines. The borderline group also continued to display clinically significant elevations in eating-attitude disturbance and emotional distress. This study provides preliminary evidence that the presence of borderline personality disorder does indeed mitigate the effects of standard treatment for eating disorders. Interestingly, those borderline patients who received the most intensive treatment showed the greatest improvement, but the absence of random assignment of subjects to treatment frequency conditions limits inferences about this finding.

Anxious-Fearful Personality Disorders

In their early report relying on clinical interview methods, Levin and Hyler (1986) found cluster C personality disorders (avoidant, dependent, compulsive, and passive-aggressive) to be relatively uncommon in their outpatient bulimic sample. In view of several recent empirical findings, however, it appears that cluster C personality disturbance is much more prominent in both bulimic and anorectic samples than was originally thought (Wonderlich & Mitchell, in press). For example, in samples that include both anorectic and bulimic patients, avoidant personality disorder has been diagnosed in 30% to 35% of eating-disordered subjects. Although it does appear that avoidant personality characteristics are more common in anorectic subtypes (Piran et al., 1988; Wonderlich et al., 1990), there is some limited evidence suggesting that prevalence in normal-weight bulimics may be nearly as high (e.g., Gartner et al., 1989). Studies attempting to examine the possible difference between restricting and bulimic anorectic subtypes in terms of concurrent avoidant personality characteristics have been contradictory. Although Piran et al. (1988) reported substantially more avoidant personality diagnoses in restricting anorexics than bulimic anorexics (60% vs. 16%), Wonderlich et al. (1990) found the opposite relationship; bulimic anorectic individuals displayed a higher frequency of avoidant personality characteristics than restrictors (60% vs. 20%). Although numerous possible methodological explanations exist for this disparity, it seems the disparity is most likely a result of differences between the two studies in diagnostic criteria for personality disorder. Although Piran et al. (1988) relied on *DSM-III* criteria for avoidant personality, Wonderlich et al. (1990) used the newer *DSM-III-R* criteria. As Widiger and Frances (1989) indicated, the newer *DSM-III-R* criteria for avoidant personality rely less on social avoidance and more on fear of risk taking and embarrassment than the *DSM-III* criteria. This may represent a parallel difference between restricting and bulimic anorexics. However, a more recent study found no differences between restricting and bulimic anorectic subtypes when *DSM-III-R* criteria for avoidant personality disorder were used (Gartner et al., 1989). This finding further complicates the possibility of an eating-disorder subtype difference in terms of avoidant personality disturbance, and further studies are clearly needed to clarify this issue.

Although early findings highlighted significant obsessionality in eating-disordered individuals (Swift & Wonderlich, 1988), evidence for an association between actual obsessive–compulsive personality disorder and the eating disorders has been quite modest. Generally, obsessive–compulsive personality disorder has been most prominent in anorectic individuals and less common in normal-weight bulimics (Wonderlich & Mitchell, in press). Efforts to identify anorectic subtype differences in terms of comorbid obsessive–compulsive personality disorder have been contradictory, and conclusions are not possible (e.g., Gartner et al., 1989; Piran et al., 1988; Wonderlich et al., 1990). Thus, although various eating-disordered individuals may display significant obsessionality, the relationship of true obsessive–compulsive personality disorder in the subtypes of anorexia nervosa and bulimia remains unclear and in need of further study.

Studies examining the presence of dependent personality disorder in the eating disorders have fairly consistently shown a moderate level of comorbidity across all eating-disorder subtypes (Wonderlich & Mitchell, in press). Early clinical literature highlighted autonomy deficits in eating-disordered individuals, and this would most likely be seen in elevated rates of dependent personality disorder. However, it is also possible that dependent personality disorder is artificially elevated when individuals are experiencing acute psychopathology, particularly depression. In fact, Wonderlich et al. (1990) reported that dependent personality disorder and borderline personality disorder were the best personality disorder predictors of self-reported dysthymia in eating-disordered subjects. Clearly, future studies of dependent personality disorder need to consider carefully confounding state effects of concurrent mood disturbance.

Passive–aggressive personality disorder has not been shown to bear a significant relationship with the eating disorders. Prevalence rates have been consistently low (0% to 5%), although Gartner et al. (1989) reported moderate rates of passive–aggressive personality disturbance in normal-weight bulimics. However, this study was based on a very small sample, and further replication is clearly indicated.

Overall, the personality disorders of cluster C are more prevalent in the eating disorders than was originally thought. There is some evidence that avoidant and obsessive–compulsive personality disorders are specifically linked to anorectic subtypes, although this is far from definitive. Dependent personality disorder appears quite common across all eating-disorder subtypes.

PERSONALITY CHARACTERISTICS AS A RISK FACTOR FOR EATING DISORDERS

A number of observations warrant comment regarding the importance of personality features as a risk factor for the onset of eating disorders. A plethora of methodological and conceptual problems accompanies any attempt to address personality issues (Wonderlich & Mitchell, in press). That the eating-disordered population is quite heterogeneous complicates these methodological and conceptual problems further. Despite the frustrating limitations of personality research, many senior clinicians continue to feel that this is a critical variable in any risk factor equation for the development of psychopathology in general (Cloninger, 1986).

How important are personality traits as risk factors more specifically for eating disorders? We speculate that one half to two thirds of the patients presenting with the symptoms of anorexia nervosa and bulimic nervosa would have been at risk for developing psychiatric symptoms of any kind at some point in their development. This figure corresponds to the percentage of patients that the initial data base seems to indicate do indeed carry an Axis II diagnosis. Although many different eating patterns could have developed, we believe that the selection of eating-related symptoms as an expression of psychological vulnerability has been socioculturally determined.

Consensus has appeared to emerge over the last several years that anorexia nervosa and bulimia nervosa are essentially "culture bound syndromes" (Devereaux, 1955; Gordon, 1990). Several criteria are necessary for a psychiatric disorder to be regarded as a culture-bound syndrome. Essentially, a culture-bound disorder expresses core conflicts and psychological tensions that are pervasive in the culture, and the symptoms of the disorder are direct extensions and exaggerations of normal behaviors and activities within the culture. Several researchers argued that the co-occurrence of several sociocultural events over the last 20 years has selectively affected the cohort at risk (adolescent and young adult females from middle- to upper-class families in Westernized cultures) and has biased them toward eating-related problems (Garfinkel & Garner, 1982; Johnson & Maddi, 1986). Obviously, however, all young women in this cohort have not developed a clinical syndrome of anorexia nervosa or bulimia nervosa. Consequently, the sociocultural factors appear to be a necessary but not a sufficient factor.

In our opinion, the primary risk factor that would make some young women develop an actual clinical syndrome would be some general vulnerability or "G-factor of coping ability" that might best be captured with the term personality. The term *personality* is used to describe the way an individual is predominantly inclined to respond or cope with the range of both daily and more global developmental challenges. This personality factor would unquestionably be a product of both an individual's biogenetic and environmental circumstances. From our perspective, an individual's psychology cannot be understood outside the context of their biology. The two are inextricably woven together and reciprocally affect each other.

In this regard we have found the revived interest in the notion of temperament to be an interesting and exciting development. In a compelling article, Strober (1991) attempted to bridge the gap between biological-psychoanalytic and personality theorists regarding the primacy of temperament in any risk factor model for eating disorders. Strober borrowed heavily from Cloninger's work (1986, 1987, 1988), which he briefly summarizes as follows:

1. The foundations of personality comprise three bipolar dimensions—namely, behavioral activation and novelty seeking; behavioral inhibition and harm avoidance; and behavioral maintenance and reward dependence. Each dimension is a superordinate structure in its own right with highly specific steering and modulating functions.

2. These dimensions are the outcome of genetic, constitutional, and learning factors; however, contrary to popular belief, the total body of evidence at hand indicates a far greater influence of genes than of environment in the foundation of these personality traits (Plomin, 1986).

3. The generality of these dimensions is quite significant; this is to say that their behavioral correlates are highly routinized and stable within individuals and across environmental situations to a remarkable degree.

4. Finally, individual differences in learning history, in the nature of response to environmental demands, and in the expression of psychopathological behavior derive from, and are readily predicted by, knowledge of the covariation of these dimensions within individuals. (Strober, 1991, pp. 358–359)

Restricting Subtype and Cluster C

It appears from the preliminary data that restricting anorexics may tend to cluster in the anxious-fearful category of *DSM-III-R*. Strober (1991) argued that these patients also fit well into Cloninger's group whose members are temperamentally harm avoidant, low novelty seeking, and reward dependent. Overall, this type of temperament configuration would be characterized as emotionally restrained, slow to change interest, excessively methodical, rigidly persistent, extreme worriers, poorly adaptable to change, demonstrating slow recovery from stress, dependent on others for emotional support, and hypersensitive to signs of approval and rejection.

Clearly if this was an enduring way of experiencing the world, then one could imagine how overwhelming the psychobiological demands of puberty would be for this type of individual. Several clinicians wrote about how the development of anorexia nervosa, or self-starvation, effectively accomplishes a retreat from the maturational demands of adolescence (Bruch, 1973; Crisp, 1980). Overall, then, cluster C traits may be a specific risk factor for developing psychiatric symptoms during the highly challenging developmental phase of adolescence. The predominance of the specific symptom selection of self-starvation (restricting type anorexia nervosa) found among young girls versus young boys may be best understood by the fact that submenstrual threshold weights among young girls returns them biologically to a prepubertal state, thus minimizing many of the psychobiological demands of adolescence. Essentially, manipulation of their body weight allows young girls to pace the onset of their puberty. The same type of psychobiological adaptation is not achievable for young boys through weight manipulation and, therefore, psychologically vulnerable boys select other symptom patterns.

Bulimia Subtype and Cluster B

Specifying a type of personality trait that might increase the risk for developing bulimia nervosa is more difficult partly because it appears that the bulimic group is more variable. Given the caveat that the bulimic group is more heterogeneous, our clinical impression is that this group tends toward cluster B traits. In previous work (Johnson, 1991), we argued that the bulimic subgroup is characterized by unstable affect, impulsiveness, rejection sensitivity, and approval seeking. Bulimics' lives are usually marked by more chaos and erraticness than their restricting anorectic counterparts, and their cognitive styles and predominant defensive style are more histrionic (diffuse, chaotic, and impressionistic). This more erratic and chaotic temperament may predispose this subgroup more to the impulsive, episodic, and action-oriented nature of bulimic behavior.

CONCLUSION

Despite the many methodological and conceptual difficulties that plague personality research, we believe that personality or temperament will eventually prove
to be highly predictive of potential psychiatric difficulties throughout the life
span. As we have argued here, we choose to view traits or temperament as a
product of the interaction between biogenetic and environmental contingencies.
Our hunch is that, ultimately, information about a patient's temperament and
cognitive or defensive style will tell us more about the type of treatment needed
and course of illness than the nature and extent of the disturbed eating behavior
(i.e., restrictors vs. binge eaters, frequency of binge–purge behavior, and so
on).

REFERENCES

American Psychiatric Association. (1987). *Diagnostic and statistical manual of
    mental disorders* (3rd ed., rev.). Washington, DC: Author.
Bruch, H. (1973). *Eating disorders: Obesity, anorexia, and the person within.*
    New York: Basic Books.
Cloninger, C. R. (1986). A unified biosocial theory of personality and its role
    in the development of anxiety states. *Psychiatric Developments, 3,* 167–
    226.
Cloninger, C. R. (1987). A systematic method for clinical description and clas-
    sification of personality variants. *Archives of General Psychiatry, 44,* 573–
    588.
Cloninger, C. R. (1988). A reply to commentaries. *Psychiatric Developments,
    6,* 83–120.
Cooper, J. L., Morrison, T. L., Bigman, O. L., Abramowitz, S. I., Blunden,
    D., Nassi, A., & Krener, P. (1988). Bulimia and borderline personality
    disorder. *International Journal of Eating Disorders, 7,* 43–49.
Crisp, A. H. (1980). *Anorexia nervosa: Let me be.* New York: Grune & Strat-
    ton.
Devereaux, G. A. (1955). *Normal and abnormal: Basic problems of ethno
    psychiatry.* Chicago: University of Chicago Press.
Docherty, J. P., Fiester, S. J., & Shea, T. (1986). Syndrome diagnosis and
    personality disorder. In A. J. Francis & R. E. Hales (Eds.), *American
    Psychiatric Association annual review, volume 5.* Washington, DC: Ameri-
    can Psychiatric Press.
Dubro, A. F., Wetzler, S., & Kahn, M. W. (1988). A comparison of three self-
    report questionnaires for the diagnosis of DSM-III personality disorders.
    Journal of Personality Disorders, 2, 256–266.
Edell, W. S. (1984). The borderline syndrome index: Clinical validity and
    utility. *Journal of Nervous and Mental Disease, 168,* 428–435.

Garfinkel, P., & Garner, D. (1982). *Anorexia nervosa: A multidimensional perspective.* New York: Brunner/Mazel.

Gartner, A. F., Marcus, R. N., Halmi, K., & Loranger, A. W. (1989). DSM–III–R personality disorders in patients with eating disorders. *American Journal of Psychiatry, 146,* 1585–1591.

Gordon, R. A. (1990). *Anorexia and bulimia: Anatomy of a social epidemic.* Cambridge, MA: Blackwell.

Johnson, C. (1991). Treatment of eating disordered patients with borderline false-self/narcissistic disorders. In C. Johnson (Ed.), *Psychodynamic treatment of anorexia nervosa and bulimia* (pp. 165–193). New York: Guilford Press.

Johnson, C., & Maddi, K. (1986). The etiology of bulimia: A bio-psychosocial perspective. *Annals of Adolescent Psychiatry, 13,* 253–273.

Johnson, C., & Connors, M. E. (1987). *The etiology and treatment of bulimia nervosa.* New York: Basic Books.

Johnson, C., Tobin, D., & Enright, A. (1989). Prevalence and clinical characteristics of borderline patients in an eating disordered population. *Journal of Clinical Psychiatry, 50,* 9–15.

Johnson, C., Tobin, D., & Enright, A. B. (1990). Differences in treatment outcome between borderline and nonborderline bulimics at one year follow-up. *International Journal of Eating Disorders, 9,* 617–627.

Kennedy, S. H., McVey, G., & Katz, R. (in press). Personality disorder in anorexia nervosa and bulimia. *Journal of Psychiatric Research.*

Levendusky, P. H., & Herring, J. (1989). *Therapeutic contract program for treatment of severe eating disorders.* Paper presented at the 97th annual meeting of the American Psychological Association, New Orleans, LA.

Levin, A. P., & Hyler, S. E. (1986). DSM–III personality diagnosis in bulimia. *Comprehensive Psychiatry, 27,* 47–53.

Norman, D. K., Herzog, D. B., & Stasior, J. (1989). *Personality characteristics of anorexia and bulimia nervosa as identified by the Millon Clinical Multiaxial Inventory* (MCMI). Unpublished manuscript.

Piran, N., Lerner, P., Garfinkel, P. E., Kennedy, S. H., & Brouillette, C. (1988). Personality disorders in anorexic patients. *International Journal of Eating Disorders, 7,* 589–599.

Plonim, R. (1986). *Development, genetics, and psychology.* Hillsdale, NJ: Erlbaum.

Pope, H. G., Frankenburg, F. R., Hudson, J. I., Jonas, J. M., Yurgelun-Todd, D. (1987). Is bulimia associated with borderline personality disorder?: A controlled study. *Journal of Clinical Psychiatry, 48,* 181–184.

Pope, H. G., & Hudson, J. I. (1989). Are eating disorders associated with borderline personality disorder? A critical review. *International Journal of Eating Disorders, 8,* 1–9.

Powers, P. S., Coovert, D. L., Brightwell, D. R., & Stevens, B. A. (1988).

Other psychiatric disorders among bulimic patients. *Comprehensive Psychiatry, 29,* 503–508.

Reich, J. H. (1987). Instruments measuring DSM–III and DSM–III–R personality disorders. *Journal of Personality Disorders, 1,* 220–240.

Sansone, R. A., Fine, M. A., Seuferer, S., & Bovenzi, J. (1989). The prevalence of borderline personality symptomatology among women with eating disorders. *Journal of Clinical Psychology, 45,* 603–610.

Strober, M. (1991). Disorders of the self in anorexia nervosa: An organismic-developmental paradigm. In C. Johnson (Ed.), *Psychodynamic treatment of anorexia nervosa and bulimia* (pp. 354–373). New York: Guilford Press.

Swift, W. J., & Wonderlich, S. A. (1988). Personality factors and diagnosis in eating disorders. In D. M. Garner & P. E. Garfinkel (Eds.), *Diagnostic issues in anorexia nervosa and bulimia nervosa* (pp. 121–165). New York: Brunner/Mazel.

Widiger, T. A., & Frances, A. J. (1989). Epidemiology, diagnosis, and comorbidity of borderline personality disorder. In A. Tasman, R. E. Hales, & A. J. Frances (Eds.), *Review of Psychiatry, Volume 8.* Washington, DC: American Psychiatric Press.

Wonderlich, S. A., & Mitchell, J. E. (in press). The comorbidity of personality disorders and the eating disorders. In J. Yager (Ed.), *Special problems in managing eating disorders.* Washington, DC: American Psychiatric Press.

Wonderlich, S. A., & Swift, W. J. (1989). *MCMI performance and eating disorder subtypes.* Unpublished manuscript.

Wonderlich, S. A., & Swift, W. J. (1990). Borderline vs. other personality disorders in the eating disorders: Clinical description. *International Journal of Eating Disorders, 9,* 618–629.

Wonderlich, S. A., Swift, W. J., Slotnick, H. B., & Goodman, S. (1990). DSM–III–R personality disorders in eating disorder subtypes. *International Journal of Eating Disorders, 9,* 607–617.

Yager, J., Landsverk, J., Edelstein, C. K., & Hyler, S. E. (1989). Screening for axis II personality disorders in women with bulimic eating disorders. *Psychosomatics, 30,* 255–262.

Yates, W. R., Sieleni, B., & Bowers, W. A. (1989). Clinical correlates of personality disorder in bulimia nervosa. *International Journal of Eating Disorders, 8,* 473–477.

Yates, W. R., Sieleni, B., Reich, J., & Brass, C. (1989). Comorbidity of bulimia nervosa and personality disorder. *Journal of Clinical Psychiatry, 50,* 57–59.

III

FUTURE DIRECTIONS

11

OVERVIEW

Deanne L. Zotter
Nancy E. Sherwood
Kent State University

Authors of previous chapters in this volume provide comprehensive discussions of the role of developmental, familial, and individual factors in the etiology of bulimia nervosa. Throughout these discussions, there is an appreciation for the heterogeneous nature of bulimia nervosa, and the challenge this complexity poses for researchers investigating the etiology of this disorder. Although significant progress has been made in our understanding of bulimia nervosa, it is clear that many important questions, including those generated by previous research, remain unanswered. Of great concern to the authors of this volume and other participants at the 1990 Kent Psychology Forum is the meaningful integration of research findings to date and the delineation of pertinent issues that should be addressed in the future. The final section of this volume provides recommendations for accomplishing these goals.

In the first chapter of this section, Striegel-Moore (Ch. 12) presents a thorough discussion concerning the area of prevention, with a particular focus on primary prevention. Within the prevention literature, a distinction is made among primary, secondary, and tertiary prevention. Whereas secondary and tertiary prevention efforts target populations already exhibiting symptoms of a disorder, primary prevention efforts are introduced before symptom development. Primary prevention encompasses two basic approaches: (1) a systems-level approach aimed at changing the environment with the intent of reducing environmental risk factors and (2) a person-centered approach aimed at enhancing an individual's capacity to adapt to and effectively cope with stressful life events. The success of primary prevention efforts is contingent on knowledge concerning environmental risk factors and stressful circumstances associated with a particular disorder.

Clearly, our understanding of bulimia nervosa is only beginning to reach a point at which effective primary prevention programs can be implemented. One of the major contributions of Striegel-Moore is her examination of several questions that need to be addressed before developing a primary prevention program. Among the questions addressed by Striegel-Moore are: (1) What should be the target of preventive efforts?; (2) Who should prevention programs be targeted toward?; and (3) How are eating-disorder prevention programs and obesity prevention programs related?

A second important contribution of her chapter is Striegel-Moore's examination of specific ways in which "noxious" environmental factors that facilitate the development of bulimia may be modified or eliminated as well as potential ways in which individuals' capacities to cope with these stressors may be augmented. Cultural expectations for thinness have been widely touted as influencing the development of eating disorders. Striegel-Moore posits that one of the ways in which this risk may be reduced is by encouraging stricter regulation of the diet and beauty industry. Moreover, she argues that particular attention needs to be given to the portrayal of children in advertisements to promote products and advertisements that target children as consumers. Striegel-Moore also suggests that educating the public about the potential dangers of dieting may be an important aspect of primary prevention efforts. Finally, Striegel-Moore focuses on the creation of supportive environments that may serve to "strengthen the host" and enhance an individual's capacity to cope with sociocultural pressures regarding appearance. Specifically, the role of school and family environments as key integrative social systems in the lives of young girls are examined as potential targets of intervention efforts .

In the final chapter of this volume, Crowther and Mizes (ch. 13) address the issue of the etiological implications of the heterogeneity of bulimia nervosa and raise important issues concerning the nature and direction of future research efforts. A central theme of their chapter is the recognition that, owing to the apparently heterogeneous nature of bulimia nervosa, there may be multiple etiological pathways to the disorder. Crowther and Mizes propose that a parsimonious way of conceptualizing the heterogeneity of bulimia nervosa may be by considering two intersecting psychological dimensions: a global psychopathology dimension and an eating-specific dimension. The heuristic model presented by Crowther and Mizes allows for the examination of meaningful subclassifications of bulimia nervosa and has important implications for the cause, maintenance, and treatment of different subgroups of bulimic individuals.

Another contribution by Crowther and Mizes is their recommendation for future research in the area of eating disorders focusing both on research design and psychometric issues. It is widely recognized that prospective research is needed to address adequately questions regarding the etiology of bulimia nervosa. Crowther and Mizes present several specific ways in which prospective research may be conducted. They posit that the appropriate selection of participants for prospective research should be guided by a theoretical framework. For example, it is argued that researchers conceptualizing restrictive dieting tendencies as increasing risk for bulimia nervosa (e.g., Heatherton & Polivy, this volume) may need to focus on highly restrained eaters as their high-risk group and conduct repetitive assessments prospectively to understand the roles that eating attitudes, self-esteem, or affective symptomatology may play in the development of bulimic symptomatology.

Finally, Crowther and Mizes argue that psychometrically sound measures of psychological constructs relevant to bulimia nervosa are crucial for progress in our understanding of this disorder. Without adequate assessment instruments, inconclusive research findings may be due to error in measurement rather than faulty theoretical models. Although numerous measurement devices have been demonstrated to have adequate psychometric properties, Crowther and Mizes strongly recommend comprehensive examination of those measures that have not been investigated. Given the growing trend toward evaluating children, Crowther and Mizes argue that particular attention needs to be paid to the psychometric capacities (i.e., reliability and validity) of measures used with younger populations.

The closing chapters of this volume provide comprehensive discussions of future directions for prevention and research in the eating-disorder field. The contributions of Striegel-Moore and Crowther and Mizes should facilitate progress in our understanding of the complex processes involved in the etiology of bulimia nervosa and its subsequent prevention.

12

PREVENTION OF BULIMIA NERVOSA: QUESTIONS AND CHALLENGES

Ruth H. Striegel-Moore
Wesleyan University

During the past two decades, we have witnessed the exponential growth of a clinical and research literature on bulimia nervosa. Considerable research efforts have been directed toward describing bulimia nervosa, documenting prevalence rates in various populations, identifying risk factors, and developing effective treatment approaches. (For summaries of this literature, the reader is referred to Fairburn, Agras, & Wilson, in press; Fairburn & Beglin, 1990; Johnson & Connors, 1987; Mitchell, 1991). In contrast, publications concerning prevention are rare. Although few in number, these articles on prevention provide detailed discussions of conceptual and practical issues involved in efforts to prevent bulimia nervosa (Clark, Levine, & Kinney, 1988–1989; Crisp, 1988; Hotelling, 1988–1989; Levine, 1987; Sesan, 1988–1989, 1989; Shisslak, Crago, Neal, & Swain, 1987; Smead, 1985; Striegel-Moore & Silberstein, 1989; Striegel-Moore, 1989). This literature focuses largely on secondary prevention (i.e., efforts to reduce the prevalence of the disorder through early identification and early intervention), and considerable attention is devoted to interventions designed to increase resilience in populations at risk for the disorder.

The scope of this chapter is limited to primary prevention (i.e., the efforts aimed at reducing the incidence of bulimia nervosa in populations that do not yet evidence any symptoms of the disorder). The chapter opens with the question of what constitutes a case or what it is that is to be prevented followed by a brief discussion of research on gender-related differences in key symptoms of bulimia nervosa. The next section summarizes current etiological models and highlights several unresolved questions of interest for a discussion of primary prevention. The remainder of the chapter explores how primary prevention can be achieved through (1) efforts aimed at reducing or eliminating factors that cause or facilitate development of the disorder ("eliminating noxious factors") and (2) efforts aimed at creating supportive environments.

DEFINING BULIMIA NERVOSA

Only recently, experts have agreed on a uniform definition of bulimia nervosa (*Diagnostic and Statistical Manual of Mental Disorders,* third edition, revised, *[DSM-III-R];* American Psychiatric Association [APA], 1987). Issues of definition are relevant to our discussion because accepted diagnostic criteria define what constitutes a case and thus what should be prevented. Furthermore, the definition determines how common the disorder is in the general population. Now widely accepted, the term bulimia nervosa has replaced terms such as *dietary chaos syndrome* (Palmer, 1979), *bulimarexia* (Boskind-Lodahl, 1976), and *bulimia (DSM-III,* APA, 1980). Earlier differences in definition reflected divergent views over the nature and distribution of the disorder.

In a comprehensive review of some 50 epidemiological studies, Fairburn and Beglin (1990) illustrated a marked difference in prevalence of bulimia nervosa when diagnostic criteria of differing levels of restrictiveness were applied. For example, the mean prevalence of bulimia *(DSM-III)* reported in these studies was almost 10%, whereas the mean prevalence of bulimia nervosa *(DSM-III-R)* was less than 3%. Relatively low prevalence rates for bulimia nervosa have been reported even for high-risk groups such as female college students (Drewnowski, Hopkins, & Kessler, 1988; Striegel-Moore, Silberstein, Frensch, & Rodin, 1989).

Commonly, claims that the disorder is widespread have been used to justify efforts toward prevention of bulimia nervosa. Fairburn and Beglin's (1990) review suggests that these claims are not easily supported when applying *DSM-III-R* criteria. Many professionals working with young women on college campuses or in high school settings, however, continue to report that these populations experience considerable problems regarding body image and eating behaviors (e.g., Dickstein, 1989; Sesan, 1989). The discrepancy between epidemiological work to date and the daily experience of professionals in the community is not simply a matter of disagreement regarding the number of individuals affected by an eating disorder. Rather, it reflects implicit or explicit differences regarding the definition of a case and the nature of the disorder. Existing diagnostic criteria were derived largely in clinical contexts and may be of limited usefulness when determining "caseness" in community samples.

Numerous studies have shown that key symptoms of bulimia nervosa have high base rates among women and have led some researchers to conceptualize bulimic behaviors on a continuum of severity of concerns with weight, food, and eating (Rodin, Silberstein, & Striegel-Moore, 1985). The continuum argument suggests a dimensional approach (i.e., what level of severity of the disorder does a person have?) to the diagnosis of bulimia nervosa. Alternatively, research comparing individuals who report some bulimic symptoms with those who meet stringent criteria for the clinical syndrome has shown that the latter group exhibits more severe psychopathology (Bunnell, Shenker, Nussbaum, Jacobson, & Cooper, 1990; Crowther & Chernyk, 1986; Lancelot, Brooks-Gunn, Warren, & Newman, 1991; Post & Crowther, 1985; R. H. Striegel-Moore, J. Rodin, & L. Silberstein, in preparation). These findings lend support to a categorical approach (i.e., does the person have the disorder?) to bulimia nervosa. As Szmukler (1985) argued compellingly, the answer to the question of whether one should favor a dimensional approach over a categorical approach and, hence, of what constitutes a case depends on the answer to another question: "a case for what?" For example, a definition appropriate for a study of cases that require treatment may be too narrow for a study directed to finding causes.

I argue that the scope and justification of prevention efforts should not be limited to a categorical approach to bulimia nervosa as represented in the current classification of the disorder in *DSM-III-R*. Rather, a dimensional approach appears more appropriate whereby prevention efforts should be directed toward a reduction in the prevalence of symptoms that constitute the three key features of bulimia nervosa: loss of control over eating; extreme attempts to control shape and weight (including self-induced vomiting, strict dieting, and misuse of purgatives and diuretics); and disturbed attitudes toward shape and weight. Some of these features are also present in anorexia nervosa and in binge-eating disorder (Spitzer et al., 1991), a new eating disorder proposed for inclusion in *DSM-IV.* Prevention programs designed to target these three key features are likely to influence favorably the incidence of anorexia nervosa and binge-eating disorder.

The syndrome of bulimia nervosa is most likely to emerge during late adolescence and early adulthood (e.g., Mitchell, 1990). Key symptoms of the disorders, however, have been identified in prepubertal children (e.g., Fosson, Knibbs, Bryant-Waugh, & Lask, 1987; Maloney, 1990; Pugliese, Lifshitz, Fort, Recker, & Ginsberg, 1987; Pugliese, Lifshitz, Grad, Fort, & Marks-Katz, 1983; Woolston, 1983). Researchers have begun to explore at what age body-image disturbance, weight-control attempts, and loss of control over eating emerge (for review, see Thelen, Lawrence, & Powell, this volume, ch. 5). This literature suggests that girls as young as 8 years of age desire to be thinner, and some of these girls engage in occasional dieting. Use of more drastic diets and purging methods are likely to surface around the time girls reach or have passed through puberty (e.g., Rosen & Gross, 1987). Many of the prevention programs described in the literature target high school and college populations. Efforts are needed to develop interventions that are appropriate for use among younger populations.

An important but unresolved question concerns how eating-disorders prevention programs and obesity prevention programs are related. The rise of anorexic and bulimic symptoms has been attributed in part to our culture's obsession with thinness. Reports of an increase in prevalence of eating disorders, however, find their paradoxical counterpart in reports of rising rates of childhood obesity. Between the first and second Health and Nutrition Examination surveys, obesity in children increased by about 40% (Raymond, 1986). Prevalence estimates for childhood obesity range from 9% among preschoolers to 15% among high school students (for reviews, see Foreyt, 1987; Sobal & Stunkard, 1989).

These prevalence rates are important for a discussion of prevention of bulimia nervosa for several reasons. Being overweight may comprise a risk factor for the development of bulimia nervosa (Striegel-Moore, Silberstein, & Rodin, 1986). If this is true, then prevention of obesity may indirectly reduce the incidence of bulimia nervosa. Concurrent increases in eating disorders and obesity raise the question of whether these conditions share in common certain etiological factors. Brumberg (1988), for example, delineated a number of cultural changes concerning eating habits that may contribute to both bulimia nervosa and obesity: the rise in consumption of fast foods, the decline of family meals, and the failure to adjust food intake to an increasingly sedentary lifestyle, to name a few. Teaching healthy eating and exercise habits—goals central to any program aimed at prevention of obesity—may positively affect both weight and eating disorders. Alternatively, one could argue that primary prevention efforts to reduce obesity carry the risk of reinforcing our culture's obesophobic climate, which in turn has been implicated in the development of eating disorders.

Finally, the public's acceptance of prevention efforts targeting eating disorders may depend in part on how the issue of obesity is handled. Because the lay public attributes obesity to overeating and because dietary restrictions are a central component in the treatment of the morbidly obese, the public may conclude that dieting is an appropriate response to any degree of weight dissatisfaction. Such beliefs are likely to result in the rejection of a message central to the prevention of bulimia nervosa, namely, that dieting is unhealthy. Johnson (1987), for example, described how, after giving a lecture aimed at raising high school students' awareness of risks associated with dieting, a number of annoyed parents called the principal to express their disapproval with the "anti-dieting" message. This anecdote suggests that it may not be enough to target populations at risk; rather, primary prevention programs may need to encompass parents and other significant members (e.g., teachers) in the social network of the target population.

BULIMIA NERVOSA: A GENDER-LINKED DISORDER

Epidemiological studies to determine the prevalence of bulimia nervosa in samples representative of the U.S. population have not yet been published. Studies of selective samples consistently find that bulimia nervosa occurs primarily among girls and young women of middle- and upper-middle-class background. Most identified patients are white women, although underrepresentation of minority women in many studies makes it hard to evaluate the extent to which bulimia nervosa is a problem among them. Prevalence studies have confirmed clinical experience that bulimia nervosa is exceedingly rare among men (Fairburn & Beglin, 1990), prompting many researchers to limit their samples to women. In a study of first-year college students, for example, we found that, based on a self-report questionnaire, only 0.2% of men met criteria for bulimia nervosa compared with 3.8% of women (Striegel-Moore et al., 1989). Among adolescent boys, bulimia nervosa appears to be even rarer: A 1990 epidemiological study of approximately 5,600 boys and girls identified only 1 boy, compared with 23 girls, who met diagnostic criteria (Whitaker et al., 1990). (Interestingly, eating-disordered men are quite similar to eating-disordered women in their clinical presentation, in their course of illness, and on measures of personality traits and associated psychopathology. For review, see Andersen, 1990.)

The question arises, then, whether boys or men should be included as target populations in prevention programs. Some argued that men, in response to increasing cultural pressure to engage in pursuit of attractiveness, are catching up with women on measures of body-image dissatisfaction (e.g., Cash, Winstead, & Janda, 1986; Mishkind, Rodin, Silberstein, & Striegel-Moore, 1986). Furthermore, in male subcultures in which thinness is emphasized as an important component of male beauty, as in the case of the gay male subculture, weight dissatisfaction and weight-control efforts are more common than among the general male population (e.g., Silberstein, Mishkind, Striegel-Moore, Timko, & Rodin, 1989).

A few studies explored body-image satisfaction and eating behaviors in male samples. Results suggest that a considerable number of men do experience weight dissatisfaction (Cash et al., 1986; Drewnowski & Yee, 1987; Silberstein, Striegel-Moore, Timko, & Rodin, 1988) and engage in episodic overeating (Spitzer et al., 1991). Of men who are weight dissatisfied, however, half want to be heavier rather than thinner, whereas women almost uniformly desire a thinner body (Silberstein et al., 1988). Even though some men pursue weight loss, men are less likely than women to resort to extreme measures. A recent survey of adults (ages 18 to 80 years) subscribing to *Psychology Today* or *Prodigy* yields information on this contrast (R. H. Striegel-Moore & A. Kearney-Cooke, manuscript in preparation). In a sample of 2,000 men and women, 71% of women and 58% of men indicated that they had been on a weight-loss diet during the past year. Examination of specific weight-loss strategies reported by these dieters revealed that men were as likely as women to engage in caloric restriction (71%) or exercise (64%) to lose weight. (Dieters could list more than one weight-loss strategy.) Purging and use of "medicines" to regulate weight were, however, decidedly more common among women;

13% of female dieters compared with 6% of male dieters had used diuretics, laxatives, or diet pills in efforts to lose weight, and self-induced vomiting was acknowledged by 4% of the female dieters and less than 1% of the male dieters. Interestingly, almost as many male dieters (19%) as female dieters (25%) used liquid diet products during the past year. Liquid diets have been marketed heavily not only for women but also for men as exemplified by a current television campaign featuring several well-known sports coaches and the past mayor of New York City. These television commercials associated the diet product with men known for their "toughness," and the advertisement thus countered the stereotype of dieting as a feminine activity. The successful promotion of liquid diets among men suggests that men too are susceptible to social pressures to achieve thinness and that preventive efforts are needed that protect men from such pressures and educate them about health risks associated with consuming these products.

Among certain male populations, however, extreme weight-control behaviors such as purging have been identified as in the case of athletes who have to maintain a certain weight (for review, see Carlat & Camargo, 1991). Research has yet to establish whether these men also experience the profound body-image dissatisfaction and sense of loss of control over their eating commonly associated with purging behaviors in women. Furthermore, whether these male athletes evidence elevated rates of the clinical syndrome of bulimia nervosa has yet to be determined. Factor analytic studies of commonly used measures of body image and of disordered eating suggest gender differences in the meaning of the body-image construct and in the affective valence of various forms of weight control (Franzoi & Shields, 1984; Smead & Richert, 1990). Research to date may have missed certain clinically significant behaviors practiced by men to achieve a certain body ideal, such as compulsive exercising resulting in sports injuries and the presumably widespread use of steroids among male high school students.

In sum, research on gender-related differences suggests that men are highly unlikely to develop the syndrome of bulimia nervosa. Clinically significant symptoms of the disorder, however, may be present among certain subgroups of men, and these subgroups should be targeted for preventive interventions. Finally, gender bias in assessment instruments may have left unidentified behaviors that could be classified within the spectrum of symptoms of eating disorders.

ETIOLOGICAL MODELS OF BULIMIA NERVOSA

Most experts espouse multifactorial models of cause, of which several have been described in the literature (e.g., Garner & Garfinkel, 1985; Johnson & Connors, 1987; Levine, 1987; Levine & Smolak, this volume, ch. 4; Striegel-Moore et al., 1986). These models share their characterizations of bulimia nervosa as the result of a complicated interplay of cultural, social, and familial factors in concert with individual predispositions. All models imply a temporal sequence whereby sociocultural factors and familial factors set the stage for a vulnerable individual to develop the disorder in response to a precipitating event (or sequence of events).

Multifactorial models have received initial empirical support from a recent prospective study of adolescent girls that found that physical changes associated with pubertal development, weight gain in particular, predicted onset of problem eating, whereas continuation of problem eating was predicted by poor body image and psychopathology (Attie & Brooks-Gunn, 1989). Increased weight was the best predictor of eating-disorder symptoms in a prospective study of high school girls (Patton, 1988). There is accumulating evidence that loss of control over eating may emerge as a result of prolonged dieting efforts (Polivy & Herman, 1985, 1987; Wardle & Beales, 1988).

On each level of analysis—sociocultural, familial, and individual (including personality and biological characteristics)—numerous variables have been proposed to contribute to the cause of bulimia nervosa. Of these, some have been confirmed empirically to be risk factors, whereas their validation as causal factors has not yet been achieved. (Risk factors are those factors that, based on epidemiological studies, have been found to be more common among disordered individuals than among nondisordered individuals.) For example, adolescent girls in competitive environments in which thinness is emphasized have been found to be at elevated risk for disordered eating (Brooks-Gunn, Burrow, & Warren, 1988); interaction patterns and relationships in bulimic patients' families have been described to be conflict laden and dysfunctional (e.g., Dolan, Lieberman, Evans, & Lacey, 1990); and affective instability and poor impulse control are personality traits observed in many bulimic patients (Johnson & Connors, 1987). The few prospective studies undertaken to date that identify etiological variables have limited their conclusions to the cause of symptoms rather than the syndrome of bulimia nervosa (e.g., Attie & Brooks-Gunn, 1989). At present, no rigorous case-control studies have been reported that would permit testing of specific hypotheses as has been begun in depression research (e.g., Brown & Harris, 1986).

The literature on risk factors for bulimia nervosa leaves unanswered several questions of interest to our discussion. One concerns the specificity of these risk factors: Which of the risk factors are unique to bulimia nervosa and which apply more generally to health-damaging behaviors or to other forms of psychopathology? For example, among women, disordered eating appears to be related to other health-damaging behaviors such as cigarette smoking, alcohol use, and drug abuse (Killen et al., 1987; Post & Crowther, 1985). Furthermore, disordered eating shares with these health-damaging behaviors certain risk factors, such as low self-esteem and peer support for the dysfunctional behaviors (e.g., Hover & Gaffney, 1988; Kaplan, Busner, & Pollack, 1988; Kaplan,

Landa, Weinhold, & Shenker, 1984). Many primary prevention programs aimed at reducing adolescent health-risk behaviors (e.g., smoking) include components that are not substance specific or disorder specific. Rather, these components are aimed at helping the individual at risk to resist the temptation of engaging in the problematic behavior by, for example, raising self-esteem, learning how to resist peer pressure, and improving affect regulation. It remains to be examined whether such nondisorder specific components can be implemented successfully to reduce bulimic symptoms.

Another question concerns the temporal dimension of these models. Typically, body-image concerns are assumed to precede disordered eating. As Rosen (this volume, ch. 9) points out, however, support for this temporal sequence, thus far, has been derived from prospective studies predicting disordered eating from measures of body-image disturbance. A prospective exploration using measures of disordered eating to predict body-image disturbance remains to be undertaken. It has been proposed that dieting leads to an increased preoccupation with body image and that unsuccessful dieting attempts serve to intensify self-loathing and shame about one's body (Silberstein, Striegel-Moore, & Rodin, 1987). One prospective study found that dieting resulted in increased stress (Rosen, Tacy, & Howell, 1990). In a prospective study of first-year college students, worsening of disordered eating was associated with increased weight dissatisfaction, increased levels of ineffectiveness, and high levels of stress (Striegel-Moore et al., 1989). These studies suggest that disordered eating may be either the cause or the result of poor body image, low self-esteem, and high stress. Alternatively, in keeping with Rosen (this volume, ch. 9), a reciprocal causal relationship may apply. Following this argument, prevention of bulimia nervosa may not necessarily require prevention of poor body esteem as a precursor of disordered eating. Rather, interventions aimed at discouraging weight-loss efforts may be quite effective in preventing binge eating and in reducing body-image dissatisfaction.

From multifactorial models of bulimia nervosa, causal variables of differing levels of complexity (i.e., societal, familial, individual) have been delineated, leaving unanswered the question of which of the various levels should be targeted in primary prevention efforts. Most experts propose prevention programs encompassing multiple levels of interventions and seeking to alter numerous variables. A major challenge involves demonstrating the effectiveness of such multicomponent interventions. To date, only one study has been published (Shisslak, Crago, & Neal, in press) that reports evaluation data for a multilevel prevention program. Conducted at a high school, the program included eight classroom presentations on eating disorders, four educational lectures for teachers, and consultation to staff and students in cases of identified eating disorders. The evaluation focused on the comparison of students who did or did not attend class lectures and found that the program was successful in instructing students about the nature and prevalence of eating disorders.

Whether increased knowledge results in attitudinal and behavioral change remains to be examined. Furthermore, research is needed to identify what particular format and style of presentation is most effective in changing relevant attitudes and behaviors. A number of educational films on eating disorders, for example, could be compared with educational lectures such as the ones described by Shisslak and colleagues.

In the following sections, I provide suggestions for preventive interventions that fall into two categories: interventions aimed at eliminating noxious factors and interventions aimed at creating lower risk environments. The suggestions are not intended to be exhaustive; rather, I wish to highlight some issues that I consider to be of significance and that, in my opinion, have not received sufficient attention.

ELIMINATING NOXIOUS FACTORS

Highly diverse "cultural themes" (Brumberg, 1988) have been considered significant for our understanding of bulimia nervosa, ranging from Western culture's particular attitudes toward the human body (e.g., valuing mind over body) to gender-related power differences (e.g., assigning greater value to the "masculine" than the "feminine"). Here I limit myself to a discussion of two cultural trends and their implications for prevention: the promotion of an ideal look and changes in our culture's eating habits.

Promoting the Ideal Look

Of various sociocultural factors implicated in the development of bulimia nervosa, our society's preoccupation with thinness has received the most attention. The historical trend toward an increasingly thin body ideal, for example, has been well established empirically and has been considered a major contributing factor in the increase in eating disorders in women (for a review, see Gordon, 1990). In addition to widespread acceptance of extreme thinness as a desirable goal, we have witnessed a trend toward acceptance of increasingly radical means of achieving the thin ideal. Despite recognition among health professionals of potential health risks, liquid diets are marketed vigorously and successfully. Even more radical, cosmetic surgery has become increasingly popular and is performed on ever younger women. Requests for liposuction, a surgical procedure to remove subcutaneous body fat, have increased exponentially over the past decade (Pruzinsky & Edgerton, 1990). According to one report, teenagers comprise as much as 25% of the clientele receiving plastic surgery (Alexander, 1990).

One strategy to combat the relentless promotion of thinness and of the radical means to achieve it involves stricter regulation of the diet and beauty industry and, relatedly, more consistent enforcement of already existing consumer-protection laws. Individuals or companies offering weight-loss programs should be required to disclose fully to their potential customers the known risks associated with dieting. Similar to the mandatory warnings for cigarette advertisements, promotional materials for diet products and programs could carry warnings such as "The Surgeon General has found that dieting is hazardous to your health" or "Repeated cycles of dieting have been found to cause long-term fat increase." The question of whether such warnings are effective in deterring health-damaging behavior awaits empirical investigation. Furthermore, consumers need to be informed about the success rates of various forms of weight-control treatments and products, and excessive claims should be investigated. One need only scan any popular teen magazine or fashion magazine to find numerous examples of advertisements promoting products promising permanent weight loss, clearly in violation of truth-in-advertising laws.

Related to tighter regulation of the diet and beauty industry in terms of the products that are being marketed, interventions are needed that are aimed at reversing two interrelated trends: Increasingly, children are portrayed in advertisements to promote products; and increasingly, advertisement campaigns target children as consumers. As the baby boomers of the 1950s mature into the "thirty-something" generation of the 1980s, the fashion and beauty industry has adjusted its marketing campaigns to this population's changing interests and consumer behaviors. As the members of this generation have settled down and are spending less money on fashion and beauty products for themselves, adult fashion companies have responded to declining sales by entering the children's market.

Marketing experts assert that the children's market is promising for at least three reasons: Today's parents spend more money on their children than any prior generation; children and adolescents have unprecedented amounts of money at their disposal, which they spend on fashion, beauty, and entertainment or leisure products; and children have gained increasing power in a wide range of purchasing decisions made by their parents. Whether these assumptions are correct is a matter of debate and, of course, research.

In view of these beliefs, it is not surprising that during the 1980s we witnessed an explosion of marketing campaigns featuring children for the promotion of both children's products and products for the adult consumer. This trend toward an increasing use of children in advertisements is problematic in several ways. Children are encouraged to consume products that contribute directly or indirectly to the development of body-image concerns and health-risk behaviors (e.g., advertisements for children's perfumes, cosmetics, or weight-loss products). The portrayal of children in advertisements for products intended for the adult consumer, exemplified by a recent campaign featuring two young girls discussing their mothers' beauty secret (a fiber pill to maintain a thin body), may lay the foundation for later consumption of these products.

(The tobacco industry and the alcohol industry have long recognized the importance of reaching potential consumers at a young age, although regulations prohibit portrayal of children in such advertisements.)

Finally, the widespread portrayal of children in advertisements provides a strong influence shaping children's attitudes about their appearance and themselves. Advertisements typically reflect and amplify existing cultural norms and stereotypes (Sullivan & O'Connor, 1988), many of which have been linked with the rise in bulimia nervosa. Social learning theory suggests that exposure to a model more similar to the observer has a greater impact on the observer's attitudes and behaviors than exposure to a model dissimilar to the observer. Hence, children may be particularly likely to attend to and be influenced more by advertisements portraying children even when the product is not directly intended for the child (e.g., as in the case of the fiber pills).

In addition to the rising frequency of children featured in advertisements, children have increasingly become targets for marketing campaigns. Furthermore, these campaigns have been developed well beyond simple advertising (i.e., a commercial on television or an advertisement in a magazine). For example, movies promote everything from candy and soft drinks to cigarettes and alcohol. The film industry, the food industry, and the toy industry frequently work together to link their products and thus raise sales as reflected in the popular practice of fast-food chains selling action figures that represent movie characters.

Perhaps the most blatant abuse of children through advertisement campaigns involves the promotion of products in the classroom in which the authority of classroom teachers and of educational materials are used to advertise to children. Whereas psychologists argued vigorously for a reduction in the amount of time children spend in front of television, in part because of the associated exposure to commercials, advertisement agencies have given this argument a new twist. *Consumer Reports* ("Selling to Children," 1990) quotes promotional material distributed by an advertisement agency: "Kids spend 40 hours each week in the classroom, where traditional advertising cannot reach them. Now you can enter the classroom." Legislation is needed to protect children from being flooded with advertisements.

In the eating-disorder literature, relatively little attention has been devoted to questions of how food preferences and eating habits are acquired. On the cultural level, several trends are worth noting because of their likely impact on the acquisition of eating habits and of appetite control: the rise in fast foods, the rise in health foods, and the "vanishing of the family meal." There has been a rise in consumption of fast foods (e.g., Roberts, 1989), a trend that has attracted the attention of public health professionals because of its potentially detrimental impact on physical health. For example, most fast foods are high in fat content, and many fast-food combination meals exceed caloric requirements for most customers. Some experts fear that regular consumption of fast-food meals may contribute to the development of excess weight or even obesity.

During the past decade, the health and fitness movement has promoted increasing interest among consumers to improve their nutrition. The concurrent rise in the consumption of health foods and of junk foods contributes to the popular classification of foods into good foods and bad foods. Furthermore, junk foods are highly palatable, which contributes to the commonly held belief that palatable foods are unhealthy ("if it tastes good, it must be bad for you"). Hence, the dichotomy of good foods and bad foods itself is ambiguous whereby bad foods are thought to be good (i.e., taste good) whereas good foods do not enjoy a high culinary reputation. Finally, many advertisements for food products promote the notion that highly palatable foods are irresistible and thus induce loss of control over eating, resulting in the belief that junk food promotes binge eating. These themes find their expression in the thoughts and behaviors of many bulimic individuals.

Some experts believe that an increasing number of children eat a significant number of their meals without some or all of the other family members (e.g., Gordon, 1990). This trend has been attributed to a number of social changes, including the unprecedented number of mothers employed full time, a pattern of increasingly long commutes to and from work, and the rising number of single-parent households. Possible implications of the decline in family meals include that parents have less control over their children's eating habits (including children's food choice, portion control, and timing of meals) and that children have fewer opportunities to observe their parents' eating behavior.

These cultural trends cannot be changed through legislative regulation. Largely, experts have attempted to influence consumers' eating habits with community-wide or school-based intervention programs. Expanding current educational programs (which already teach children how to make healthy food choices) to include components dealing with the dichotomization of foods into good and bad and the myth of our inability to control our eating when confronted with highly palatable foods will help counter the cultural trends that may contribute to binge eating.

A major preventive strategy to eliminate noxious factors involves mass media campaigns to educate the general public about the potential dangers of certain substances (Schinke & Gilchrist, 1985) as widely practiced in the case of alcohol and drug abuse. Some experts argued that such campaigns have been highly overrated in terms of their success, although more recent campaigns often involve highly evocative imagery (e.g., an egg being fried in a pan to symbolize a brain on drugs), which may be more effective.

At present, public service announcements focus primarily on health conditions such as heart disease and obesity. There seems to be little recognition that eating patterns that may be appropriate or even essential for certain medical conditions (e.g., adhering to a strict dietary regimen for individuals with metabolic or endocrine disorders) may be inappropriate or even detrimental for healthy individuals. In 1990, for example, the American Heart Association sponsored the following public service announcement in various magazines. In the center of the page was a plate with morsels of leftover food and a fork, and a caption reading: "You are looking at a lethal weapon." In our society's climate of unquestioning acceptance of the virtues of dietary restraint, few may worry that this message fuels the already pervasive fear of obesity and the widespread belief that only overeating rather than also undereating is a common cause of ill health. Research is needed to determine what type of public service announcement can be used effectively to promote healthy eating habits without contributing to obesophobia. Research is also needed to evaluate whether public service announcements are successful in deterring consumption of liquid diet products, diet pills, and other purgatives.

In our free economy, any effort to achieve a reduction of noxious factors through legislative action (e.g., to reduce the availability or promotion of health-damaging products) will likely encounter powerful resistance by those industries benefiting from the sale of these products. Furthermore, it is unlikely that all potential causal factors can be eliminated. Therefore, additional preventive strategies are needed.

CREATING SUPPORTIVE ENVIRONMENTS

Even though the theoretical literature attributes considerable importance to social variables such as the school setting and the family climate, relatively few empirical studies have explored the role of these factors in the development of bulimia nervosa.

The college environment has been implicated in the development of bulimia nervosa because of its implicit norms around food and eating, its achievement pressures and high levels of competitiveness, and its pressures regarding dating (e.g., Dickstein, 1989). A few studies have been published that suggest that during the early stages of their college career female students undergo eating and weight-related changes that may promote or intensify body dissatisfaction and disordered eating. One study found that female college students gained significantly more weight during their first year in college than age-matched peers who did not attend college (Hovell, Mewborn, Randle, & Fowler-Johnson, 1985). Another study reported that a considerable number of men and women began dieting or binge eating during their freshman year (Striegel-Moore et al., 1989), although the specific mechanisms contributing to these changes are yet to be explored. In a prospective study of first-year college students, Crandall (1988) documented a social contagion effect for dieting and binge eating. Students who entered social groups in which dieting and binge eating were deemed acceptable were significantly more likely to report engaging in these behaviors than students who entered social groups in which these behaviors were not normative.

Completely unexplored is the question of how continued exposure to the college environment affects women's body-image concerns and eating behaviors. In my clinical experience, I have found that the prospect of college graduation, for example, contributes to a worsening of bulimic symptoms, especially among students from highly competitive campuses. College environments differ in terms of the amount of support provided for students to tackle this important life transition. To date, research has focused largely on predictors of symptom worsening. Improvement of symptoms, however, has also been recorded (Drewnowski et al., 1988; Striegel-Moore et al., 1989; Yager, Landsverly, & Edelstein, 1987), although predictors of symptom improvement are not yet clearly delineated.

Several of the prevention programs described in the literature contain components aimed at creating environments that facilitate high body esteem and healthy eating habits, mostly focusing on high school and college settings. Interventions range from peer-support programs to consultation with sports coaches (e.g., Levine, 1987; Whitacker & Davis, 1990). However, a major emphasis of these programs involves attempts to change individuals at risk for developing bulimia nervosa, whereas efforts to change the particular environment appear to play a minor role.

FAMILY ENVIRONMENT

A growing literature speaks to the importance of family factors in the development of disordered eating (e.g., Strober & Humphrey, 1987; Wonderlich, this volume, ch. 6). A controlled family study of anorexia nervosa (Strober, Morell, Burroughs, Salkin, & Jacobs, 1985) documented familial aggregation of the disorder (i.e., anorexia probands were more likely to have other female relatives with an eating disorder than were control subjects) and found that the aggregation was by subtype of anorexia nervosa (e.g., among the female relatives of binge-eating anorexics, binge eating was more common than among the female relatives of restricting anorexics). The mechanisms underlying this aggregation phenomenon remain to be explored.

Several familial factors deserve further attention in explanations of the development of disordered eating including parents' own body image and eating behavior, family rules and practices regarding food and eating, and parents' role as mediators and interpreters of their children's larger social content. Each of these factors is considered briefly.

Several studies found relationships between mothers' body-image concerns and eating behaviors and their daughters' dieting behaviors (Attie & Brooks-Gunn, 1989; Drewnowski & Yee, 1987; R. H. Striegel-Moore & A. Kearney-Cooke, manuscript in preparation). The transmission of body-image dissatisfaction and disordered eating may occur though various mechanisms, including modeling, instruction, and instrumental learning. Most girls are growing up with female role models who express body-image dissatisfaction. One survey reported, for example, that only 13% of respondents thought their mothers were satisfied with their bodies (Wooley & Wooley, 1984). Parents who dieted themselves were found to be more likely to encourage dieting behavior in their children than were parents who did not diet (R. H. Striegel-Moore & A. Kearney-Cooke, manuscript in preparation). Too little is known about the potential role of fathers in the development of body-image concerns and disordered eating in young girls. A weight-preoccupied father, for example, may contribute to an intensification of pressures toward thinness by being an additional role model for weight dissatisfaction and for weight-control strategies and by making weight a more salient issue for everyone in the family. Primary prevention efforts need to include components aimed at raising parents' consciousness of how their own body-image concerns and related behaviors affect their children's body image and eating behaviors.

Relatively few empirical data exist that help explain how eating habits are acquired in the family context. An important question for our discussion is, for example, how children learn self-regulatory skills regarding food and eating. It has been speculated that parents resort to a more controlling style of parenting around issues deemed highly important to the parents. Many parents consider their children's weight and appearance important (A. Kearney-Cooke & R. H. Striegel-Moore, manuscript in preparation). Parents of overweight daughters are likely to take control over the amount and types of food their daughters are permitted to eat (Costanzo & Woody, 1985). Imposing such external controls may minimize the child's opportunities for learning self-control skills regarding food intake. Consistent with this argument, maintenance of weight loss in obese children was found directly related to the degree of self-control of the child's eating behavior (Cohen, Gelfand, Dodd, Jensen, & Turner, 1980). Research is needed to understand more fully how family rules and practices regarding food and eating contribute to the development of eating disorders. Parents may benefit from learning how to facilitate self-regulatory skills around food and eating in their children.

Another way in which parents influence their children's body image and related behaviors is through the role of mediator and interpreter of the children's larger social context. Families differ in the degree to which they endorse the prevailing cultural norms. Some families may amplify cultural norms that place a child at risk for the development of bulimia nervosa; others may downplay the importance of these norms. The literature on the influence of television on children's behavior, aggressive behavior in particular, suggests that parents can attenuate the impact of television viewing by watching and then discussing the programs with their children. By being aware of what their children are watching, parents gain an opportunity to help their children make sense and evaluate the images and messages to which they are being exposed. Similarly, parents can help their children deal with social pressures to achieve an ideal look by being aware of the various ways in which the attractiveness stereotype is reinforced, by helping their children put attractiveness into perspective, and by supporting development of body esteem that is not limited to physical appearance.

CONCLUSION

Multifactorial models of bulimia nervosa suggest that primary prevention needs to encompass multiple levels of intervention and, within each level, to target numerous variables. This poses enormous challenges in terms of implementation and evaluation. Several comprehensive prevention programs have been described in the literature. Research is now needed to evaluate the effectiveness of these programs. This chapter focused on selected themes and issues that have received relatively little attention to date yet that promise fruitful avenues for research and intervention.

REFERENCES

Alexander, S. (1990, September). Egged on by moms, many teenagers get plastic surgery. *The Wall Street Journal*, p. A1-2, p. A16.

American Psychiatric Association. (1980). *Diagnostic and statistical manual of mental disorders* (3rd ed.). Washington, DC: Author.

American Psychiatric Association. (1987). *Diagnostic and statistical manual of mental disorders* (3rd ed., rev.). Washington, DC: Author.

Andersen, A. E. (1990). *Males with eating disorders*. New York: Brunner/ Mazel.

Attie, J., & Brooks-Gunn, J. (1989). Development of eating problems in adolescent girls: A longitudinal study. *Developmental Psychology, 25,* 70–79.

Boskind-Lodahl, M. (1976). Cinderella's stepsisters: A feminist perspective on anorexia nervosa and bulimia. *Signs, 2,* 342–356.

Brooks-Gunn, J., Burrow, C., & Warren, M. P. (1988). Attitudes towards eating and body weight in different groups on female adolescent athletes. *International Journal of Eating Disorders, 7,* 749–757.

Brown, G. W., & Harris, T. O. (1986). Depression. In H. Katschnig (Ed.), *Life events and psychiatric disorders* (pp. 107–187). Cambridge, England: Cambridge University Press.

Brumberg, J. J. (1988). *Fasting girls*. Cambridge, MA: Harvard University Press.

Bunnell, D. W., Shenker, I. R., Nussbaum, M. P., Jacobson, M. S., & Cooper, P. (1990). Subclinical versus formal eating disorders: Differentiating psychological features. *International Journal of Eating Disorders, 9,* 357–362.

Carlat, D. J., & Camargo, C. A. (1991). Review of bulimia nervosa in males. *American Journal of Psychiatry, 148,* 831–843.

Cash, T. F., Winstead, B. A., & Janda, L. H. (1986, April). The great American shape-up. *Psychology Today,* pp. 30–37.

Clark, L. V., Levine, M. P., & Kinney, N. E. (1988–1989). A multifaceted and integrated approach to the prevention, identification, and treatment of bulimia on college campuses. *Journal of College Student Psychotherapy, 3,* 257–298.

Cohen, E., Gelfand, D., Dodd, D., Jensen, J., & Furner, C. (1980). Self-control practices associated with weight loss maintenance in children adolescents. *Behavior Therapy, 11,* 26–87.

Costanzo, P. R., & Woody, E. Z. (1985). Domain specific parenting styles and their impact on the child's development of particular deviance: The examples of obesity proneness. *Journal of Social and Clinical Psychology, 3,* 425–445.

Crandall, C. S. (1988). The social contagion of binge eating. *Journal of Personality and Social Psychology, 55,* 588–589.

Crisp, A. H. (1988). Some possible approaches to prevention of eating and body weight/shape disorders, with particular reference to anorexia nervosa. *International Journal of Eating Disorders, 7,* 1–17.

Crowther, J. H., & Chernyk, B. (1986). Bulimia and binge eating in adolescent females: A comparison. *Addictive Behaviors, 11,* 415–424.

Dickstein, L. J. (1989). Current college environments: Do these communities facilitate and foster bulimia in vulnerable students? In L. C. Whitacker & W. N. Davis (Eds.), *The bulimic college student* (pp. 107–134). New York: Haworth.

Dolan, B. M., Lieberman, S., Evans, C., & Lacey, J. H. (1990). Family features associated with normal body weight bulimia. *International Journal of Eating Disorders, 9,* 639–647.

Drewnowski, A., Hopkins, S. A., & Kessler, R. C. (1988). The prevalence of bulimia nervosa in the U.S. college population. *American Journal of Public Health, 78,* 1322–1325.

Drewnowski, A., & Yee, D. K. (1987). Men and body image: Are males satisfied with their body weight? *Psychosomatic Medicine, 49,* 626–634.

Fairburn, C. G., Agras, W. S., & Wilson, G. T. (in press). The research on the treatment of bulimia nervosa: Practical and theoretical implications. In G. H. Anderson & S. H. Kennedy (Eds.), *The biology of feast and famine: Relevance to eating disorders.* New York: Academic Press.

Fairburn, C. G., & Beglin, S. J. (1990). Studies of the epidemiology of bulimia nervosa. *American Journal of Psychiatry, 147,* 401–408.

Foreyt, J. P. (1987). Issues in the assessment and treatment of obesity. *Journal of Consulting and Clinical Psychology, 55,* 677–684.

Fosson, A., Knibbs, J., Bryant-Waugh, R., & Lask, B. (1987). Early onset anorexia nervosa. *Archives of Disease in Childhood, 62,* 114–118.

Franzoi, S. L., & Shields, S. A. (1984). The Body Esteem Scale: Multidimensional structure and sex differences in a college population. *Journal of Personality Assessment, 48,* 173–178.

Garner, D. M., & Garfinkel, P. E. (Eds.). (1985). *Handbook of psychotherapy for anorexia nervosa and bulimia.* New York: Guilford Press.

Gordon, R. A. (1990). *Anorexia and bulimia: Anatomy of a social epidemic.* Cambridge, MA: Basil Blackwell.

Hotelling, K. (1988–1989). A model for addressing the problem of bulimia on college campuses. *Journal of College Student Psychotherapy, 3,* 241–255.

Hovell, M. F., Mewborn, C. R., Randle, Y., & Fowler-Johnson, S. (1985). Risk of excess weight gain in university women: A three-year community controlled analysis. *Addictive Behaviors, 10,* 15–28.

Hover, S. J., & Gaffney, L. R. (1988). Factors associated with smoking behavior in adolescent girls. *Addictive Behaviors, 13,* 139–145.

Johnson, C. (1987, September). *The treatment of bulimia nervosa* (training workshop). Newington, CT: Newington Children's Hospital.

Johnson, C., & Connors, M. (1987). *The etiology and treatment of bulimia nervosa: A biopsychosocial perspective.* New York: Basic Books.

Kaplan, S. L., Busner, J., & Pollack, S. (1988). Perceived weight, actual weight, and depressive symptoms in a general adolescent sample. *International Journal of Eating Disorders, 7,* 107–113.

Kaplan, S. L., Landa, B., Weinhold, C., & Shenker, I. R. (1984). Adverse health behaviors and depressive symptomatology in adolescents. *Journal of the American Academy of Child Psychiatry, 23,* 595–601.

Killen, J. D., Taylor, C. B., Telch, M. J., Saylor, K. E., Maron, D. J., & Robinson, T. N. (1987). Evidence for an alcohol-stress link among normal weight adolescents reporting purging behavior. *International Journal of Eating Disorders, 6,* 349–356.

Lancelot, C., Brooks-Gunn, J., Warren, M. P., & Newman, D. L. (1991). Comparison of DSM–III and DSM–III–R bulimia nervosa classifications for psychopathology and other eating behaviors. *International Journal of Eating Disorders, 10,* 57–66.

Levine, M. P. (1987). *Student eating disorders: Anorexia nervosa and bulimia.* Washington, DC: National Educational Association.

Maloney, M. J. (1990, April). *Children's eating attitudes and dieting behaviors.* Paper presented at the 4th International Conference on Eating Disorders, New York.

Mishkind, M., Rodin, J., Silberstein, L. R., & Striegel-Moore, R. H. (1986). The embodiment of masculinity: Cultural, psychological, and behavioral dimensions. *American Behavioral Scientist, 29,* 545–562.

Mitchell, J. E. (190). *Bulimia nervosa.* Minneapolis: University of Minnesota Press.

Palmer, R. L. (1979). The dietary chaos syndrome: A useful new term? *British Journal of Medical Psychology, 52,* 187–190.

Patton, G. C. (1988). The spectrum of eating disorder in adolescence. *Journal of Psychosomatic Research, 32,* 579–584.

Polivy, J., & Herman, C. P. (1985). Dieting and bingeing: A causal analysis. *American Psychologist, 40,* 193–201.

Polivy, J., & Herman, C. P. (1987). Diagnosis and treatment of normal eating. *Journal of Consulting and Clinical Psychology, 55,* 635–644.

Post, G., & Crowther, J. H. (1985). Variables that discriminate bulimic from non-bulimic adolescent females. *Journal of Youth and Adolescence, 14,* 85–98.

Pruzinsky, T., & Edgerton, M. T. (1990). Body-image change in cosmetic plastic surgery. In T. F. Cash & T. Pruzinsky (Eds.), *Body images: Development, deviance, and change* (pp. 217–236). New York: Guilford Press.

Pugliese, M., Lifshitz, F., Fort, P., Recker, B., & Ginsberg, L. (1987). Pituitary-hypothalamic response in adolescents with growth failure due to fear of obesity. *Journal of the American College of Nutrition, 6,* 113–120.

Pugliese, M., Lifshitz, F., Grad, G., Fort, P., & Marks-Katz, M. (1983). Fear of obesity: A cause of short stature and delayed puberty. *New England Journal of Medicine, 309,* 513–518.

Raymond, C. A. (1986). Biology, culture, and dietary changes conspire to increase incidence of obesity. *Journal of the American Medical Association, 256,* 2157–2158.

Roberts, C. (1989). Sounding board: Fast-food fare. Consumer guidelines. *New England Journal of Medicine, 321,* 752–755.

Rodin, J., Silberstein, L. R., & Striegel-Moore, R. H. (1985). Women and weight: A normative discontent. In T. B. Sonderegger (Ed.), *Nebraska symposium on motivation: Vol. 32. Psychology and gender* (pp. 267–307). Lincoln: University of Nebraska Press.

Rosen, J., & Gross, J. (1987). Prevalence of weight reducing and weight gaining in adolescent girls and boys. *Health Psychology, 6,* 131–147.

Rosen, J., Tacy, B., & Howell, D. (1990). Life stress, psychological symptoms, and weight reducing behavior in adolescent girls: A prospective analysis. *International Journal of Eating Disorders, 9,* 17–26.

Schinke, S. P., & Gilchrist, L. D. (1985). Preventing substance abuse with children and adolescents. *Journal of Consulting and Clinical Psychology, 53,* 596–602.

Selling to Children. (1990, August). *Consumer Reports,* pp. 518–521.

Sesan, R. (1988–1989). Peer education: A creative resource for the eating disordered college student. *Journal of College Student Psychotherapy, 3,* 221–240.

Sesan, R. (1989). Eating disorders and female athletes: A three-level intervention program. *Journal of College Student Development, 30,* 568–570.

Shisslak, C. M., Crago, M., & Neal, M. E. (in press). Prevention of eating disorders among adolescents. *Journal of Health Promotion.*

Shisslak, C. M., Crago, M., Neal, M. E., & Swain, B. (1987). Primary prevention of eating disorders. *Journal of Consulting and Clinical Psychology, 55,* 660–667.

Silberstein, L. R., Mishkind, M., Striegel-Moore, R. H., Timko, C., & Rodin, J. (1989). Men and their bodies: A comparison of homosexual and heterosexual men. *Psychosomatic Medicine, 51,* 337–346.

Silberstein, L. R., Striegel-Moore, R. H., & Rodin, J. (1987). Feeling fat: A woman's shame. In H. Lewis (Ed.), *The role of shame in symptom formation* (pp. 89–108). Hillsdale, NJ: Erlbaum.

Silberstein, L. R., Striegel-Moore, R. H., Timko, C., & Rodin, J. (1988). Behavioral and psychological implications of body image dissatisfaction: Do men and women differ? *Sex Roles, 19,* 219–232.

Smead, V. S. (1985). Considerations prior to establishing preventive interventions for eating disorders. *Ontario Psychologist, 17,* 12–17.

Smead, V. S., & Richert, A. J. (1990). Eating attitude test factors in an unselected undergraduate population. *International Journal of Eating Disorders, 9,* 211–215.

Sobal, J., & Stunkard, A. J. (1989). Socioeconomic status and obesity: A review of the literature. *Psychological Bulletin, 105,* 260–275.

Spitzer, R. L., Devlin, M., Walsh, T. B., Hasin, D., Wing, R., Marcus, M., Stunkard, A., Wadden, T., Yanovski, S., Agras, S., Mitchell, J., & Nonas, C. (1991). *Binge eating disorder: A multisite field trial of the diagnostic criteria.* Unpublished paper, Biometrics Research Department, 722 West 168th Street, New York, NY 10032.

Striegel-Moore, R. H. (1989). Prävention der Bulimia nervosa. In A. Kammerer & B. Klingensport (Eds.), *Bulimie: Zum Verstaendnis einer geschlechts-spezifischen Esstoerung* (pp. 138–149). Stuttgart: Kohlhammer.

Striegel-Moore, R. H., & Silberstein, L. R. (1989). Early identification of bulimia nervosa. In W. Johnston (Ed.), *Advances in eating disorders, Vol. II. Bulimia nervosa: Conceptualization, assessment, and treatment* (pp. 267–281). Greenwich, CT: JAI Press.

Striegel-Moore, R. H., Silberstein, L. R., Frensch, P., & Rodin, J. (1989). A prospective study of disordered eating among college students. *International Journal of Eating Disorders, 8,* 499–509.

Striegel-Moore, R. H., Silberstein, L. R., & Rodin, J. (1986). Toward an understanding of risk factors for bulimia. *American Psychologist, 41,* 246–263.

Strober, M., & Humphrey, L. L. (1987). Familial contributions to the etiology and course of anorexia nervosa and bulimia. *Journal of Consulting and Clinical Psychology, 55,* 654–659.

Strober, M., Morrell, W., Burroughs, J., Salkin, B., & Jacobs, C. (1985). A controlled family study of anorexia nervosa. *Journal of Psychiatric Research, 19,* 239–246.

Sullivan, G. L., & O'Connor, P. J. (1988). Women's role portrayals in magazine advertising. *Sex Roles, 18,* 181–188.

Szmukler, G. I. (1985). The epidemiology of anorexia nervosa and bulimia nervosa. *Journal of Psychiatric Research, 19,* 143–153.

Wardle, J., & Beales, S. (1988). Control and loss of control over eating: An experimental investigation. *Journal of Abnormal Psychology, 97,* 35–40.

Whitacker, L. C., & Davis, W. N. (Eds.). (1990). *The bulimic college student.* New York: Haworth.

Whitaker, A., Johnson, J., Schaffer, D., Rappaport, J. L., Kalikow, K., Walsh, B. J., Davies, M., Braiman, S., & Dolinsky, A. (1990). Uncommon troubles in young people. *Archives of General Psychiatry, 47,* 487–496.

Wooley, S. C., & Wooley, O. W. (1984, February). Feeling fat in a thin society. *Glamour,* pp. 190, 252.

Woolston, J. (1983). Eating disorders in infancy and early childhood. *Journal of the American Academy of Child Psychiatry, 22,* 114–121.

Yager, J., Landsverk, J., & Edelstein, C. K. (1987). A 20-month follow-up study of 628 women with eating disorders. I: Course and severity. *American Journal of Psychiatry, 144,* 1172–1177.

13

ETIOLOGY OF BULIMIA NERVOSA: CONCEPTUAL, RESEARCH, AND MEASUREMENT ISSUES

Janis H. Crowther
Kent State University

J. Scott Mizes
MetroHealth Medical Center

Given that bulimia nervosa was not formally recognized as a diagnostic category until 1980 (American Psychiatric Association [APA], 1980), it is not surprising that research has only recently focused on the etiology of this eating disorder. Although its cause is generally recognized to be complex, considerable speculation remains regarding the relative impact and interaction of various individual, familial, and sociocultural factors. Early chapters in this volume address the role of puberty, with its inherent physiological and psychological changes, as a critical developmental transition point for the development of eating problems and eating disorders. As well, the individual and familial factors that may increase an individual's vulnerability during this time period are considered. Later chapters focus more specifically on individual psychological characteristics that may increase the likelihood that an adolescent girl will develop subsequent eating disturbance. Across the chapters, there is variability as to whether the authors discuss characteristics that distinguish bulimic versus non-eating-disordered populations as opposed to bulimic versus subclinical eating-disordered populations. As a result, authors differ on the etiological significance they ascribe to those factors that predict maladaptive eating attitudes and behaviors and whether these attitudes and behaviors are conceptualized as precursors to the clinically more severe eating pathology. Underlying all of these chapters is a growing recognition of the need for additional research regarding the cause of bulimia nervosa.

Although it was the intent of this volume to highlight individual and familial factors, it was not its intent to neglect the role of sociocultural factors. Indeed, it was widely recognized within the chapters of this volume and among the participants at the Kent Psychology Forum that sociocultural pressures toward extreme thinness play an important role in the cause of bulimia nervosa. However, for us the question became, "If adolescent and young adult women are exposed to the same sociocultural pressures, what individual and familial factors increase their vulnerability toward developing bulimia nervosa? In addition, how does this occur and how should we investigate it?" To this end, we address the following issues. First, we discuss the heterogeneity of bulimia nervosa and its etiological implications. Second, we raise several research issues including the need for prospective research and psychometrically sound measurement instruments.

In developing this chapter, we have drawn extensively from the literature on bulimia nervosa, from the chapters in this volume, and from the stimulating discussions among the chapters' authors and other invited guests at the 1990 Kent Psychology Forum. Although we have done the actual writing of this chapter, the issues that we raise are the results of collaborative efforts by forum participants.

HETEROGENEITY OF BULIMIA NERVOSA

Early models of bulimia presented a monolithic view of the disorder (Hudson, Wentworth, Hudson, & Pope, 1985; W. G. Johnson & Brief, 1983; Mizes, 1985) focusing primarily on normal-weight women who binged and purged. However, increasing evidence exists that meaningful subclassifications may be present within the syndrome of bulimia nervosa. Clearly, identification of these subclassifications would facilitate greater understanding of the variability in bulimics' clinical presentation and the potential etiological pathways to this disorder. To provide a foundation for understanding the heterogeneity within the syndrome of bulimia nervosa, we first discuss bulimia nervosa within the context of its relationships to anorexia nervosa, binge eating, and subclinical eating disturbances (including weight preoccupation, body dissatisfaction, and chronic dieting). Of interest here are the similarities and differences among these groups with respect to symptom presentation, maladaptive eating and weight-related attitudes, and global psychopathology. Second, we focus on two additional dimensions that appear relevant to an understanding of the heterogeneity of bulimia nervosa: the presence or absence of personality disorder with particular attention to borderline personality disorder and the presence or absence of affective disorder.

HETEROGENEITY OF EATING DISORDERS: THE "CONTINUUM NOTION" REVISITED

Since Nylander (1971) first proposed the "continuum hypothesis," many researchers raised questions regarding the continuity or discontinuity of dieting, subclinical eating disturbances, and frank eating disorders, the latter including bulimia nervosa and anorexia nervosa (e.g., Button & Whitehouse, 1981; Garner, Olmstead, & Garfinkel, 1983; Polivy & Herman, 1987; Striegel-Moore, Silberstein, & Rodin, 1986). Typically, comparisons are drawn between these groups on similarities and differences in symptom presentation, eating-related pathology, and related psychopathology.

Although both bulimia nervosa and anorexia nervosa are considered clinical eating disorders, there has long been a conceptual blurring between bulimia nervosa and anorexia nervosa in terms of the symptom presentation and related psychopathology of the two disorders (e.g., see Crowther, Wolf, & Sherwood, this volume, ch. 1). Although some argued that bulimia nervosa and anorexia nervosa should be viewed on a continuum, sharing the common pathology of fear of weight gain (Fairburn & Garner, 1986), the question remains regarding whether a meaningful demarcation point on the continuum exists. Historically, the demarcation has focused on the absence or presence of extremely low weight and amenorrhea, primarily because of the medical complications and risk of mortality associated with anorexia nervosa.

However, in terms of related psychopathology, growing evidence exists that on some dimensions distinctions in symptom presentations are better achieved based on the presence or absence of binge eating and purging rather than normal or underweight status. Growing evidence supports the conclusion that bulimics and bulimic anorexics are more similar to each other than they are to restricting anorexics on variables such as eating attitudes, personality characteristics, impulse control problems, and familial psychopathology (e.g., Garner, Garfinkel, & O'Shaughnessy, 1985; Johnson & Wonderlich, this volume, ch. 10; Wonderlich, this volume, ch. 6). For example, with respect to associated personality disturbance, the bulimic groups appear to have more dramatic-erratic personality diagnoses, whereas anorexics have more anxious-fearful personality styles. Initial research also suggests that the families of anorexics are more enmeshed and overprotective, whereas the families of the two bulimic groups experience more conflict, hostility, disorganization, and emotional isolation (Strober & Humphrey, 1987).

The relationship between normal-weight bulimia nervosa and obesity has received less research attention. In comparing bulimics with overweight persons, a distinction must be drawn between comparisons to the obese versus obese binge eaters. It appears that normal-weight bulimics have greater overall psychopathology, both global and eating disorder specific, than obese persons (Prather & Williamson, 1988; Williamson, Kelley, Davis, Ruggiero, & Blouin, 1985). Similarly, obese binge eaters appear to have greater restraint, more global psychopathology, and more depressive disorders than do the obese (Marcus, Wing, & Hopkins, 1988; Marcus et al., 1990). Because both normal-weight bulimics and obese binge eaters share the recurrent episodes of binge eating and appear to have more pathology than the obese control groups, one could infer the potential for significant similarities in the psychopathology of normal-weight bulimics and obese binge eaters. However, a study by Lowe and Caputo (1991) suggests that obese binge eaters and the obese are best discriminated by eating disorder rather than global psychopathology; therefore, the global psychopathology of obese binge eaters may be secondary to the primary eating pathology. Unfortunately, there have not been any direct comparisons of bulimia nervosa patients and obese binge eaters (e.g., Marcus & Wing, 1987). Until additional research is conducted, it is important to recognize that there may be important quantitative and qualitative differences in these two groups as well.

Finally, a growing body of research compared bulimics with individuals with various forms of subclinical eating disturbances, including restrained eaters, chronic dieters, or those who are preoccupied and dissatisfied with their weight and appearance. In an early analysis of available research, Polivy and Herman (1987) concluded that normal dieters may resemble individuals with eating disorders on their drive for thinness, concern about weight and dieting, body-image dissatisfaction, and the behavioral manifestations of bulimia (including bingeing with or without purging). However, dieters do not necessarily exhibit the perceptual disturbances in body image and interoceptive awareness and the pervasive sense of ineffectiveness, interpersonal distrust, and low self-esteem that characterize clinical samples of bulimics and anorexics (e.g., Bruch, 1973; Selvini-Palazzoli, 1978). These conclusions were largely based on cross-sectional research using the Eating Disorders Inventory (e.g., Garner, Olmstead, & Polivy, 1983; Garner, Olmstead, Polivy, & Garfinkel, 1984; Olmstead & Garner, 1986).

Several more recent studies compared bulimics with restrained eaters, chronic dieters, and non-eating-disordered comparison groups on the Eating Disorders Inventory and other measures as well. Research has clearly shown that bulimics can be distinguished from nonpsychiatrically impaired normals (Mizes, 1988) and non-eating-disordered psychiatric patients (Mizes, 1990) on certain food and weight-related attitudes. Research also found that although the scores of bulimics on diverse measures of body image were significantly more pathological than those of nonrestrained controls, their scores resembled those of restrained eaters (Lindholm & Wilson, 1988). Rossiter, Wilson, and Goldstein (1989) found that, although bulimic subjects did not differ significantly from nonbulimic restrained eaters on measures of fear of weight gain, drive for thinness, body dissatisfaction, and dietary restraint, bulimic subjects had significantly more bulimic symptomatology and disinhibited eating and reported more severe depression, ineffectiveness, lack of interoceptive awareness, and global psychological distress than restrained eaters. Wilson and Smith (1989) used the Eating Disorder Examination (Cooper & Fairburn, 1987) to compare bulimics and restrained eaters. In contrast to previous research, they found that although both groups had similar levels of dietary restraint bulimic patients could be distinguished from this subclinical group of restrained eaters in a greater intensity of their shape, weight, and eating-related concerns.

One other study deserves mention. In a comparison of clinical and subclinical bulimics, Bunnell and colleagues (Bunnell, Shenker, Nussbaum, Jacobson, & Cooper, 1990) found that the two groups differed on only one subscale— Ineffectiveness—of the Eating Disorders Inventory (EDI), suggesting much similarity in eating-related pathology. However, consistent with previous research (e.g., Dykens & Gerrard, 1986; Rossiter et al., 1989), they found that the clinical bulimics scored much higher on several dimensions of global psychopathology. Unfortunately, this study did not compare subclinical bulimics to clinical bulimics with and without personality disorders. It is conceivable that such a comparison might reveal substantial similarities between subclinical and nonpersonality disorder clinical bulimics but wide differences compared with personality disorder bulimics. Also this study appeared to include in the subclinical group persons who barely missed the *Diagnostic and Statistical Manual of Mental Disorders* (third edition, revised; *DSM-III-R)* criteria for bulimia nervosa, which may result in a less dramatic comparison than a comparison group of "garden-variety" normal-weight binge eaters or frequent dieters. Finally, one must be cautious in interpreting the lack of differences in eating-related pathology because the sample size was small.

Taken together, this body of research suggests considerable heterogeneity in the symptom presentation of eating disorders in general. Although persons may be distributed on a continuum resulting in normal, subclinical, and, ultimately, clinically disturbed eating attitudes and behaviors, the essential argument offered here is that an understanding of the heterogeneity of eating disorders is best brought into focus by examining psychological dimensions including eating-related and global psychopathology, with less emphasis on weight status or presence or absence of bingeing or purging.

We are aware of only one study using cluster analytic techniques that addresses this question. Welch, Hall, and Renner (1990) were able to separate a sample of restricting anorexics, bulimic anorexics, and bulimics into two meaningful clusters. Notably, the two clusters differed in eating-related and global psychopathology; the more severe group exhibited substantially greater drive for thinness, body dissatisfaction, bulimic symptomatology, depression, and secondary pathology on the relevant scales of the EDI (e.g., Interpersonal Distrust, Perfectionism, and so on). The two clusters did not differ significantly on dimensions such as weight, percentage of ideal weight, length of illness, or history of anorexia or obesity. The authors originally hypothesized that the clusters would separate on the basis of restricting versus bulimic behaviors; however, this hypothesis was only partially supported. Although the restricting anorexics were approximately equally divided among the two clusters, two thirds of the bulimics and all but one of the bulimic anorexics were in the more severe cluster. In our opinion, this study is consistent with our contention that the heterogeneity of eating disorders can be viewed along psychological continua as well as the observations that more pathology tends to be associated (although not exclusively so) with the bulimic forms of eating disorders.

HETEROGENEITY OF BULIMIA NERVOSA: ASSOCIATED PSYCHOPATHOLOGY

Within the syndrome of bulimia nervosa, researchers began to investigate the co-occurrence of personality disorders and affective disorders. Growing evidence suggests that bulimia nervosa occurs with and without concurrent personality disorder and that there may be significant differences between the groups in terms of cause and prognosis (e.g., Johnson & Wonderlich, this volume, ch. 10). For example, initial research suggests that family pathology may be more associated with concurrent personality disturbance rather than eating pathology per se. In their sample of bulimics, Head and Williamson (1990) found that family pathology was associated with neuroticism and introversion but not measures of eating pathology. Several studies suggested that although borderline and nonborderline bulimics do not differ in severity of eating pathology, borderline bulimics have evidence of family pathology, which may have etiological significance (Johnson, Tobin, & Enright, 1989; Wonderlich, this volume, ch. 6; Wonderlich & Swift, 1990). Finally, borderline bulimics appear to have a much poorer prognosis than nonborderline bulimics (Garner et al., 1990; Johnson, Tobin, & Dennis, 1990).

Although historically there has been much debate on the role of depression in bulimia nervosa, it appears that approximately half of some bulimic samples suffer some mild dysphoria, whereas one quarter experience significant depression (Lee, Rush, & Mitchell, 1985; Wilson & Lindholm, 1987). A review of the research literature strongly suggests that although dysphoria may be a consequence of the disruption of bingeing and purging (Hinz & Williamson, 1987), depression may be due to the co-occurrence of bulimia nervosa and affective disorder. The presence of depression has not been found to have prognostic significance.

However, different etiological pathways may exist when affective disorder is present. Although there is evidence of high rates of affective disorder in the families of bulimics, research suggests that the bulimics with concurrent affective disorder have a family history of depression (Wilson & Lindholm, 1987). In addition to family history of depression, some research shows that depressed bulimics have more global family disruption than nondepressed bulimics (Blouin, Zuro, & Blouin, 1990). As with personality disorder, bulimics with and without a family history of depression have essentially equivalent eating pathology (Wilson & Lindholm, 1987).

CONCEPTUAL MODEL FOR UNDERSTANDING THE HETEROGENEITY OF BULIMIA NERVOSA

We have argued that there is heterogeneity not only among eating disorders in general but also among the syndrome of bulimia nervosa as well. Although the conceptual model we are proposing here may be relevant for understanding the heterogeneity among eating disorders generally, we limit our discussion here to bulimia nervosa. This is in part because the focus of the present volume is bulimia nervosa but also because it helps simplify the variables to be considered. It is hypothesized that two intersecting psychological continua—reflecting eating pathology and global psychopathology—provide a means for conceptualizing the heterogeneity of bulimia nervosa. Progression along the eating-pathology continuum moves from normal adjustment to various forms of subclinical eating disturbance to clinical bulimia nervosa (Figure 1). The second continuum represents a progression along other dimensions of psychopathology; at present the most relevant are personality and affective disorders. Progression along this continuum moves from normal to subclinical to clinical forms of the various disorders.

For the current discussion, two "clusters" emerge as significant. The first cluster, represented in the upper left quadrant of the model, represents a group of bulimics uncomplicated by other forms of psychopathology. Some from this

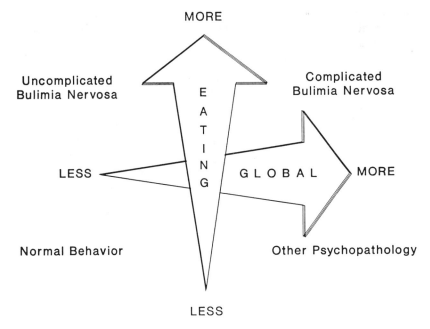

FIGURE 1 A conceptual model of the influence of eating specific and global pathology in the heterogeneity of bulimia nervosa.

group may present for treatment, and among all treatment-seeking bulimics, this group may be the most responsive to therapy. In particular, they may be maximally responsive to short-term, focused therapy. The second cluster, represented in the upper right quadrant, represents those bulimics who have moved to the pathological ends of both continua and reflects those cases of bulimia nervosa complicated by other forms of psychopathology. This group is likely to predominate among those bulimics presenting for treatment because they will likely seek help in response to the distress of the other psychopathology as much if not more than that of their eating pathology. It is likely that this complicated bulimia nervosa group has the poorest prognosis in magnitude with the prognosis of the complicating condition.

A few caveats merit discussion. First, this model does not suggest that uncomplicated bulimia nervosa has no psychological sequelae. They are likely to be present but are probably consequences of the primary eating disorder (e.g., secondary dysphoria). Second, the model does not suggest that the influence of the two variables is always purely orthogonal. At times, this may be the situation because a complicated case of bulimia nervosa may represent a co-occurrence of psychopathologies that add to one another. At other times, there may be a dynamic interaction between bulimia nervosa and other psychopathology such that a particularly severe symptom presentation results. This may be the case with bulimic borderlines in whom the unstable self-structure, affective instability, and impulsiveness of borderline personality disorder may interact synergistically with the fundamental disruption in self-structure (i.e., weight as the basis of self-esteem) characteristic of bulimia nervosa.

Viewing bulimia nervosa as a heterogeneous disorder influenced by two pathological continua also provides a heuristic model for examination of multiple etiological pathways. Thus, for example, the eating pathology continuum may point more toward the etiological roles of societal pressures or adolescent developmental concerns such as pubertal weight gain that coincides with greater concerns about social acceptance and dating (e.g., Levine & Smolak, this volume, ch. 4). The global psychopathology continuum may highlight etiological influences such as family psychopathology or affective instability (e.g., Johnson & Connors, 1987; Johnson & Wonderlich, this volume, ch. 10; Wonderlich, this volume, ch. 6). In short, by viewing bulimia nervosa as multifaceted, one can adopt a multifaceted view of the etiological pathways to the disorder.

NEED FOR PROSPECTIVE RESEARCH

Despite the difficulty of conducting prospective research, we contend that additional prospective research is needed to answer adequately questions regarding the etiology of bulimia nervosa. Indeed, when one examines the limited prospective research that has been performed (e.g., Attie & Brooks-Gunn, 1989;

J. H. Crowther, P. Crawford, & K. Shepards, manuscript in preparation; Drewnowski, Yee, & Krahn, 1988; Levine & Smolak, this volume, ch. 4; Patton, 1988; Rosen, Tacy, & Howell, 1990; Striegel-Moore, Silberstein, Frensch, & Rodin, 1989), there appears to be considerable variability among the studies regarding (1) whether the emphasis is placed on familial characteristics, individual psychological characteristics, or both as risk factors and (2) whether the dependent variable is a clinical case (e.g., Patton, 1988) or the problematic eating attitudes or dieting behaviors that are conceptualized as precursors to the actual case (e.g., Attie & Brooks-Gunn, 1989; Levine & Smolak, this volume, ch. 4; Rosen, Tacy, & Howell, 1990). Although many risk factors have been proposed for bulimia nervosa, Striegel-Moore (this volume, ch. 12) argues that research has yet to validate which risk factors are causally related to the onset of the actual disorder. The issue becomes even more complicated when one recognizes that, as a result of the apparent heterogeneity of bulimia nervosa, there may be several different etiological pathways to this disorder. Fortunately, the literature has begun to yield testable models to guide our endeavors (see, e.g., Levine & Smolak, this volume, ch. 4; Heatherton & Polivy, this volume, ch. 8; Rosen, Tacy, & Howell, 1990). We propose that future prospective research focus on the following areas.

Prospective Research on Bulimic Populations

Two epidemiological studies followed identified bulimic individuals over time, usually over a period of less than 1 year (e.g., Drewnowski et al., 1988; Striegel-Moore et al., 1989). Both of these studies found point prevalence rates of 2.9% (Drewnowski et al., 1988) and 3.8% (Striegel-Moore et al., 1989) for bulimia nervosa among women and reported that these prevalence rates remained stable over time. However, these studies also reported that whereas some of the women surveyed met the diagnostic criteria for bulimia nervosa during the fall and spring, new cases emerged and initial cases demonstrated partial remission, the latter often occurring in the absence of professional intervention (e.g., Drewnowski et al., 1988). The relatively small numbers of incident cases, chronic cases, and partial remission cases in these studies may have precluded further statistical analyses. However, comparisons of larger samples of these cases on factors thought to be etiologically relevant might be one step toward increasing our understanding of the cause and course of eating disorders at least among college-aged women. Of particular interest would be comparisons of the chronic cases and cases that demonstrate partial or full spontaneous remission, because it can be hypothesized that different etiological pathways may be operative for cases with different clinical courses.

There are, of course, methodological advantages and disadvantages to this approach. The major advantage is that once the cases of bulimia nervosa have been identified, a much more select group of subjects can be followed. With this type of approach, subjects can be assessed more frequently over shorter time periods to investigate the course of the disorder. The major disadvantage is that this approach is based on the assumption that those factors that are associated with the maintenance of bulimia nervosa are also etiologically related to the more severe and chronic manifestations of this disorder. Some evidence shows that this may be the case. For example, compared with nonborderline bulimic individuals, bulimic individuals who also received an Axis II borderline personality disorder diagnosis showed a poorer response to treatment and continued to display significant elevations in eating-attitude disturbance and emotional distress at 1-year follow-up (Johnson et al., 1990). It has also been hypothesized that, within the context of a dysfunctional familial environment, the personality traits that are often characteristic of borderline personality disorders, including affective instability and low self-esteem, also may predispose a young woman to an eating disorder (e.g., Johnson & Connors, 1987; Johnson & Wonderlich, this volume, ch. 10; Wonderlich, this volume, ch. 6). The other major disadvantage to this approach involves the fact that once bulimic patients are identified, they may be referred for treatment or seek treatment on their own. In this case, patients in remission may in fact represent patients who have responded positively to treatment. Despite these disadvantages, this approach may provide important clues to the role of various individual and familial characteristics in the cause of bulimia nervosa.

Prospective Research on High-Risk Populations

Conducting large-scale prospective research on populations at risk for bulimia nervosa represents a second avenue for researchers interested in the cause of this disorder. Here the questions become: "What groups constitute high-risk populations?", "At what age do we begin to follow these individuals?", and "On what aspects of their lives should we focus?" Although many risk factors for bulimia nervosa have been proposed, epidemiological evidence indicates that postpubertal white women who come from families with upwardly mobile value systems are at greatest risk for eating disorders in general and bulimia nervosa more specifically. With respect to timing, although Wooley and Kearney-Cooke (1986) argued that bulimia represents difficulties in the passage out of adolescence and into adulthood, epidemiological research indicated that bulimia is already prevalent among high school adolescent girls (e.g., for review, see Crowther, Wolf, & Sherwood, this volume, ch. 1; Fairburn & Beglin, 1990). Conducting large-scale prospective research projects that follow young white women from puberty through young adulthood represents an enormous investment of time and money. We discuss some of the assumptions that may characterize etiological research on bulimia nervosa and present a conceptual framework to guide future research in this area.

First, inherent in most etiological models (e.g., Crowther, Wolf, & Sherwood, this volume, ch. 1; Johnson & Connors, 1987; Mizes, 1985) is the assumption that maladaptive eating attitudes and chronic, restrictive dieting tendencies increase risk for the development of bulimic symptomatology. Indeed, the spiral model proposed by Heatherton and Polivy (this volume, ch. 8) is based on this assumption. Individuals with bulimia often report retrospectively that periods of severely restrictive dieting occurred 6 months to a year before the onset of bingeing and purging (e.g., Dally & Gomez, 1979; Pyle, Mitchell, & Eckert, 1981). However, with few exceptions (e.g., Attie & Brooks-Gunn, 1989; Patton, 1988), little prospective research established temporal relationships between maladaptive eating attitudes, dieting behaviors, and bulimic symptomatology. It has been proposed that body dissatisfaction, self-esteem, and depression may be intricately involved in the gradual descent from repetitive dieting to the development of bulimic symptomatology (e.g., Heatherton & Polivy, this volume, ch. 8; Rosen, this volume, ch. 9). Prospective research is needed that investigates the temporal relationships between maladaptive eating attitudes, dieting behaviors, and bulimic symptomatology as well as the mechanisms of change. This research may need to focus on repetitive dieters or highly restrained eaters as their high-risk group and conduct repetitive assessments over an extended time period to understand the roles that eating and weight-related attitudes or self-esteem and affective symptomatology play in the development of bulimic symptomatology.

Second, inherent in the belief that there are different etiological pathways to bulimia nervosa is the assumption that there may be variability in the familial backgrounds or personality characteristics that increase a young woman's risk for moving down the diet spiral (e.g., Heatherton & Polivy, this volume, ch. 8) to severe eating pathology. To illustrate this point, we suggest two possible etiological pathways to bulimia nervosa: one for an adolescent girl who might develop an uncomplicated case of bulimia nervosa and the second for an adolescent girl who might develop a complicated case of bulimia nervosa (see Figure 1). For example, as a result of a biological predisposition toward being overweight, one adolescent girl may experience increased body dissatisfaction and low self-esteem in response to the weight gain associated with puberty. To cope with these feelings, she may begin dieting initially with the support and encouragement of her family. When repeated diets do not result in weight loss, she may move to more extreme weight-control efforts and eventually begin bingeing and purging. In contrast, another adolescent girl who comes from a severely dysfunctional familial environment and experiences chronic mood swings, feelings of ineffectiveness, and extremely low self-esteem may also begin dieting as a way of bolstering her low self-esteem and increasing feelings of control over her internal and external environment. Again repetitive failures may lead to bingeing and purging. Both of these young women might fall within a high-risk group for bulimia nervosa on the basis of their maladaptive eating attitudes and repetitive dieting attempts, yet they arrived at their risk status in very different ways. Researchers interested in the cause of bulimia nervosa may need to determine whether or not individuals who are at risk for bulimia nervosa or who are already bulimic fall into clusters characterized by different familial and personality characteristics.

Finally, the last assumption is that there may be several different high-risk groups that, over time, will develop bulimic symptomatology at higher rates than the general population. If researchers can identify two or more clusters of characteristics that potentially confer risk for the development of bulimia nervosa, the next step would be to identify and follow these adolescent girls to determine whether they are at greater risk for bulimic symptomatology than the general population. Several issues arise here. The first involves identifying the age at which you preselect the high-risk population. From the perspective of developmental psychopathology, puberty, with its physiological changes and associated psychological demands, appears to be the developmental period posing the greatest risk for eating-related problems (e.g., Attie & Brooks-Gunn, 1989, this volume, ch. 3). Thus, prospective researchers might begin to follow adolescent girls who have just begun experiencing the physiological changes associated with puberty. Second, it is likely that interactions between familial and personality characteristics may be etiologically significant particularly in view of the changes in the parent–child relationship during adolescence (see Attie & Brooks-Gunn, this volume, ch. 3). To investigate such interactions in a prospective study, researchers need to conduct familial and personality assessments at the onset and during the course of the research project. A final issue concerns whether one is predicting the presence or absence of a clinical case or a continuous measure of bulimic symptomatology. Although a conservative epidemiological approach would argue for the use of a dichotomous variable, it has been argued that much information regarding risk factors and their etiological significance might be lost if researchers choose not to use continuous measures (e.g., Drewnowski et al., 1988).

Prospective Research on Prepubertal Children

Although it was originally believed that body-image dissatisfaction and maladaptive eating attitudes and dieting behaviors were not prevalent until the junior high and high school years, recent research indicated that substantial proportions of elementary school-aged children (aged 10 to 12 years) express dissatisfaction with their bodies and report engaging in dieting behaviors (e.g., for review, see Thelen, Lawrence, & Powell, this volume, ch. 5). These data suggest that, to the extent researchers hypothesize that body-image dissatisfaction and chronic dieting are risk factors for more serious eating pathology, we need to have some understanding of the manifestations of these phenomena in younger populations.

However, currently researchers know very little about the nature and stability of body-image dissatisfaction and dieting among elementary school children. For example, it is possible that body-image dissatisfaction reflects concerns about facial features or height rather than current dissatisfaction with normative weight and shape. Moreover, it is not clear whether these younger populations confuse dieting behaviors (e.g., caloric restriction to promote weight loss) with eating a healthy diet (e.g., consumption of healthy foods and restriction of junk foods with no concern regarding weight loss). Although it can be argued that even transient perceptions of body-image dissatisfaction or the need to diet may be important, we need more information about the stability of body image among elementary school-aged children and the relationship between self-report of dieting and eating behaviors.

In summary, additional prospective research is needed to answer questions more adequately regarding the cause of bulimia nervosa. We have suggested that prospective research might focus on bulimic populations, populations at risk for the development of bulimia, and populations of prepubertal children. However, in conducting prospective research with these populations, measurement issues may arise.

MEASUREMENT ISSUES

Prospective research on bulimia nervosa may be partially hampered by the lack of adequate measurement instruments and strategies. There apparently is a strong tendency among researchers to be less interested in the more mundane but tedious task of developing psychometrically sound assessment strategies than the more intriguing topics such as pursuing treatment outcome studies. Even when a promising new assessment strategy is introduced, there tends to be little continuing research on its psychometric adequacy after the initial exploratory study or two.

There are, however, some noteworthy exceptions. For prospective researchers interested in predicting maladaptive eating attitudes or bulimic symptomatology in adolescent and young adult populations, a growing body of research established the psychometric properties of the Eating Attitudes Test (EAT; Garner & Garfinkel, 1979); EDI (Garner & Olmstead, 1984) and its revision, the EDI-2 (Garner, 1991); and the Bulimia Test (BULIT; Smith & Thelen, 1984) and its revision, the BULIT-R (Thelen, Farmer, Wonderlich, & Smith, 1991). Of particular interest to prospective researchers is research establishing the stability over a 1-year period of many of the EDI subscales, including Drive for Thinness, Body Dissatisfaction, Ineffectiveness, Perfectionism, and Interpersonal Distrust (Crowther, Lilly, Crawford, & Shepherd, in press). Although these instruments were originally developed for late adolescent and young adult populations, research on the etiology of bulimia nervosa tends to focus on much younger populations, including junior high and high school populations. However, Rosen, Silberg, and Gross (1988) published norms for adolescent girls and boys, ages 14 through 18, for the EAT and EDI, whereas Shore and Porter (1990) reported normative and reliability data for adolescent girls and boys, ages 11 through 18, on the EDI. Shore and Porter (1990) noted that analyses of the internal consistency of the Bulimia and Maturity Fears subscales failed to demonstrate adequate reliability for either girls or boys. They concluded that the lower reliability of these two EDI subscales may reflect their limited relevance for this age group.

Of greater concern to researchers who are interested in investigating eating attitudes, body-image concerns, and dieting behaviors among prepubertal children is the virtual absence of instruments for use with late elementary school-aged children. One common strategy is to ask elementary school-aged children whether they are currently on a diet or have dieted at some point in the past. Yet if children indicate they are currently dieting, there is very little information regarding the validity of their self-report. Research with adolescents has tested the external validity of questions assessing weight-reducing and weight-gaining attempts and found a high degree of correspondence between self-reported weight control and independent ratings completed by parents, siblings, or friends (e.g., Jerome, 1991; Rosen & Poplawski, 1987). Rosen and Poplawski (1987) also found that on a 7-day food and exercise diary, weight reducers reported consuming less food, skipping more meals, exercising more often, and using more diet pills than those who reported they were not trying to change their weight. If research is going to focus on dieting among elementary school children, similar strategies may need to be used with this population. Meanwhile, self-report questionnaires for use with this population are becoming available. For example, Maloney, McGuire, Daniels, and Specker (1989) published a children's version of the EAT with adequate internal consistency and test–retest reliability for use with children in the third through sixth grades; a children's version of the EDI is also being developed (D. M. Garner, personal communication).

Although many constructs are theoretically relevant yet present measurement dilemmas in this area (e.g., body-image distortion or disturbance), we briefly discuss measurement issues related to cognitive distortions. (For discussions of the measurement issues related to the construct of body image, refer to Cash & Brown, 1987; Hsu & Sobkiewicz, 1991; Rosen, this volume, ch. 9). Garner and Bemis (1982) suggested that eating-disordered patients' cognitions reflect rigid beliefs about food and weight regulation, an evaluation of personal worth on the basis of weight and appearance, and an overemphasis on self-control of food and weight as a determinant of self-worth. Fairburn (1985), who believed that distorted beliefs are not merely symptomatic of bulimia nervosa but rather are its core pathology, noted that the disrupted eating behavior of bulimics is understandable once it is appreciated that shape and weight are of fundamental importance to the self-esteem of these women.

Despite the intuitive appeal of these ideas, there is very little supportive research because, at least partially, of the lack of valid assessment approaches.

Two cognitively oriented questionnaires have been recently introduced: the Bulimia Cognitive Distortions Questionnaire (Schulman, Kinder, Powers, Prange, & Gleghorn, 1986) and the Bulimic Thoughts Questionnaire (Phelan, 1987). Although they may eventually prove useful, at present there has only been initial investigation of their reliability and validity. More extensive research has been performed on the psychometric properties of the Mizes Anorectic Cognitions Questionnaire (MAC; Mizes & Klesges, 1989; for summary of research, see Mizes, 1991). However, the MAC clearly needs more research investigating its properties in large samples of clinical patients. Portions of the Eating Disorders Examination, a structured interview, are designed to assess cognitive distortions or "overvalued" ideas, and initial research on its psychometric properties is favorable (e.g., Cooper, Cooper, & Fairburn, 1989; Cooper & Fairburn, 1987; Rosen, Vara, Wendt, & Leitenberg, 1990; Wilson & Smith, 1989). Finally, a few recent efforts have been made to apply other methodologies to cognitive assessment, such as in vivo sampling (Zotter & Crowther, 1991) or assessment of cognitive schema (for overview, see Vitousek & Hollon, 1990).

Although assessment of these cognitive variables appears important on theoretical grounds, the current state of the art is that all the specific instruments and methodologies are in their infancy. Until the methodologies improve, we will not be able to define the essential psychopathology of bulimia, investigate the role of cognitive factors in etiological models, or identify relevant indexes that might indicate premorbid risk, predict response to treatment, or project likelihood of relapse.

CONCLUSION

In this chapter, we have offered a conceptual model for understanding the heterogeneity of bulimia nervosa and have identified some priorities for prospective research in this area. As research increases our understanding of the individual and familial factors that confer risk for an eating disorder in general and bulimia nervosa, more specifically, the next challenge facing health professionals in the area will be the implementation as well as the evaluation of primary prevention programs to foster more healthy attitudes regarding eating attitudes, body image, and dieting while reducing the incidence of eating disorders.

REFERENCES

American Psychiatric Association. (1980). *Diagnostic and statistical manual of mental disorders* (3rd ed.). Washington, DC: Author.

American Psychiatric Association. (1987). *Diagnostic and statistical manual of mental disorders* (3rd ed., rev.). Washington, DC: Author.

Attie, I., & Brooks-Gunn, J. (1989). Development of eating problems in adolescent girls: A longitudinal study. *Developmental Psychology, 25,* 70–79.

Blouin, A. G., Zuro, C., & Blouin, J. H. (1990). Family environment in bulimia nervosa: The role of depression. *International Journal of Eating Disorders, 9,* 649–658.

Bruch, H. (1973). *Eating disorders: Anorexia nervosa, obesity, and the person within.* New York: Basic Books.

Bunnell, D. W., Shenker, I. R., Nussbaum, M. P., Jacobson, M. S., & Cooper, P. (1990). Subclinical versus formal eating disorders: Differentiating psychological features. *International Journal of Eating Disorders, 9,* 357–362.

Button, E. J., & Whitehouse, A. (1981). Subclinical anorexia nervosa. *Psychological Medicine, 11,* 509–516.

Cash, T. F., & Brown, T. A. (1987). Body image in anorexia nervosa and bulimia nervosa. *Behavior Modification, 11,* 487–521.

Cooper, Z., Cooper, P., & Fairburn, C. G. (1989). The validity of the Eating Disorder Examination. *British Journal of Psychiatry, 154,* 807–812.

Cooper, Z., & Fairburn, C. G. (1987). The Eating Disorder Examination: A semi-structured interview for the assessment of the specific psychopathology of eating disorders. *International Journal of Eating Disorders, 6,* 1–8.

Crowther, J. H., Lilly, R. S., Crawford, P., & Shepherd, K. (in press). The stability of the Eating Disorder Inventory. *International Journal of Eating Disorders.*

Dally, P., & Gomez, J. (1979). *Anorexia nervosa.* London: William Heinemann.

Drewnowski, A., Yee, D. K., & Krahn, D. D. (1988). Bulimia in college women: Incidence and recovery rates. *American Journal of Psychiatry, 145,* 753–755.

Dykens, E. M., & Gerrard, M. (1986). Psychological profiles of purging bulimics, repeat dieters, and controls. *Journal of Consulting and Clinical Psychology, 54,* 283–288.

Fairburn, C. G. (1985). A cognitive-behavioral treatment of bulimia. In D. M. Garner & P. E. Garfinkel (Eds.), *Handbook of psychotherapy for anorexia nervosa and bulimia* (pp. 160–192). New York: Guilford Press.

Fairburn, C. G., & Beglin, S. J. (1990). Studies of the epidemiology of bulimia nervosa. *American Journal of Psychiatry, 147,* 401–408.

Fairburn, C. G., & Garner, D. M. (1986). The diagnosis of bulimia nervosa. *International Journal of Eating Disorders, 5,* 403–419.

Garner, D. M. (1991). The Eating Disorder Inventory—2. Odessa, FL: Psychological Assessment Resources, Inc.

Garner, D. M., & Bemis, K. M. (1982). A cognitive-behavioral approach to anorexia nervosa. *Cognitive Therapy and Research, 6,* 123–150.

Garner, D. M., & Garfinkel, P. E. (1979). The Eating Attitudes Test: An index of the symptoms of anorexia nervosa. *Psychological Medicine, 9,* 273–279.

Garner, D. M., Garfinkel, P. E., & O'Shaughnessy, M. (1985). The validity of the distinction between bulimia with and without anorexia nervosa. *American Journal of Psychiatry, 142,* 581–587.

Garner, D. M., & Olmsted, M. P. (1984). *The Eating Disorder Inventory manual.* Odessa, FL: Psychological Assessment Resources.

Garner, D. M., Olmsted, M. P., Davis, R., Rockert, W., Goldbloom, D., & Eagle, M. (1990). The association between bulimic symptoms and reported psychopathology. *International Journal of Eating Disorders, 9,* 1–15.

Garner, D. M., Olmsted, M. P., & Garfinkel, P. E. (1983). Does anorexia nervosa occur on a continuum: Subgroups of weight-preoccupied women and their relationships to anorexia nervosa. *International Journal of Eating Disorders, 2,* 11–20.

Garner, D. M., Olmsted, M. P., & Polivy, J. (1983). Development and validation of a multidimensional eating disorder inventory for anorexia and bulimia. *International Journal of Eating Disorders, 2,* 15–34.

Garner, D. M., Olmsted, M. P., Polivy, J., & Garfinkel, P. E. (1984). Comparison between weight-preoccupied women and anorexia nervosa. *Psychosomatic Medicine, 46,* 255–265.

Head, S. B., & Williamson, D. A. (1990). Association of family environment and personality disturbances in bulimia nervosa. *International Journal of Eating Disorders, 9,* 667–674.

Hinz, L. D., & Williamson, D. A. (1987). Bulimia and depression: A review of the affective variant hypothesis. *Psychological Bulletin, 102,* 150–158.

Hsu, L. K. G., & Sobkiewicz, T. A. (1991). Body image disturbance: Time to abandon the concept for eating disorders? *International Journal of Eating Disorders, 10,* 15–30.

Hudson, J. I., Wentworth, S. M., Hudson, M. S., & Pope, H. G. (1985). Prevalence of anorexia nervosa and bulimia among young diabetic women. *Journal of Clinical Psychiatry, 46,* 88–89.

Jerome, L. W. (1991). *Primary intervention for bulimia: The evaluation of a media presentation for an adolescent population.* Unpublished doctoral dissertation, Kent State University, Kent, OH.

Johnson, C., & Connors, M. E. (1987). *The etiology and treatment of bulimia nervosa: A biopsychosocial perspective.* New York: Basic Books.

Johnson, C., Tobin, D. L., & Dennis, A. (1990). Differences in treatment outcome between borderline and nonborderline bulimics at one-year follow-up. *International Journal of Eating Disorders, 9,* 617–628.

Johnson, C., Tobin, D. L., & Enright, A. (1989). Prevalence and clinical characteristics of borderline patients in an eating disordered population. *Journal of Clinical Psychiatry, 50,* 9–15.

Johnson, W. G., & Brief, D. J. (1983). Bulimia. *Behavioral Medicine Update, 4,* 16–21.

Lee, N. F., Rush, A. J., & Mitchell, J. E. (1985). Bulimia and depression. *Journal of Affective Disorders, 9,* 231–238.

Lindholm, L., & Wilson, G. T. (1988). Body image assessment in patients with bulimia nervosa and normal controls. *International Journal of Eating Disorders, 7,* 527–540.

Lowe, M. R., & Caputo, G. C. (1991). Binge eating in obesity: Toward the specification of predictors. *International Journal of Eating Disorders, 10,* 49–56.

Maloney, M. J., McGuire, J., Daniels, S. R., & Specker, B. (1989). Dieting behavior and eating attitudes in children. *Pediatrics, 84,* 482–489.

Marcus, M. D., & Wing, R. R. (1987). Binge eating among the obese. *Annals of Behavioral Medicine, 9,* 23–27.

Marcus, M. D., Wing, R. R., Ewing, L., Kern, E., Gooding, W., & McDermott, M. (1990). Psychiatric disorders among obese binge eaters. *International Journal of Eating Disorders, 9,* 69–78.

Marcus, M. D., Wing, R. R., & Hopkins, J. (1988). Obese binge eaters: Affects, cognitions and responses to behavioral weight control. *Journal of Consulting and Clinical Psychology, 56,* 433–439.

Mizes, J. S. (1985). Bulimia: A review of its symptomatology and treatment. *Advances in Behavior Research and Therapy, 7,* 91–142.

Mizes, J. S. (1988). Personality characteristics of bulimic and non-eating-disordered female controls: A cognitive-behavioral perspective. *International Journal of Eating Disorders, 7,* 541–550.

Mizes, J. S. (1990). Validity of the Mizes Anorectic Cognitions scale: A comparison between anorectics, bulimics, and psychiatric controls. Manuscript submitted for publication.

Mizes, J. S. (1991). Development and validation of the Mizes Anorectic Cognitions questionnaire. *Behavior Therapist, 14,* 81–82.

Mizes, J. S., & Klesges, R. C. (1989). Validity, reliability,and factor structure of the Anorectic Cognitions questionnaire. *Addictive Behaviors, 14,* 589–594.

Nylander, J. (1971). The feeling of being fat and dieting in a school population: An epidemiologic interview investigation. *Acta Socio-Medica Scandinavica, 3,* 17–26.

Olmsted, M. P., & Garner, D. M. (1986). The significance of self-induced vomiting among non-clinical samples. *International Journal of Eating Disorders, 5,* 683–700.

Patton, G. C. (1988). The spectrum of eating disorder in adolescence. *Journal of Psychosomatic Research, 32,* 579–584.

Phelan, P. W. (1987). Cognitive correlates of bulimia: The Bulimic Thoughts Questionnaire. *International Journal of Eating Disorders, 6,* 593–607.

Polivy, J., & Herman, C. P. (1987). Diagnosis and treatment of normal eating. *Journal of Consulting and Clinical Psychology, 55,* 635–644.

Prather, R. C., & Williamson, D. A. (1988). Psychopathology associated with bulimia, binge eating, and obesity. *International Journal of Eating Disorders, 7,* 177–184.

Pyle, R. L., Mitchell, J. E., & Eckert, E. D. (1981). Bulimia: A report of 34 cases. *Journal of Clinical Psychiatry, 42,* 60–64.

Rosen, J. C., & Poplawski, D. (1987). The validity of self-reported weight losing and weight gaining in adolescence. *International Journal of Eating Disorders, 6,* 515–523.

Rosen, J. C., Silberg, N. T., & Gross, J. (1988). Eating Attitudes Test and Eating Disorders Inventory: Norms for adolescent girls and boys. *Journal of Consulting and Clinical Psychology, 56,* 305–308.

Rosen, J. C., Tacy, B., & Howell, D. (1990). Life stress, psychological symptoms, and weight reducing behavior in adolescent girls: A prospective analysis. *International Journal of Eating Disorders, 9,* 17–26.

Rosen, J. C., Vara, L., Wendt, S., & Leitenberg, H. (1990). Validity studies of the Eating Disorders Examination. *International Journal of Eating Disorders, 9,* 519–528.

Rossiter, E. M., Wilson, G. T., & Goldstein, L. (1989). Bulimia nervosa and dietary restraint. *Behaviour Research and Therapy, 27,* 465–468.

Schulman, R. G., Kinder, B. M., Powers, P. S., Prange, M., & Gleghorn, A. (1986). The development of a scale to measure cognitive distortions in bulimia. *Journal of Personality Assessment, 50,* 630–639.

Selvini-Palazzoli, M. (1978). *Self-starvation: From individual to family therapy in the treatment of anorexia nervosa.* New York: Jason Aronson.

Shore, R. A., & Porter, J. E. (1990). Normative and reliability data for 11 to 18 year olds on the Eating Disorder Inventory. *International Journal of Eating Disorders, 9,* 201–207.

Smith, M. C., & Thelen, M. H. (1984). Development and validation of a test for bulimia. *Journal of Consulting and Clinical Psychology, 52,* 863–872.

Striegel-Moore, R. H., Silberstein, L. R., Frensch, P., & Rodin, J. (1989). A prospective study of disordered eating among college students. *International Journal of Eating Disorders, 8,* 499–509.

Striegel-Moore, R. H., Silberstein, L. R., & Rodin, J. (1986). Toward an understanding of risk factors for bulimia. *American Psychologist, 41,* 246–263.

Strober, M., & Humphrey, L. L. (1987). Familial contributions to the etiology and course of anorexia nervosa and bulimia. *Journal of Consulting and Clinical Psychology, 55,* 654–659.

Thelen, M. H., Farmer, J., Wonderlich, S., & Smith, M. (1991). A revision of the Bulimia Test: The BULIT-R. *Psychological Assessment: A Journal of Consulting and Clinical Psychology, 3,* 119–124.

Vitousek, K. B., & Hollon, S. D. (1990). The investigation of schematic content and processing in the eating disorders. *Cognitive Therapy and Research, 14,* 191–214.

Welch, G., Hall, A., & Renner, R. (1990). Patient subgrouping in anorexia nervosa using psychologically based classifications. *International Journal of Eating Disorders, 9,* 311–322.

Williamson, D. A., Kelley, M. L., Davis, C. J., Ruggiero, L., & Blouin, D. C. (1985). Psychopathology of eating disorders: A controlled comparison of bulimic, obese, and normal subjects. *Journal of Consulting and Clinical Psychology, 53,* 161–166.

Wilson, G. T., & Lindholm, L. (1987). Bulimia nervosa and depression. *International Journal of Eating Disorders, 6,* 725–732.

Wilson, G. T., & Smith, D. (1989). Assessment of bulimia nervosa: An evaluation of the Eating Disorders Examination. *International Journal of Eating Disorders, 8,* 173–179.

Wonderlich, S. A., & Swift, W. J. (1990). Borderline versus other personality disorders in the eating disorders: Clinical description. *International Journal of Eating Disorders, 9,* 629–638.

Wooley, S. C., & Kearney-Cooke, A. (1986). Intensive treatment of bulimia and body-image disturbance. In K. D. Brownell & J. P. Foreyt (Eds.), *Handbook of eating disorders: Physiology, psychology, and treatment of obesity, anorexia, and bulimia* (pp. 476–502). New York: Basic Books.

Zotter, D. L., & Crowther, J. H. (1991). The role of cognitions in bulimia nervosa. *Cognitive Therapy and Research, 15,* 413–426.

Index

245